The Encyclopedia of Home Recording

by Mark Garrison

Copyright © 2011 Mark Garrison

All rights reserved. Unauthorized reproduction or distribution of any part of this publication in any format, digital or mechanical, is an infringement of copyright. This includes photocopying, photographic reproduction, audio recording, video recording, or storage in a database or retrieval system. Authorization must be given by written consent from the publisher.

Questions and concerns can be directed to info@homerecordingbook.com

ISBN-13: 978-1461090427

ISBN-10: 1461090423

Disclaimer:

The author and fact checkers have endeavored to ensure this book is as complete and correct as possible, but no warranty is made or implied. Recording equipment should always be used according to the manufacturers specifications and manuals should always be read thoroughly. The author and publisher shall not be responsible nor liable for any loss or damage resulting from information contained in this book.

To my lovely wife, Pia

Thank you for all of your love and support during the writing and production of this book.

How To Use This Book

This book was written to be a quick and easy reference for people who record in home studios and small project studios. The main section of the book is written in the format of an encyclopedia, with alphabetically organized entries covering the tools, techniques, and terminology of the recording studio. Many of the entries will refer you to other entries to help you learn more.

Unlike most books on home recording, the *Encyclopedia of Home Recording* is not meant to be read front-to-back. It's sections are meant to be read individually, so that you can get on with recording. You can keep it on hand in your home studio and use it for ideas and answers whenever they're needed.

At the back of the book you will find three appendices: The Basics of Sound, a Studio Setup Guide, and a Microphone Placement Guide. If you are new to recording, I recommend you start by reading the first appendix to gain a basic understanding of how sound propagates. This will help you better understand and apply the information in the rest of the book.

If you already have a basic understanding of sound and recording, you can jump right in by flipping to a subject you are interested in.

Good luck and happy recording!

Mark Garrison

Absorption

Absorption refers to the amount of acoustic energy absorbed into a surface. All surfaces partially reflect and partially absorb sound. In recording studios, acoustic foam and other acoustic materials are used to both absorb sound energy, and control how reflected sound moves within the room. Placement, shape, quantity, and density of acoustic materials will affect the overall sound of a room. While proper acoustic treatment is a specialized field, some basic treatment can easily be done in the home studio.

Soft, textured surfaces (such as carpet or blankets) are good at absorbing sound and can be an inexpensive way to gain basic control over reflections. It is important to be aware, however, that high frequencies are more easily absorbed than low frequencies. It is not uncommon for beginners to absorb too much high frequency energy and find themselves left with muddy sounding recordings.

See also *Acoustics, Acoustic Foam, Bass Trap*.

Acoustics

The term acoustics refers to the properties that affect how sound moves around a room or space. From live performance to recording, the acoustics of a room have a significant effect on what we hear. The amount of reflected sound, when it occurs in relation to the original (or direct) sound, and the balance of frequencies in those reflections combine to make the acoustic properties of a space.

Factors that affect a room's acoustics include:
- size
- shape
- angles of walls/ceiling
- materials the walls/ceiling/floor are made from
- size/shape/material/placement of objects in the room

We rarely have control over all of these factors, but we usually have control over some. Keeping these factors in mind and strategically manipulating them can dramatically improve your recordings.

The prime component of acoustics is reverberation. Reverberation can be broken down into three elements (see *Fig. 1*). Sound waves that travel directly from the sound source to your ear (or microphone) are referred to as direct sound. Sound waves that reach your ear by way of reflection off of a surface are called early reflections. Early reflections generally happen within 10–100 milliseconds of the direct sound (depending on the size of the room and placement within it). The third element is reverberation, which is made up of sound waves that travel around the room reflecting off of multiple surfaces. The length of reverberation will vary depending on the size of the room and the nature of the surfaces in it. In a large cathedral, for example, sounds may reverberate for 4 or 5 seconds whereas a small room may only have a couple of hundred milliseconds of reverberation.

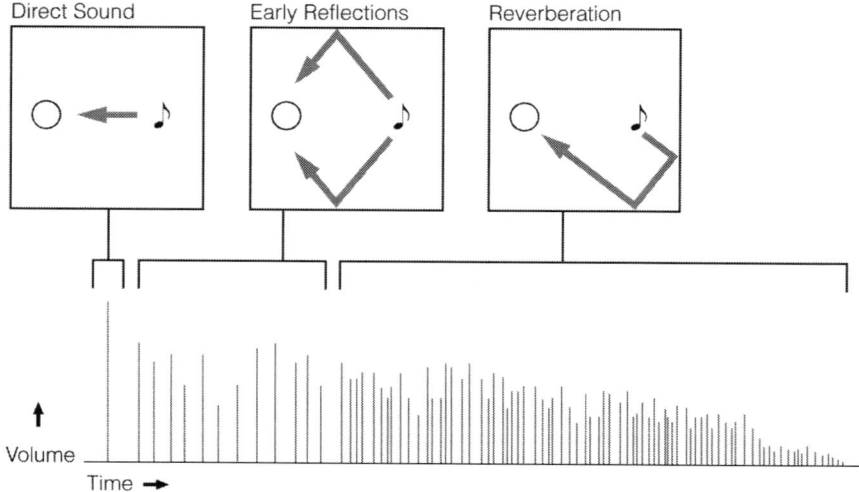

Figure 1: Elements of Reveberation

When treating a room acoustically, there are three main factors to consider: absorption, reflection, and standing waves. Absorption is the amount of sound energy that is absorbed by a surface. It is common practice to have rugs in a studio space that can be moved or removed as required. It is also common to use acoustic foam on the walls, ceiling, or on movable panels to absorb and break up reflections. On a budget, a similar result can be achieved using egg cartons. Their shape works very well for trapping high frequency reflections (see *Fig. 2*).

Low frequencies can be more difficult to control, so bass traps are frequently used to keep them in check. Bass traps absorb low-frequency energy that can build up in a room causing muddy sounding recordings. They come in a variety of styles, most of which are designed to be placed in the corner of the room (see *Bass Trap*)

A room with very few reflections is referred to as sounding "dead". Conversely a "live" sounding room has many reflections. Both of these environments are useful in the recording process. Voice-over work is frequently done in a dead room to make the speaker seem very close to the listener, whereas many engineers prefer a live room for acoustic instruments or vocals because of the added high frequency "sparkle" it can add (much like the effect of singing in the shower).

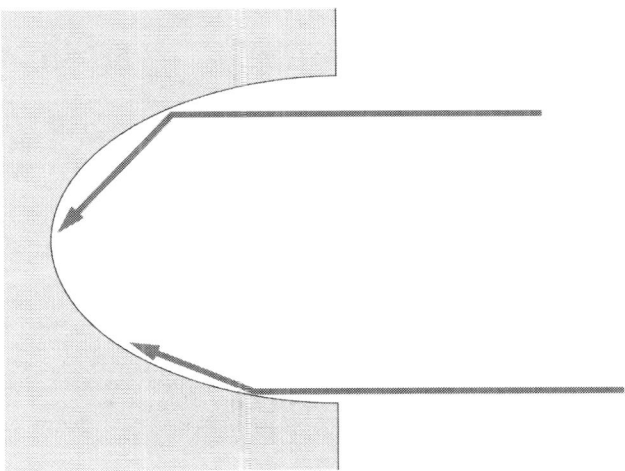

Figure 2: Egg Carton Shape Traps Reflections

Reflection is the opposite of absorption. Reflected sounds and their tonal characteristics have a significant effect on the sound of a recording and should be considered when choosing a room to record in or where in a room to place the performer and microphone(s). A basic empty room (four parallel walls with nothing on them) provides uninteresting reflections as sound travels out to the walls and then reflects straight back. These reflections can be made more complex (and therefore more acoustically pleasing) by use of diffusers (panels designed to create a variety of reflections), dividers (movable, freestanding panels), and by strategically placing available objects within the room for sound to reflect off of.

The material a surface is made from will affect the frequencies it reflects. Hard, smooth surfaces (such as wood or tile) will reflect most high frequencies, whereas soft or porous surfaces will absorb them. Mid-range and low frequencies will be absorbed to some degree, but not as easily as high-frequencies. The frequency range of the instruments being recorded should be kept in mind when considering reflections in a room.

Standing waves occur when a sound reflects off of parallel surfaces (such as walls, or floor and ceiling) then back into each other. Where the reflected sounds meet they begin to cancel each other out. This cancellation occurs in different locations for different frequencies, so moving the performer or microphone to different parts of a room can yield different sounds. In order to avoid standing waves and their effects, many studios are built in a way that specifically avoids parallel surfaces. Since it is rare in a home studio environment that we have the option of using a room without parallel walls, we must rely on diffusers, dividers, and other methods of breaking up reflections.

Acoustics in Your Recordings

When beginning a recording it can be a good idea to take a mental (or even written) inventory of the acoustic environments you have available to record in and their individual strengths and weaknesses. For example most bathrooms are full of surfaces that reflect a lot of high frequencies (tile, porcelain, glass, linoleum, etc.) and are reasonably small. This means plenty of bright, short reflections and may be a good choice as a location for recording vocals or acoustic instruments. If a room has too much reflected sound, blankets or carpets can be added to absorb some of the sound energy.

Another example of a possible recording space to consider would be a stairwell. The close walls and high ceiling will give a range of reflections, some quick (off of the close walls) and some longer (off of the high ceiling). A carpeted stairwell will be mellower sounding, whereas wooden stairs will sound brighter. This can be an interesting space to record percussion instruments.

A common way to take stock of the acoustic qualities of a space is to move around the room while clapping your hands, singing, or whistling to get a feel for its sound. Not only will different spaces have different acoustic qualities, but the sound of your recordings may differ greatly depending in where the performer and the microphone(s) are placed within an individual room or space. The proximity of walls and objects in the room can affect the reflected sound as well as the tonal content of these reflections (see *Standing Waves*). For this reason it is important to use care when choosing where to position the performer and the microphone(s).

See also *Diffuser, Reverberation, Standing Wave*.

Acoustic Envelope

The term acoustic envelope refers to how the volume of a sound changes over the span of its occurrence. Along with timbre, the acoustic envelope is one of the main reasons that two different instruments will sound different, even when playing the same note.

The acoustic envelope is broken into four sections: attack, decay, sustain and release (see *Fig. 3*). The attack is the initial burst of sound as the note goes from silence to its loudest peak. After the peak, there is a quick decay down to the volume at which the note sustains, and then eventually releases to silence.

We can manipulate the acoustic envelope to some extent through the careful use of compression.

See also *Compression, Timbre*.

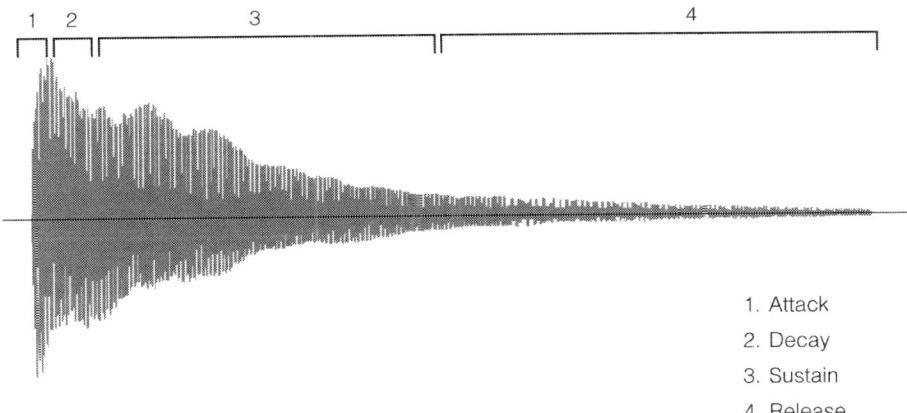

Figure 3: The Acoustic Envelope

Acoustic Foam

Acoustic foam is high-density foam manufactured in specific shapes to control the reflections of sound within a room. The soft, porous material absorbs high frequencies while the curves and angles on the panels scatter the remaining reflections.

Low frequencies are not as easily absorbed, so bass traps must be used to control them. Bass traps come in a few different designs, including large, corner-mounted wedges designed to absorb bass frequencies that tend to build up in corners.

See also *Acoustics, Bass Trap, Diffuser*.

Acoustic Isolation

Acoustic isolation refers to a situation where the effects of outside noise have been removed from an environment. This can refer to external noises such as traffic as well as internal factors such as the fan on your computer.

In an ideal recording situation we would have complete acoustic isolation for our live room (the room in which the performers are playing) from both the outside word and from the control room (the room where the recording equipment is operated). It is also common for studios to have one or more isolation rooms or isolation booths to allow more than one instrument to be recorded at the same time while keeping them isolated from each other. In a situation like this, the performers are given headphones in order to hear each other, any recorded tracks they are playing along to, as well as instructions from the engineer or producer than can be given through a "talkback microphone". The rooms are usually separated by glass to allow for communication through visual cues.

Unfortunately, in the home studio we rarely have the luxury of such an environment and often find ourselves in the same room as the performer. In a case like this we must be creative in order to create as much acoustic isolation as possible with the resources available.

Computer fan noise is a common problem in a situation like this. Low noise fans can be installed in the computer in order to reduce the noise at its source. Placing solid objects around the computer itself can help but should be done carefully in order to allow enough air flow for the computer to cool itself. Other options include using long cabling to allow the computer tower to be outside the room while the monitor, keyboard and mouse are inside, or placing the computer tower around a corner.

Computers and other equipment are not the only source of background noise in the studio. The amount of noise a person makes when they think they are being quiet should not be underestimated. Heavy breathing, rustling of clothes, squeaking of chairs, and general movement all add noise to the room. On a recording of a quiet instrument, the effect can be quite significant. It is a good practice to have as few people in the room as possible to keep the amount of noise in the recording to a minimum.

See also *Soundproofing*.

Active DI

The term DI is short for direct injection or direct input. It is a method of recording an electric instrument directly, without a microphone. A DI takes an unbalanced, high-impedance, instrument-level signal and converts it into a balanced, low-impedance, microphone-level signal, allowing it to be plugged into a standard mic preamp or mixing board.

An active DI is a direct injection box that contains a preamplifier, providing a stronger signal output. Active DIs require power which can be supplied by an AC adaptor, phantom power, or an internally mounted battery.

See also *Direct Injection, Phantom Power*.

Active Monitors

Active monitors are studio reference speakers that have amplifiers built into them, eliminating the need for a separate power amp.

See also *Monitors*.

A/D

See *Analog to Digital Converter*.

ADAT

ADAT is an acronym for Alesis Digital Audio Tape, a recording format that was released in 1991 which is capable of recording 8 tracks simultaneously onto an SVHS tape. Multiple ADAT machines can be synchronized together to allow up to 24 tracks simultaneously.

Several models of ADAT were released over the years offering 16- or 20-bit recording at a sample rate of 44.1 kHz or 48 kHz. The original tape-based ADAT machines have been replaced by a 24 channel version that records onto hard disc.

ADAT Optical Interface

The ADAT Optical Interface (sometimes referred to as "lightpipe") is a standard used to transfer digital information by use of a fiber optic cable. ADAT Optical allows transfer of 8 channels of 24-bit, 48kHz audio. Though designed by Alesis specifically for use with their ADAT recorders, ADAT Optical is frequently found on equipment from other manufacturers. The cable itself is identical to an optical S/PDIF or TOSLINK cable.

ADSR

See *Acoustic Envelope*.

AES/EBU

AES/EBU is an acronym for American Engineering Society/European Broadcasters Union. The acronym is used to refer to the digital audio standard developed by these two groups that describes the transmission of two channels of digital audio from one device to another over a single XLR cable.

In the early 1990s, Sony and Phillips introduced S/PDIF (Sony/Phillips Digital Interface) as a consumer-level alternative to AES/EBU. S/PDIF uses a 75Ω coaxial RCA cable or a TOSLINK optical cable to transmit digital audio data. The main practical difference between the two formats is S/PDIF's ability to transmit track markers and copy protection information.

See also *SCMS, S/PDIF*.

AIFF

AIFF (Audio Interchange File Format) is a standard uncompressed file format for digital audio. Because it was co-developed by Apple Computers it sees more common usage on the Mac operating system. AIFF, WAV, and SDII are all uncompressed (or lossless) file formats, making them more suitable choices than MP3 (a "lossy" file format) when file size is not of great concern. AIFF files use the file extensions .aif or .aiff.

See also *File Compression*.

Ambient Microphone Placement

Ambient microphone placement is when microphones are placed at a distance from the sound source to pick up reverberated, ambient sound from the room or space. This is usually used in conjunction with close miking to take advantage of natural reverberation in a space or to pick up crowd noise in a live recording. Frequently a stereo pair of microphones is used either in an X-Y pattern or as a spaced pair.

See also *Stereo Miking Techniques*.

Amp Emulator

An amp emulator is a digital processor that imitates the sound of a guitar amplifier for the purpose of direct recording. These can be found as either software or hardware, and in some cases are built right into an amplifier.

Direct recording an electric guitar without an amp emulator often yields poor results when the guitar is overdriven. The reason for this is that an overdriven guitar creates some rather harsh harmonics. Electric guitar amps are built with this in mind and use speakers designed to smooth out some of these harsh tones. Amp emulators can improve direct-recorded guitar sounds by approximating the tonal effects of an amplifier and speaker.

Some amp emulators are designed to recreate the sound of classic amplifiers and speakers. These are referred to as amp modelers, and they can be a valuable tool for the home studio because they provide tonal variety without a huge investment in equipment.

Amp Modeler

See *Amp Emulator*.

Amplitude

When referring to a physical environment, amplitude refers to the amount of compression and rarefaction in the air (or, more practically, the volume of sound). This translates directly to an electrical equivalent when the sound has been picked up by a transducer such as a microphone.

The most common usage of the word amplitude in recording is to refer to a graphic representation of sound. We represent sound with a baseline, or zero line, indicating silence, and a curve which shows how far from silence the sound is. When the sound is above the baseline it is referred to as "positive amplitude" (which indicates compression) and it is referred to as "negative amplitude" when it is below (indicating rarefaction) (see *Fig. 4*).

See also *Cycle, Frequency, Appendix A: The Basics Of Sound*.

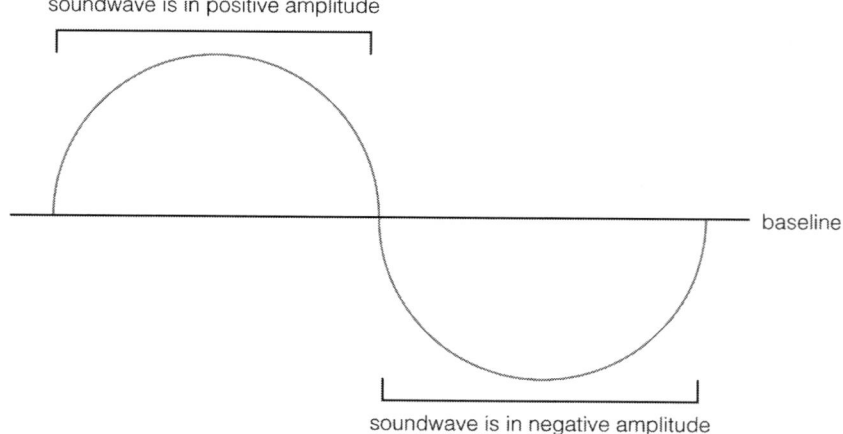

Figure 4: A Sound Wave

Analog to Digital (A/D) Converter

An A/D converter is a device that converts analog signal into digital signal for recording and/or processing. A/D converters may be standalone units or part of another device such as a digital audio workstation (DAW). Most computer-based recording setups use an audio interface that contains A/D converters, D/A converters, and, in some cases, microphone preamplifiers.

An A/D converter can be as simple as a soundcard with a single input or a more elaborate audio interface with multiple inputs and outputs. The number of A/D converters an interface or DAW has will determine the number of simultaneous tracks that can be recorded.

Interfaces with A/D converters usually have D/A (digital to analog) converters as well, which are used for playback and for routing signals to external analog equipment. Some audio interfaces can be "piggybacked" (more than one can be used simultaneously) to increase the number of inputs and outputs on a workstation.

Angle of Most Rejection

The direction from which a microphone picks up the least sound is called its angle of most rejection, or null point. Where this point sits depends on the pickup pattern of the microphone. For example, the angle of most rejection on a cardioid microphone is directly behind the microphone, whereas on a bi-directional pattern, it's directly from the side.

See also *Microphones, Pickup Pattern*.

Attack

The term attack can refer to two things in the realm of audio: a control on a compressor or the initial segment of a sound's acoustic envelope. Both are covered below.

Attack (compressor)

A compressor's attack control sets how quickly, once the compression threshold has been passed, the compressor begins to work. A fast attack setting will begin to work immediately, compressing the initial transient (or "attack" – see other definition of attack below) of the sound. Alternatively, a compressor with a slow attack setting will allow the initial transient sound to pass before starting to compress, affecting only the sustain of the sound. Slow attack settings will allow short peaks of volume to pass through unaffected, while a fast attack would engage the compressor briefly to control them.

See also *Compression*.

Attack (acoustic envelope)

When referring to the acoustic envelope (which represents the volume of a sound over time) the term attack means the initial rise in volume of a sound (see *Fig. 5*). The attack (sometimes referred to as the transient) of most natural sounds is short and decays quickly into the sustain of the note.

See also *Acoustic Envelope*.

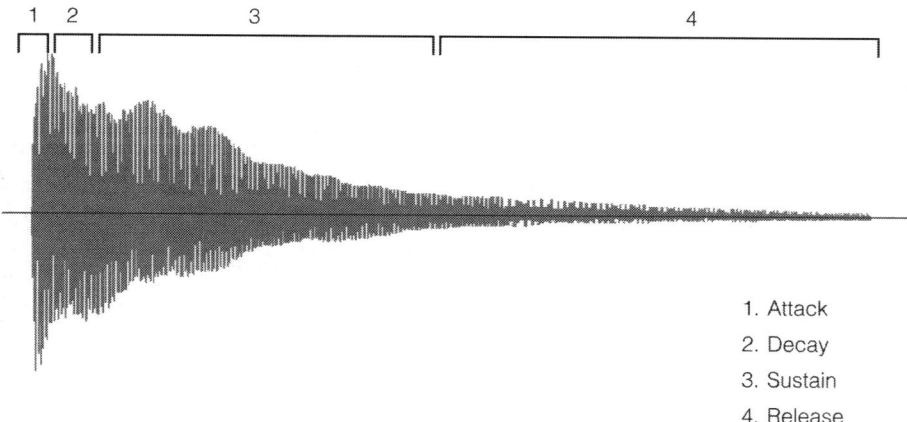

1. Attack
2. Decay
3. Sustain
4. Release

Figure 5: The Acoustic Envelope

Attenuate

The term attenuate means to reduce the volume of a signal. This can be done at various points in the signal flow. Methods of attenuating a signal include using a pad, a preamp, or a volume control.

See also *Signal Flow*.

AU

See *Audio Units*.

Audible Range

The audible range of human hearing is roughly 20 Hz–20,000 Hz (20kHz). Most people tend to lose a little of their hearing in the high frequencies with age, so the adult range of hearing is generally closer to 20 Hz–16 kHz. Sounds below 20 Hz (called subsonic frequencies) do not register in our ears, but can be perceived through our sense of touch if the volume is great enough. Studies have suggested that supersonic frequencies (those above 20 kHz) can be perceived by listeners as well even though they are not consciously aware of them.

See also *Appendix A: The Basics of Sound*.

Audio Engineer

The term audio engineer (also sound engineer or recording engineer) refers to a professional who deals with recording and/or reproducing sound. The term is often used interchangeably with the term producer, though this is somewhat inaccurate.

In the early days of the record industry, the engineer worked for the music studio and the producer worked for the record company. The engineer's job was to accurately record the performers according to the vision of the producer, and he or she was also responsible for maintaining the recording equipment.

The producer was responsible for making sure that the record company would have a marketable product in the end. He or she would work closely with the performers, helping them make decisions about what songs to perform, arrangement, etc. Ultimately the producer had the decision making power by means of controlling the money that was paying for the recording.

In the modern studio, however, the roles of engineer and producer are changing and becoming more blurred as we see many producers getting behind the mixing board, many artists producing and/or engineering their own work, and many record companies allowing artists to hire their own producers.

Audio engineering blends both creative and technical skills. The engineer incorporates knowledge and skills from the fields of electrical engineering, acoustics, psychoacoustics, and music to be able to effectively do his or her job.

Unlike other areas of technical expertise, audio engineering does not have a universally accepted form of accreditation. This has both positive and negative implications, as it allows many different approaches to learning (including apprenticeship, formal schooling, and self-directed study). The lack of a clearly defined accreditation process, however, can leave those looking to enter the profession unsure of how to proceed, and those looking to hire an engineer without an objective way to distinguish between the qualified and unqualified.

Audio Interface

An audio interface is a method of getting sound in or out of a digital recording device or computer. Sometimes referred to as a soundcard or a I/O Module, audio interfaces come in many sizes and styles, with a variety of different forms of connectivity, and with a wide range of features.

A very basic interface will have 2 inputs and 2 outputs. This means that two distinct signals can be recorded at the same time (or one stereo signal) and played back in stereo. It is not uncommon to find audio interfaces with as many as 24 inputs and outputs, allowing many tracks to be recorded at once and leaving options for routing signals out of the recording unit, into external effect processors, then back into the device.

A feature that is quite common for computer interfaces is to have one or more microphone preamplifiers (preamps) built in. These are very convenient because they can be used without any other equipment and, when combined with a portable computer, make location recording very easy. When mic preamps are not included in the interface, a standalone preamp or mixing board must be placed before the input to attain proper signal level and control.

Other features that may or may not be included in an audio interface are MIDI in and out, Word Clock, digital inputs and outputs (usually via S/PDIF or ADAT Optical), signal metering, and even effects.

See also *ADAT Optical Interface, Preamplifier, S/PDIF, Word Clock.*

Audio Units

Audio Units (AU) is the name of a software plug-in architecture developed by Apple and in their software, such as Logic and Garage Band, as well as a variety of programs from other developers.

See also *Plug-In*.

Aural Exciter

The Aural Exciter is a signal processor designed and manufactured by the Aphex company. The Aural Exciter was designed to add clarity and "sparkle" to recordings by use of phase shifting and by adding synthesized harmonics in the high-mid frequency range. In other words, brightness is achieved by making the frequency range fuller rather than louder (as an equalizer would).

Aphex has also introduced their "Big Bottom" circuit in newer models which works in a similar manner but targets low frequencies instead. It is meant to fill out the low end, making it seem louder without significantly adding to the signal's output.

Auto-Tune

See *Pitch Correction*.

Automation

The ability to automate mixes is a relatively new development in recording. Before the development of automation, if an engineer wanted the volume of an instrument, the equalization of a signal, or the settings on an effect to change over the course of a song, he or she needed to manually make those changes during the final mixdown. This was not a big deal if a song had one or two changes, but in a situation with a lot of changes, it was not uncommon practice for the entire band and anyone else that was available to line up at the mixing desk and each memorize a series of changes they had to make during the mixdown. The mixdown would be repeated until everyone got it exactly right.

Most modern digital workstations allow for mix automation. This means that changes that need to be made over the course of a song can be recorded into the workstation and will happen automatically during playback or mixdown. Depending on the recording setup, these changes might be made by entering values manually or by putting the unit into "automation record" mode and then performing the changes in real time. Some workstations, digital mixers, and software control surfaces even have motorized faders that will move on their own as they perform the automation changes.

Auxiliary Return

When an auxiliary send is used for routing signals from a mixing board to an external effect processor, the wet signal (signal with effect on it) needs to be returned to the mixing board to be added to the mix. This can be achieved by plugging the output of the effect unit into an available channel on the mixer. Most mixers, however, will provide an auxiliary return for this exact purpose.

An auxiliary return functions just like an ordinary channel on the mixer with some of the controls missing (such as an equalizer and routing options). For almost all applications this is not a problem, but in some cases an engineer may choose to use a full channel to return the wet signal, providing greater control over its tone.

See also *Auxiliary Send, Channel Strip, Mixing Board, Signal Flow.*

Auxiliary Send

An auxiliary send allows us to take a signal from a channel on the mixing board and send it out of the mixer to an external destination. The two most common uses for an auxiliary send are for external effects and for creating multiple mixes (such as monitor mixes for a live performance). The number of auxiliary sends per channel will vary from mixer to mixer.

While the auxiliary send and the insert are both methods of sending a signal to an external device, they do so in different ways. The insert takes the entire signal out of the channel strip, sends it to an external device, then returns the processed signal to the channel strip at the same point from which it was taken. Auxiliary sends, on the other hand, maintain the original signal path through the channel strip but also send a copy of that signal to the aux output. The signal from the auxiliary is then sent to the external device, and the processed signal is returned to the mixing board to be blended with the original signal.

An effect placed on an insert is called a serial effect because the path moves through the devices in a series: first part of channel strip, external device, then second part of channel strip. Routing in this manner is used for processors that require the entire signal to be processed, such as compressors and equalizers. An effect used via an auxiliary send is called a parallel effect because it creates two copies of the signal (one processed, one unprocessed) that take parallel paths through the mixing board (see *Fig. 7* below). Parallel routing is used for effects where the original and processed signals are to be blended together, such as reverb or delay. Running effects through an auxiliary send has the added benefit that multiple channels can be routed to the same processor (for example, all channels can use the same reverb).

In the signal path, the auxiliary send usually comes after the insert point and before the equalizer. On the channel strip it will be controlled by a knob or fader usually marked "Aux" or "Aux Send" (see *Fig. 6*). The mixer will also have an output to match each aux send. Each auxilary send will be accessible on every channel, meaning that more than one channel can be sent to the same auxiliary output. Turning up the aux send on a channel will increase the amount of signal from that channel that will be sent to the aux output. The auxiliary output can then be plugged into the input of an effect processor or amplifier (for a monitor mix).

Figure 6: Auxiliary Sends

In the case of using an auxiliary for effects, the "wet" signal (with effect) needs to be returned to the mixing board to mix with the "dry" signal (without effect). This is achieved by plugging the output of the effect processor in to the auxiliary return (see *Fig. 7*). The aux return will also have a volume control to dictate how much of the wet signal is blended back into the mix. So, the aux send knobs

The Encyclopedia of Home Recording

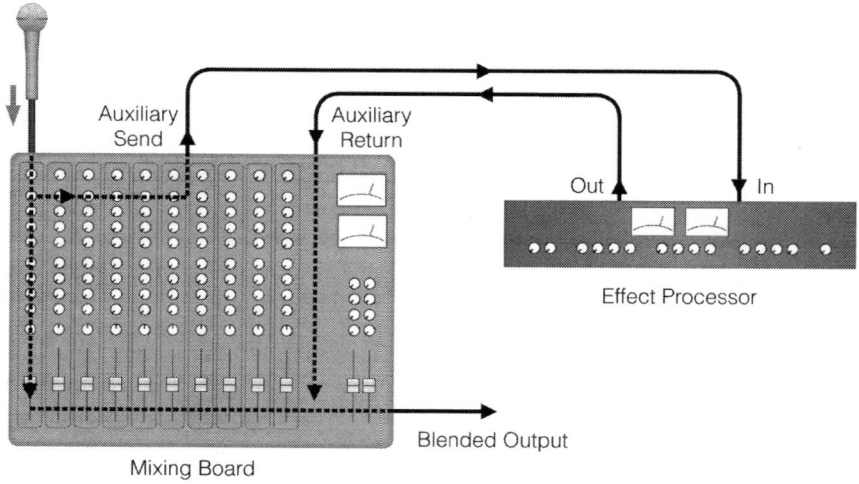

Figure 7: Connecting Effects to an Auxiliary Send

control how much of each channel goes into the effect, and the aux return knob controls how much of the wet signal is added back into the mix.

Pre- and Post-Fader Sends

One factor that makes the aux send more versatile, but also a little more confusing, is the ability to make a send "pre-fader" or "post-fader". If a send is pre-fader, then the volume fader on the channel will have no effect on the output of the send. That is to say that even if the volume on the channel is all the way down, or the channel is muted, signal will still be sent out of the aux send. If the send is post-fader, then any changes to the channel's volume will change the send's volume.

It is important, if you are using a send to create a separate mix, to have your send pre-fader because otherwise any changes to the main mix would also change the aux mix. By using a pre-fader send, the output of the send is not affected by the main mix.

If a send is being used for an effect, it is generally best to use a post-fader send so that the send does not have to be adjusted every time the channel volume is changed. Having a send set as pre-fader when using effects can be a problem because turning a channel down will still leave the processed version of the signal in the mix at the same volume.

See also *Auxiliary Return, Channel Strip, Mixing Board, Signal Flow.*

Balanced Cabling

Audio cabling comes in two varieties: balanced, which has three wires in it (positive, negative, and ground) and three leads on the connectors at each end; and unbalanced, which uses only two wires, the ground sharing the same wire as the positive lead. The difference between balanced and unbalanced cabling is similar to the difference between grounded (3-prong) and ungrounded (2-prong) electrical plugs in your home.

The two types of jacks (connectors) primarily used for balanced cabling are XLR (used on most microphones) and TRS (Tip Ring Sleeve – a balanced version on the ¼" jack) (see *Fig. 8*). The most common connectors for unbalanced cabling are RCA and ¼".

The advantages of a balanced connection include reduced noise, reduced interference, and stronger signal level. It is generally advisable to use balanced cabling wherever possible, though it is necessary for the equipment being connected to have balanced inputs and outputs. An electric guitar, for example, has an unbalanced output, and a guitar amplifier has an unbalanced input, therefore an unbalanced cable should be used.

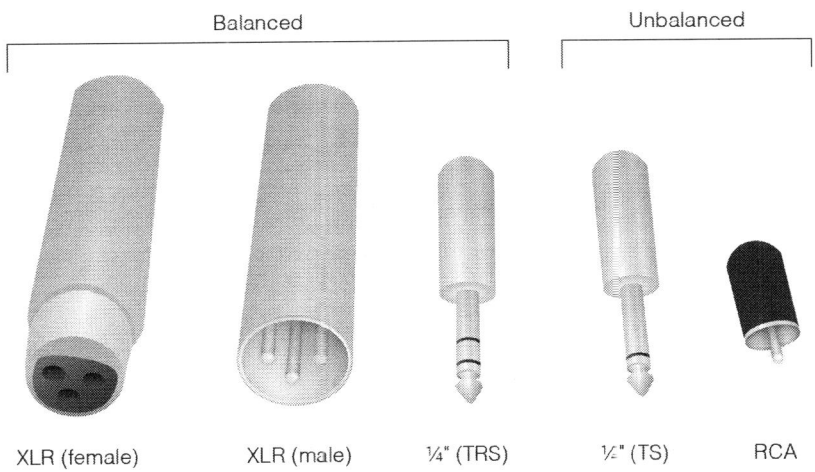

Figure 8: Jacks for Balanced and Unbalanced Cabling

The Encyclopedia of Home Recording

Band-Pass Filter

A band-pass filter is achieved by combining a high-pass filter (which cuts everything below a given frequency) with a low-pass filter (which cuts everything above a given frequency). The result is a frequency band between the two filters that is allowed to pass through while everything on either side of the band has been cut (see *Fig. 9*).

Pass filters are labelled with their target frequency, which is the point at which the signal has been cut by 3 dB. Depending on the equipment being used, the target frequency may be fixed or the user may be able to choose it.

One application of a band-pass filter is the "telephone voice" effect. By combining a band-pass filter with a sharp (high Q) boost at around 2.5 kHz, a voice sounds as if it were coming through a telephone or a low-quality radio.

See also *Equalizer, High-Pass Filter, Low-Pass Filter*.

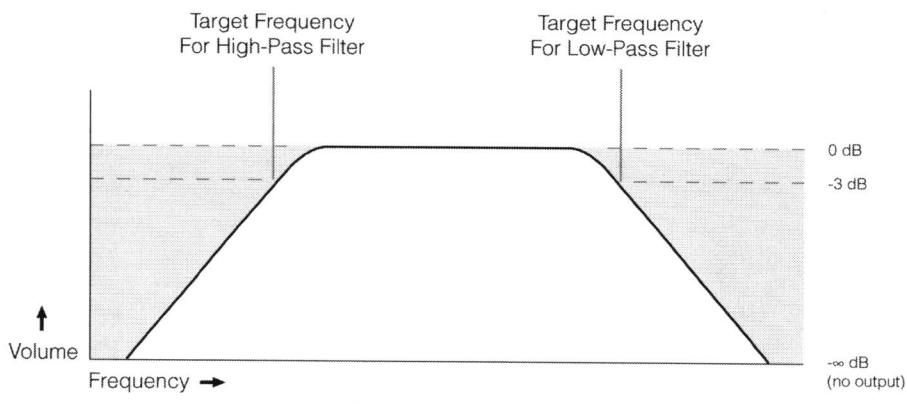

Figure 9: A Band-Pass Filter

Bass Trap

Bass traps absorb low-frequency sound energy. They are used to prevent low frequencies from building up in a room, causing muddy recordings. Because bass frequencies tend to build up in corners, this is the most common placement for bass traps. There are a variety of bass trap designs available commercially, constructed from high density foam, fiberglass, or similar materials.

One of the most common bass trap designs is the functional trap, or "tube trap". The functional trap is constructed of a thick, medium-density fibreglass tube placed in a corner. Low frequencies reflect into the tube and are absorbed into its surface. In some cases the half of the tube that faces the room will be covered with a harder surface to reflect high frequencies back into the room (see *Fig. 10*). This can be approximated on a budget with some degree of success by standing rolls of carpet in the corners of the room.

For those who are inclined towards do-it-yourself projects, plans for a variety of bass trap designs can be found online or in books devoted to acoustic treatment.

See also *Acoustics, Acoustic Foam*

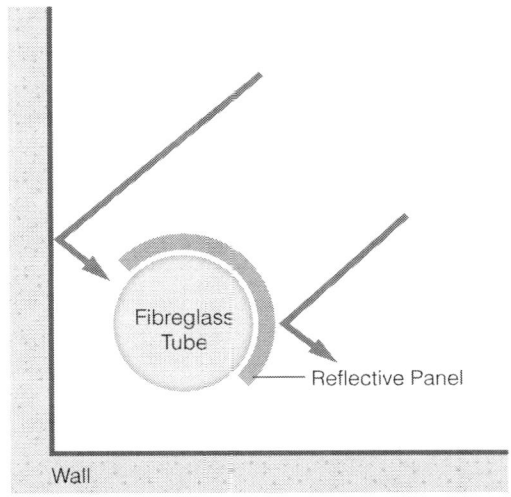

Figure 10: Overhead View of a Functional Bass Trap

Bed Track

A common approach to recording a song is to begin by recording just the rhythm tracks, then overdubbing the rest of the instruments over top. These initial rhythm tracks are referred to as "bed track" and lay the foundation for the song. This method allows greater control over the tone of each instrument because they can be recorded with no other performers in the room. This technique also allows the engineer to concentrate on getting the right tone for each instrument one at a time.

One drawback to this method is that it can be difficult to achieve the same level of energy in the performance as would be achieved by recording an entire group at once. Performers often feel awkward or self-conscious when recording their part individually and do not have the energy of the other members of the group to play off of. This is when the engineer or producer's ability to get the best possible performance out of the musicians is very important.

See also *Overdubbing*.

Bi-Amplification

We use the term bi-amplification to describe a situation where a full-range speaker or speaker system has its high-frequency driver (tweeter) and low frequency driver (woofer) powered by separate amplifiers. This is achieved by running the signal into a crossover circuit which separates it into two frequency ranges and routes each of those frequency ranges into its own amplifier. Bi-amplified speakers provide a cleaner overall sound and also have the benefit that if one frequency range begins to distort due to excessive signal level, the other range will not be affected.

Most models of active (self-powered) studio monitors currently available are bi-amplified.

Bi-Directional Pickup Pattern

A bi-directional, or figure-8, microphone picks up equally from the front and the back while rejecting sound from the sides, top, and bottom (see *Fig. 11*). This means that the angle of most rejection is 90° from the front or back of the microhone. On most bi-directional mics, the front side of the mic gives a brighter sound than the rear, though the volume is equal.

Unlike uni-directional microphones, bi-directional microphones are not subject to proximity effect, an increased bass response that occurs as the mic is placed closer to the sound source.

A bi-directional mic may be a good choice for miking two vocalists at the same time, adding some of the sound of the room to a recording, or avoiding proximity effect.

See also *Microphones, Pickup Pattern*.

Binaural Miking

The word binaural means "two ears". Binaural miking refers to stereo microphone placement that is meant to approximate our ears. This can be achieved through careful placement of a pair of microphones or by use of a specially designed binaural microphone array. There have even been cases where

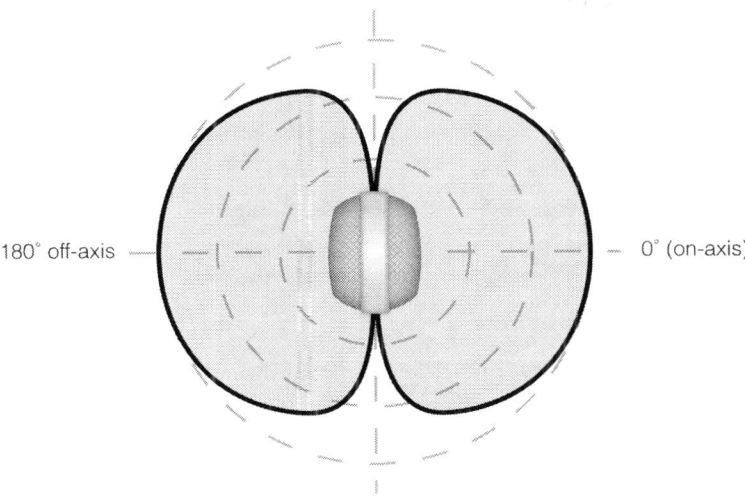

Figure 11: Pickup Pattern of a Bi-Directional (Figure-8) Microphone

engineers have placed specially designed microphones within their own ears and recorded from them.

One of the simplest and most popular binaural miking techniques is called ORTF (an acronym for Office de Radiodiffusion-Télévision Française) for the French broadcasting commission who developed it. This technique uses two cardioid microphones placed 7" (17 cm) apart at an angle of 110° (see *ORTF*).

Techniques such as ORTF approximate the spacing and angle of our ears but do not account for the fact that the listener's head blocks sound from reaching the ear on the opposite side. There are a variety of binaural microphones on the market that use a head sized disc or sphere between two microphones to simulate this acoustic shrouding. Some manufacturers have taken this a step further and incorporate an actual dummy head with the microphones in the ears. In some cases the ears even have pinnae (the outer ear) to take advantage of the way they affect our hearing.

Binaural miking has the distinct advantage that mic placement can be as simple as moving around the room as the performer plays, finding the spot where you think is sounds best, and putting the binaural mic (or ORTF pair) there.

See also *Microphones*.

Bit Depth

Digital recording is achieved by converting analog audio signal into binary code. Binary code is a numerical made up of a series of ons and offs (or signal and no-signal) which are usually represented as ones and zeros. Each of these ones and zeros is referred to as a bit, and these bits form digital words. Bit depth refers to the length of each digital word.

Digital recordings consist of a series of static samples which are played back rapidly to create sound (see *Fig. 12*). This is very similar to the way motion pictures are made up of static photos shown fast enough to fool our eyes into thinking the picture is moving. A CD has a sample rate of 44.1 kHz which means that it has 44,100 digital samples for every second of audio.

The bit depth of a CD recording is 16-bit which means that each of those digital samples is made up of 16 ones and zeros (see *Fig. 13*). This means that for every second of audio, a CD has 705,600 ones and zeros (44,100 × 16) for each channel (left and right). That's a grand total of 1,411,200 bits (ones and zeros) per second of audio.

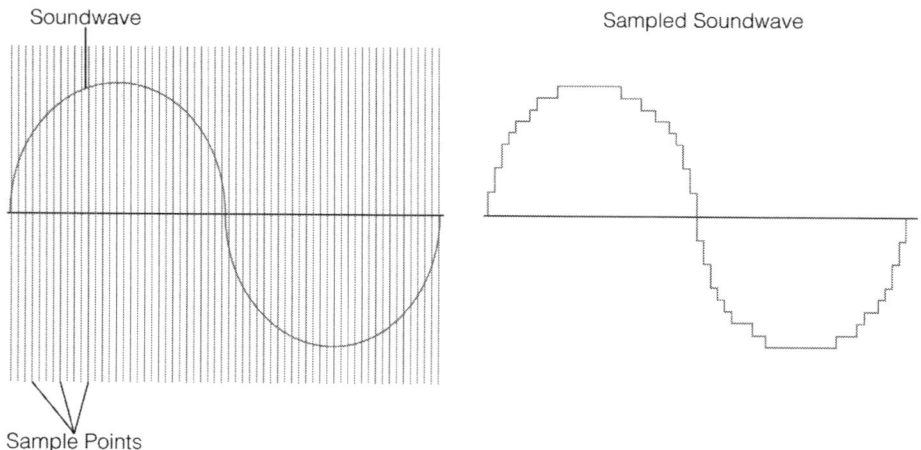

Figure 12: Digital Sampling of a Sound Wave

DVD audio uses a sample rate of 96 kHz at a bit depth of 24-bits. So, a string of code for DVD audio has a 24-bit word 96,000 times per second per channel (a total of 2,304,000 ones and zeros per second per channel, and a combined total of 4,608,000 bits for every second of audio).

The Practical Results of Bit Depth

There are two practical benefits of higher bit depth. First, the longer digital word allows for a more precise measurement of the amplitude of the signal at the time of the sample. This means a more accurate recording.

A 16-Bit Digital Word: 1001100001001101

A 24-Bit Digital Word: 011001001101001001000100

Figure 13: Digital Words

The second reason is that any errors that occur during recording or playback will be less significant. If there is an error resulting in two of the bits in a 16-bit recording being completely lost then 1/8 of the sample is missing. In a 24-bit recording, losing two bits would only be 1/12 of the sample. Fewer errors effectively means less noise in a recording.

The downside of using a higher bit depth is greatly increased file size. As hard drives and other digital storage mediums get cheaper, however, this becomes less and less of an issue.

Most engineers will choose to record using the highest bit depth and sample rate available even if the recording is eventually going to be released on a medium that does not support it. This allows them to somewhat "future-proof" their recordings so they can take advantage of more advanced mediums down the road.

Blumlein Technique

The Blumlein technique (named after Alan Dower Blumlein who pioneered stereo miking techniques in the 1930s) uses a coincident pair (two mics placed together) of bi-directional microphones. These microphones are placed one above the other with their pickup patterns at 90° to each other and 45° to the sound source (see *Fig. 14*). With the microphones in this pattern, one microphone will pick up the left of the sound source and the back right of the room while the other picks up the right of the sound source and the back left of the room. The two signals are then panned hard left and right.

See also *Stereo Miking*.

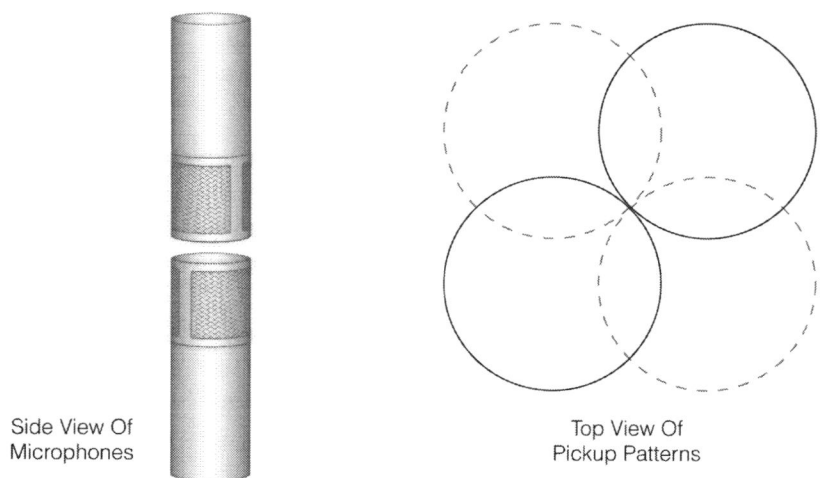

Figure 14: Blumlein Microphone Placement

Bouncing

Bouncing, or ping-ponging, is the technique of taking multiple tracks and recording them together onto a single available track in order to free up the initial tracks to be recorded over (see *Fig. 15*).

For example, if we had a 4-track recording unit and wanted to record six distinct instruments. We could begin by recording the first three of these instruments each onto a different track. We would then do any editing or processing we would like to these tracks and set their relative volume levels. Next, we would take these three tracks, route them all to the unused fourth track, and record a mix of the three onto it. We can now erase the first three tracks and record three more instruments, effectively recording six tracks on a 4-track recording unit. This process can be repeated if necessary to further increase the number of tracks we can record.

There are two main concerns that come from the act of bouncing. The first is that once a set of tracks has been bounced we no longer have control of them individually. Any changes we make to the bounced track will affect all instruments that have been recorded onto it. This means that a variety of mixing decisions have to be made before the rest of the tracks have even been recorded, which can be a big limitation.

The second problem with bouncing is only really a big concern in the area of analog recording. This is the problem of quality degradation as the tracks are re-recorded from one track to another. Each generation of bounce will cause further loss of quality. In the realm of digital recording this is not really an issue as bouncing from one track to another will theoretically result in a perfect digital copy.

Figure 15: Bouncing Tracks on a 4-Track Recording

Boundary Mic

The boundary mic, or PZM (Pressure Zone Microphone), is a flat microphone that picks up reflections from the surface (or "boundary") on which it is placed. They can be placed on a table, wall, the soundboard of a piano, or any other flat surface. Because of this unique positioning, boundary mics have a hemispherical pickup pattern, meaning they pick up everything to one side of the surface on which they are placed and tend to give significant "room sound".

The term PZM is a trademark of Crown International, though it sees more common usage than the term boundary mic.

See also *Microphones*.

Buss

A buss (also spelled bus) is a signal path used to connect one or more channels of a mixer to a common destination such as another channel (for submixing) or an output. If channels can be thought of as traveling vertically on a mixing board, then busses can be thought of as traveling horizontally.

Basic mixers have a single stereo buss that goes to its main outputs. Channels can be removed from this buss by using the mute switch. Larger mixers have multiple busses, allowing for more complex signal routing (such as routing multiple combinations of channels to different destinations).

Fig. 16 shows a live mix that uses two stereo busses. The main buss (marked here as 1-2) goes to the front of house to be heard by the audience and has all of

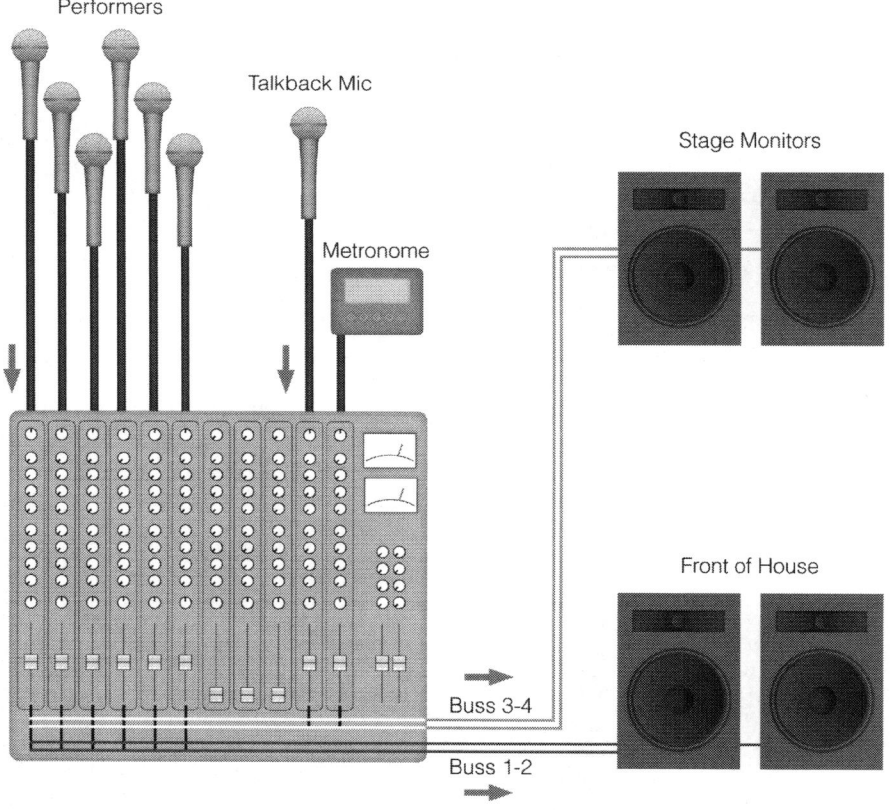

Figure 16: A Mix Using Two Stereo Busses

the performers in the mix. The other buss (marked 3-4) goes to the stage monitors for the performers. In addition to the performer's own sound, the stage monitors also include the click track and the engineer's talkback mic, allowing him or her to communicate with the performers without going through the main speakers.

Fig. 17 shows 3 stereo busses being used to feed signal into a 4-track recorder and to mix the signals as they come out into a stereo mix. Note that on the stereo pairs being used as an input mixer, the channels are panned hard left and right in order to have just one channel per buss.

See also *Mixing Board, Signal Flow*.

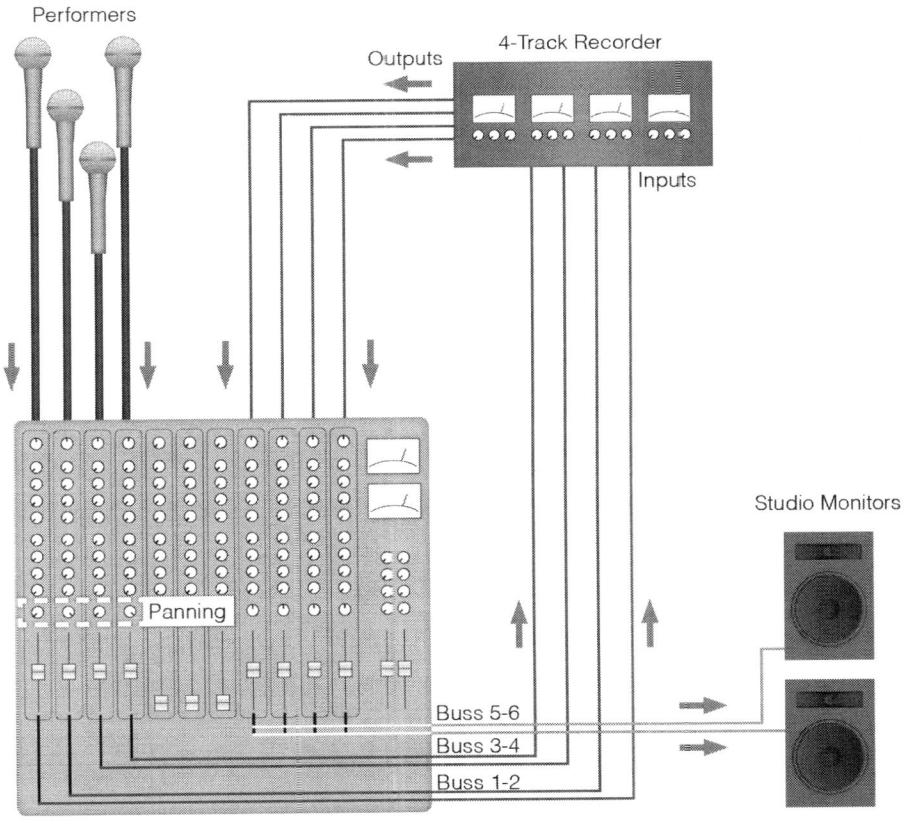

Figure 17: An Input Mix and an Output Mix for a 4-Track Recorder

Buss Assign

On mixers with multiple busses, each channel will have a buss assign area (usually located at the bottom of the channel by the volume fader) allowing the engineer to select which busses each channel is routed to. The buss assign usually consists of a set of buttons, each sending the channel's signal to a different buss or stereo pair of busses. When busses are only assignable in stereo pairs, a channel can be routed to a single buss by turning the pan knob all the way to one side. In these situations, panning the signal to the left will usually send it to the odd-numbered busses while panning right will send it to the even-numbered busses.

See also *Buss, Channel Strip, Mixing Board.*

Cannon Jack

See *XLR.*

Cardioid Pickup Pattern

Cardioid is a unidirectional microphone pickup patten that is named for its slightly heart-like shape. Cardioid mics are most sensitive directly in front, somewhat less sensitive from the side, and reject the most sound from directly behind (see *Fig. 18*).

To take full advantage of this pickup patten, the desired sound source should be placed directly in front of the microphone, and any undesirable sounds should be placed directly behind. That being said, placing the sound source at a slight angle to a cardioid mic will alter the mic's tone and so should be experimented with when choosing mic placement. This is referred to as off-axis miking, and its results will vary depending on the mic, instrument, and room.

See also *Microphones, Pickup Pattern.*

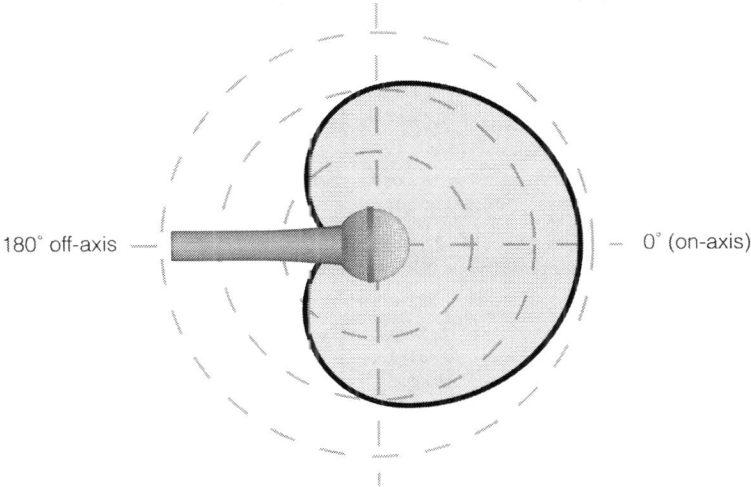

Figure 18: Cardioid Pickup Pattern

Chamber Reverb

Chamber reverb is usually created by playing a signal through a speaker placed in a highly reflective room (often tiled) and rerecording the sound through a series of microphones placed facing different directions in different parts of the room. The varied microphone placements result in a wide variety of reflections. The resulting recording is usually quite natural sounding.

In the home studio we often have a wide variety of spaces we can play with to make temporary echo chambers including bathrooms, stairwells, and basements. Experimenting with this technique in various spaces can add depth and interest to your recordings.

Les Paul created a famous design for a reverb chamber that consists of multiple trapezoid-shaped rooms, each with a microphone and a speaker placed in different positions.

Many digital reverb units will have a setting that is meant to approximate the sound of a chamber reverb.

See also *Reverberation*.

Channel

When referring to a mixing board, a channel is the input and signal path for a single source. See *Channel Strip*.

In the context of MIDI, a channel is a discrete stream. of MINI information. A MIDI file consists of multiple channels. See *MIDI*.

Channel Strip

A channel strip is the signal path taken by a single input on a mixing board or recording unit. A basic channel strip consists of a preamplifier, an equalizer, and volume control, and will often have routing controls including auxiliary sends, insert points, and buss assignment.

Fig. 19 shows a fairly standard channel strip. Signal travels from top to bottom, and all controls (with the exception of the aux send as noted below) are placed in the order in which they sit in the signal path. Adjusting a control on the channel strip will affect the signal reaching all controls below it and none above (e.g., the equalizer does not affect the preamp, but the gain, at the top of the strip, affects everything else).

The elements of the channel strip (as shown in *Fig. 19*) are listed and described below. For further explanation, please see the entries indicated for each control.

1. Gain/Trim: This provides control over the preamp. It is a means of controlling how "hot" your signal is. It is best to get as much signal at this stage as possible without the signal clipping (distorting). Some channel strips will have a "clip light" to indicate when the signal is beginning to distort. See *Preamplifier*.

2. Insert Point: This allows you to send the entire signal to an external device (such as a compressor or

Figure 19: A Channel Strip

equalizer) and return it to the channel on the same cable (called an insert cable or a send/retur cable). See *Insert*.

3. Aux Sends: These knobs control how much signal is sent to an auxiliary output. An auxiliary send is used for parallel effects (effects where the processed signal is blended with the original, dry signal), or for creating separate monitor mixes. When using an aux send for effects, the aux output is plugged into the input of the effect unit and the output of the effect is plugged into the auxiliary return. See *Auxiliary Send*.

4. Pre-fader Select: This button controls whether the sends are "pre-fader" or "post-fader". If sends are pre-fader, then the master fader will not affect the output of the send (better for creating monitor mixes). If a send is "post-fader" then the output of the send will go up or down with the master fader (better for effects). See *Auxiliary Send*.

5. Equalizer: Like the equalizer on your stereo, these knobs control the tonal qualities of your signal. Each knob will cut or boost the frequency range specified. See *Equalizer*.

6. Pan: The pan, or panorama, control allows you to place the signal anywhere in the stereo field by adjusting the amount of the signal that goes to either speaker. Turning this knob all the way to one side will send the signal only to one speaker. See *Stereo Mixing*.

7. Mute: As the name suggests, this removes the channel from the mix and from any post-fader sends. This will not affect pre-fader sends.

8. Buss Assignment: These allow you to choose where you send your signal. Busses are most frequently used to select outputs but can allow for more complex routing as well, such as sub mixes. See *Buss*.

9. Fader: This controls the volume for the channel going into its assigned buss.

See also *Mixing Board*.

Chorus

Chorus is an effect achieved by blending a copy of a signal, which has been slightly delayed and detuned, with the original sound. The difference of timing and pitch between the two signals gives the illusion of multiple instruments playing in unison. When used subtly, chorus can add richness and depth to a sound, and is popular for acoustic instruments, clean electric guitar, and even voice. When used more heavily, chorus creates an ethereal, washy effect.

Click Track

A click track is a metronome for the performers to play to. The term click track originated from the metronome sound being recorded onto a free track on the tape, though on most modern workstations it is a function of the workstation itself.

Recording to a click track assures consistent timing in the performance. Editing is greatly aided when recording to a click track because it adds the ability to easily and seamlessly copy and paste one part of a track to another (such as duplicating the first chorus to replace a sloppier second).

One concern when using a click track is bleed from a performer's headphones into the microphones being used to record them. This is particularly problematic when recording vocals since the headphones are directly in front of the microphone. Closed-back headphones can help to minimize the amount of click track that bleeds out, however vocalists are often uncomfortable singing with closed back headphones because it limits their ability to hear themselves naturally in a room. The close proximity of the speaker to the singer's ear when using headphones can also play tricks on the vocalist's perception of sound, causing problems with the pitch of his or her singing. Removing one ear of the headphones from their ear can help to counteract this problem but can increase click track bleed

Many recording devices allow a choice of tones to be used for the beat of the click track. Lower and mellower tones will generally bleed less but can be harder to hear amid other instruments. Ultimately this choice comes down to the best trade-off for the performer and the song.

Clipping

When the volume, or amplitude, of a signal gets too high for the circuit it is passing through, the top and bottom of the waveform will be cut off, resulting in distortion. This is called clipping. *Fig. 20* shows a simple waveform as well as the result that clipping has on that waveform.

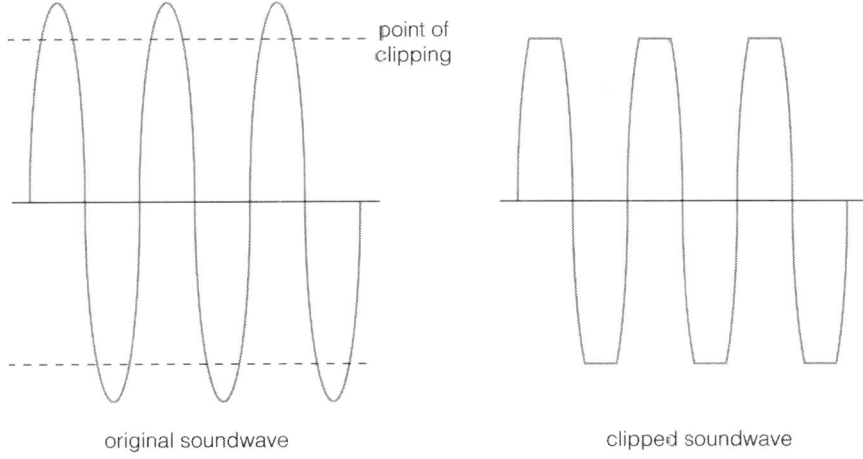

Figure 20: Clipping

Allowing a signal to clip slightly when recording onto magnetic tape can result in a gritty or growly sound. This is called "soft clipping" and is sometimes intentionally used when recording rock bass or drums. Soft clipping is unique to analog tape, however, as clipping in the digital realm is much more destructive.

Coincident Pair

A coincident pair is a pair of microphones placed together to create a stereo image. Stereo miking techniques that use a coincident pair include X-Y, ORTF, Blumlein, and Mid-Side techniques. The opposite of a coincident pair is a spaced pair.

See also *Appendix C: Microphone Placement Guide*.

Compansion

The compansion process is a form of noise reduction often used in wireless technologies. Upward compression is used on the signal before it is transmitted (the volume of quieter sounds is increased to make them closer to the loud sounds), then the receiver uses downward expansion to return the signal to its original dynamics. The benefit of this is that any noise that was added to the signal during the transmission is then reduced in volume during the process of downward expansion (see *Fig. 21*).

See also *Compression, Expansion.*

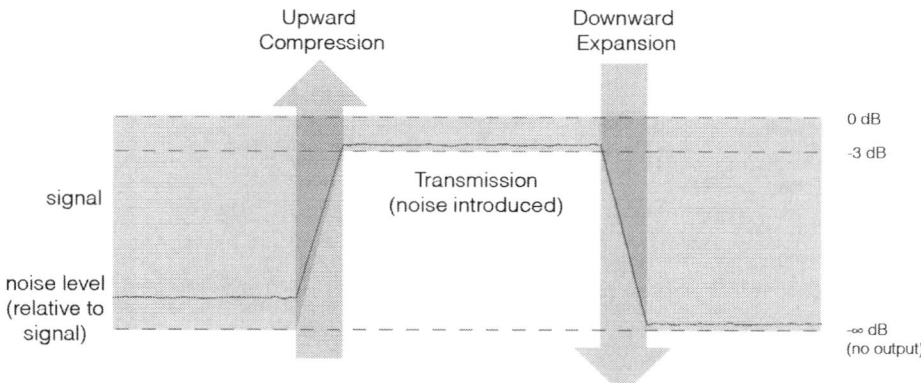

Figure 21: The Compansion Process

Composite Track

A composite track is a track made up of parts from multiple different takes. To do this, the performer records multiple takes to a click track or previously recorded bed tracks. The engineer then goes through the performance, copying and pasting the best parts of each take onto a new track, creating one take that is better than any of the originals.

Compression

Compression is a way of controlling the dynamics (the difference between the loudest parts and the quietest parts) of a signal. This is done by reducing the volume of the louder parts of the signal, which allows the volume of the whole signal to be increased accordingly (see *Fig. 22*). The result is more overall volume without the signal distorting at the louder points.

Some find compression easier to understand if they think of it as an automated volume control. It reduces the output during volume peaks, resulting in a more consistent output volume.

The reasons for using compression include, among others, reducing the risk of distortion while tracking, dealing with an overly dynamic performance (i.e., a vocalist who is too loud in the loud parts and too quiet in the soft parts), making an instrument sit more evenly in the mix (such as percussion), fattening up a sound, and increasing perceived volume.

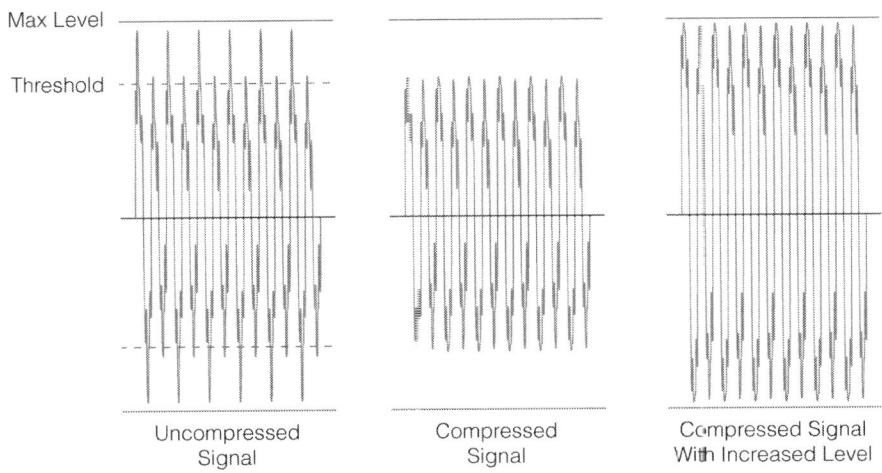

Figure 22: Compression Reducing Peaks

Compressors are referred to as "transparent" if they have little effect on the instrument's tone and "non-transparent" if there is a noticeable change in tonal quality. Depending on the application, an engineer may choose one style or the other. When budget is a concern, a transparent compressor can be a more versatile choice for the home studio.

While compression is an extremely useful tool, and is used extensively in popular music styles, it should be used carefully. Too much, or poorly implemented, compression can rob a performance of its natural dynamics.

It is also important to be aware that when the overall volume of a signal is raised after compression, any noise in the signal will be increased as well. Therefore, every decibel of compression will add a decibel of noise. This is less of a concern when recording with digital equipment, which does not have the self-noise that we experience with tape, but computer fans, traffic, heating systems, and other ambient noise from the recording environment will become more prominent when compression is used.

The Encyclopedia of Home Recording

Threshold and Ratio

The threshold is the volume level at which the compressor begins to work. Once the threshold has been exceeded, all signal above threshold will be reduced according to the compression ratio, which determines the ratio of input signal to output signal. For example, if we have a ratio of 2:1, for every 2 decibels (dB) of input above the threshold we will get 1 decibel of output (see *Fig. 23*).

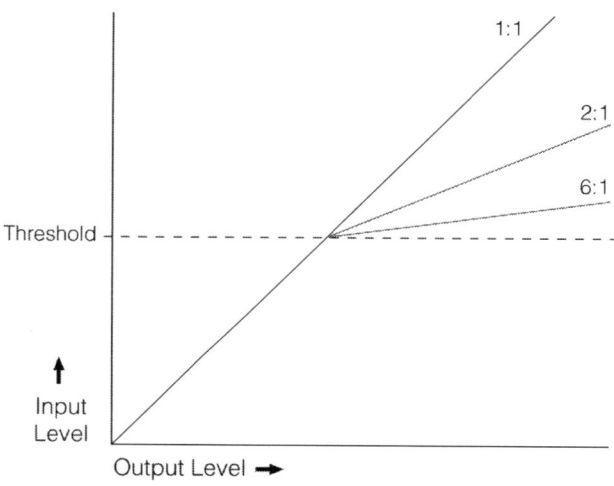

Figure 23: Compression – Threshold and Ratio

For the sake of illustration, here is an example using round numbers: If we have the threshold set to begin compressing at 2 dB of input signal and have set the compression ratio to 4:1, then 6 dB of input would result in 3 dB of output (2 dB are below the threshold, and the 4 dB above the threshold have been reduced to 1 dB).

A compressor with a ratio of 10:1 or greater is called a limiter because the out signal will only ever barely exceed the threshold.

Attack and Release: Controlling the Acoustic Envelope

The attack control on a compressor affects how quickly, once the threshold is exceeded, the compressor begins to work. A slow attack will allow transient peaks (short bursts of sound) to pass by without triggering the compressor, whereas a fast attack will catch them.

The release controls how quickly compression stops once the signal has fallen below the threshold again. A slow release time will allow dips in volume to go by without the compressor dropping out and in again.

One advantage of the attack and release controls is the way they allow us to control the envelope of the sound (see *Acoustic Envelope*). By carefully setting the attack and release, we can manipulate the acoustic envelope to increase or decrease perceived sustain and accentuate or smooth the attack of the instrument (see *Fig. 24*).

The first example in *Fig. 24* shows how a long attack time and a long release time will compress just the sustain of the instrument, leaving the transient peak of the sound unaffected. The second example shows a short attack time and a short release time compressing the transient and not the sustain of the sound.

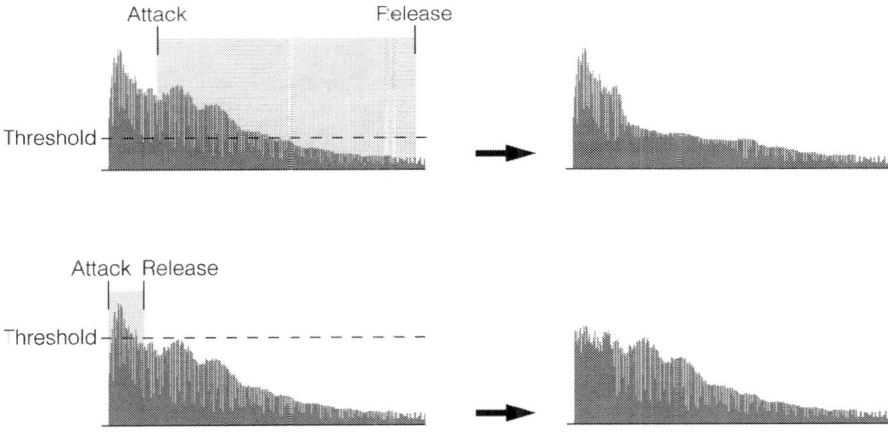

Figure 24: Compression – Attack and Release

Knee

Knee is a frequently misunderstood aspect of compression. Knee refers to how quickly the compressor reaches its full compression ratio once it has engaged. With hard-knee compression, once the compressor kicks in, it will compress at its full ratio almost immediately. With a soft-knee compressor there is a transition period as the compressor smoothly eases into full compression (see *Fig. 25*).

Knee is frequently confused with attack time. Here is an analogy that may make the difference more clear. Consider a car driving at 50 kph that needs to slow to 30 kph. Once the instruction is given to the driver to slow down, there

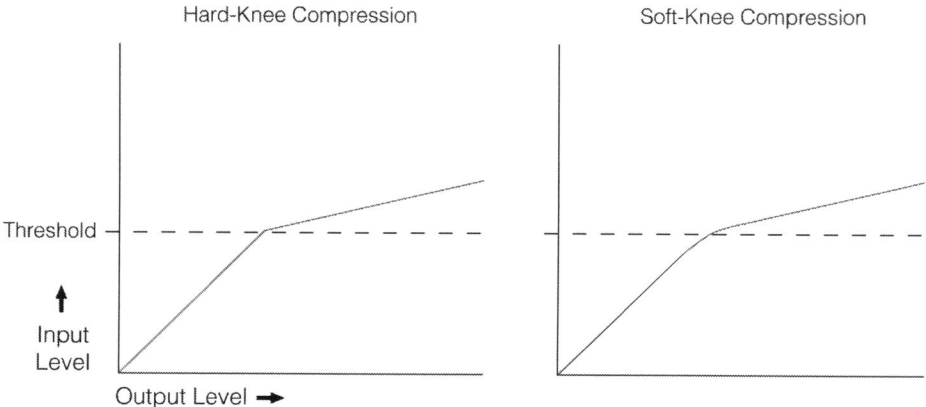

Figure 25: Compression – Knee

will be two factors that will affect how long it takes for the car's speed to reach 30 kph: the driver's reaction time (the attack time on a compressor) and the car's rate of deceleration (the knee on a compressor). So, in this analogy, hard-knee compression would be a car that slowed from 50 kph to 30 kph in the blink of an eye, while soft-knee compression would gradually slow until the car had reached 30 kph.

As a basic rule of thumb, hard-knee compression tends to be preferred for rhythmic, staccato instruments (such as percussion), and soft-knee compression is more often used for smooth, legato instruments (such as voice or violin).

Side Chain

Some compressors have a second input called the side chain. The side chain allows us to trigger a compressor with a signal other that the signal being compressed. For example, if a DJ wished to have the music she is playing reduce in volume whenever she speaks (a technique called "ducking"), she can run the music through a compressor and route a copy of the signal from her mic into the side chain input of the compressor. The result is that an increase in the signal from her mic will trigger the compressor, reducing the volume of the music running through it.

Limiters

A limiter is a compressor with a compression ratio of 10:1 or higher. With such heavy compression, they can be thought of as somewhat of a brick wall for sound since the output signal will not move far above the threshold. Limiters can be very useful to avoid clipping during tracking, mixdown, and mastering.

Dynamic Range

Dynamic range is a measurement of the difference between the quietest possible sound (silence) and the loudest possible sound that can be handled by a given medium. The potential dynamic range of music in an acoustic environment is as high as 120 decibels (dB). The dynamic range of a CD is closer to 80 dB, FM radio is only about 50 dB, and AM radio a mere 30 dB. With these severe limitations on dynamic range, compression becomes necessary in order to allow the changing dynamics in music to be heard.

Another reason for limiting the dynamic range of a recording is consideration of the listening environment. Many people listen to music in environments with a lot of background noise, such as in their car or at work. In these situations quieter passages will be masked by the background noise. Careful compression can be used to reduce this problem.

Multi-Band Compression

Multi-band compression breaks the signal into different frequency ranges and compresses each range separately. This is a bit of a middle-ground between compression and equalization. The signal is broken up into frequency bands, just like with an equalizer, but rather than boosting or attenuating the volume of these bands like an equalizer, a multi-band compressor applies compression to the bands separately.

Multi-band compressors are most commonly used in the mastering process, when instruments can no longer be affected separately. Because the frequency bands are compressed separately, an overly dynamic instrument in one range will not affect the amount of compression in other ranges.

Compression and Mastering

During the mastering process, compression is usually added to the completed mix. This is done with the dynamic limitations of different mediums in mind (as mentioned above), but is also used to increase the perceived volume of the mix. In modern music there is a bit of an unspoken competition to make louder mixes, the reasoning being that if your song is just a bit louder than any other on the radio, it will be noticed more.

The advertising industry uses this same technique, which is why television commercials are often far louder that the programs themselves.

When To Compress

It has been said that the sound of modern music is the sound of compression. By the time we hear a sound in a modern recording it has generally been compressed multiple times.

During the tracking process, a little bit of compression can act as a safety net, preventing the signal from clipping. This can save a good take that may otherwise have been unusable due to distortion.

Depending on the style of music, instruments may be compressed again (sometimes quite heavily) during the mixing process in order to have them all sit nicely in the mix. This is also a first chance to get the overall volume of the mix higher.

Once the track is mixed, it will usually be compressed again during the mastering process to further increase its perceived volume. This needs to be done carefully as it is very easy at this point to lose the natural dynamics of the song.

If the track is then broadcast over the radio, it is compressed again (rather heavily) in order to deal with the limited dynamic range of radio broadcasting.

Significant amounts of compression have become not only accepted but expected in modern recordings.

Compression Ratio

The compression ratio sets the relationship between input volume and output volume (above the threshold) on a compressor. So, for example, if we have a ratio of 2:1, for every 2 decibels (dB) of input above the threshold we will get 1 decibel of output. If we have a ratio of 6:1, then 12 dB of input will equal 2 dB of output (see *Fig. 26*).

Also see *Compression*.

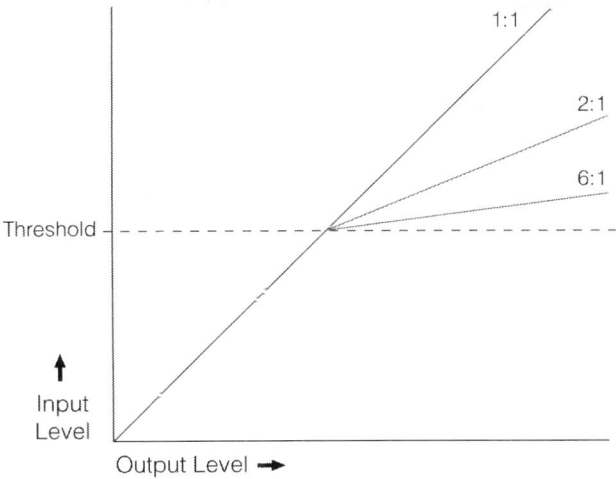

Figure 26: Compression Ratio

Condenser Microphone

A condenser microphone is a microphone that works through the process of electrical induction. The capsule of a condenser mic is made up of a positively charged, fixed plate and a negatively charged, movable diaphragm. As sound pressure hits the movable diaphragm, it moves closer to and farther from the plate, creating the electrical flux that makes up the microphone's output (see *Fig. 27*).

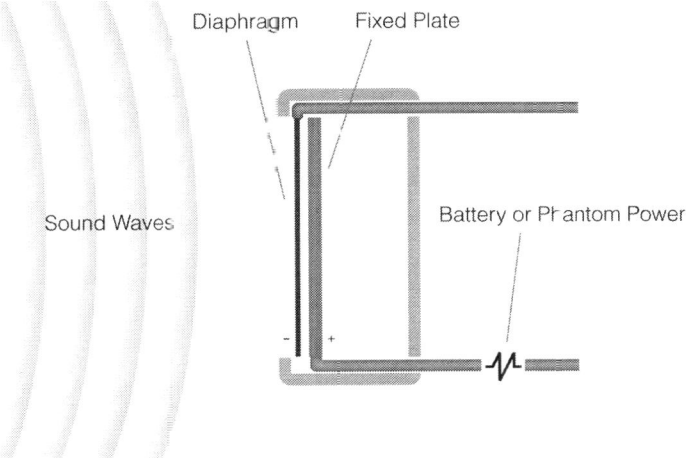

Figure 27: Capsule of a Typical Condenser Microphone

Condenser mics are more sensitive than dynamic microphones and tend to pick up more of the acoustics of the room it is being used in. In the recording studio, condenser mics tend to be favored, particularly for acoustic instruments, vocals, and room mics. Condenser mics are not as rugged as dynamic microphones, so care should be taken if they are going to be used for miking high sound pressure levels such as those from electric guitar amps and close-miked drums.

Because the capsule of the mic gives off a very low signal, a small amplifier is built into condenser mics to boost their output to an acceptable level. This amplifier requires power to function, which can be supplied from one of two sources: some condenser microphones allow for a battery to be mounted inside, but most rely on phantom power.

Phantom power is a current that is supplied through an XLR microphone cable from the mixer or preamplifier. In situations where a mixer or preamp does not have phantom power capability, a phantom power supply can be purchased at a reasonably low cost and is then placed between the mic and the mixer.

See also *Microphones, Phantom Power*.

Control Room

In a recording studio, the control room is the room in which the engineer works. This room will generally contain the mixing board, most of the recording equipment, and in some cases a couch or two for the producer and/or band members who are not currently recording to sit on during the session. In most studios, the control room will be separated from the live room by a large window, allowing the engineer to have visual contact with the performers.

It is important that the control room be as acoustically isolated as possible from the live room in order for the engineer to be able to hear the sounds being recorded without hearing them acoustically.

Because the control room is a critical listening environment in which all decisions about a recording are made, great care is usually taken to treat the acoustics of the control room to provide an effective mixing environment. The control room should be symmetrical to the left and right of the mix position because any asymmetry will affect the engineer's perception of stereo imaging. Reverberation within the control room can also influence the engineer's decisions, so acoustic foam and diffusers are usually placed strategically within the space to ensure it is not too reflective but also not entirely devoid of natural reverberation.

See also *Isolation Room, Live Room, Mix Position*.

Control Surface

A control surface is a device that controls digital recording software in a tactile manner. Most control surfaces look like mixing boards with a series of knobs and faders, each of which can be assigned to control various software functions. Some control surfaces have motorized faders which move on their own when automated volume changes are played out in the software. Many engineers and home recordists prefer to use a control surface because they find it more satisfying to manipulate physical faders and knobs than a mouse.

Convolution Reverb

Convolution reverbs are digital reverbs that reproduce the acoustic behavior of actual environments. To create a convolution reverb, a control signal is played in an acoustic space, and the resulting reverberation is recorded. The timing and frequency content of the resulting reflections are then analyzed and programmed into the convolution reverb. When the reverb is applied to a signal, it mathematically reproduces the effect of the sample environment.

See also *Reverberation*.

Crossfade

Crossfading is the act of fading one signal out (reducing its volume until it reaches silence) while simultaneously fading another signal in (bringing its volume up from silence until it reaches the desired level).

When editing together two different takes, or two different audio segments of the same instrument, we often hear a click caused by the incomplete waveforms at the point where one transitions into the other. This can usually be remedied by crossfading them, making the splice far more subtle.

The term crossfade is used slightly differently when referring to a DJ mixer. DJ mixers have a crossfader that allows the DJ to fade smoothly from one channel of the mixer to another. While the process is essentially the same, the application differs from that of editing.

Crossover

A crossover is a circuit used to separate a signal into different frequency bands. The frequency that marks the cutoff between bands is called a crossover point. The response at the end of each band slopes off, overlapping slightly (see *Fig. 28*).

Crossover circuits are used in loudspeaker setups to send each frequency range to the appropriate speaker, and in multi-band compressors, they allow different frequency bands to be compressed independently of each other.

See also *Multi-Band Compression, Pass Filter*.

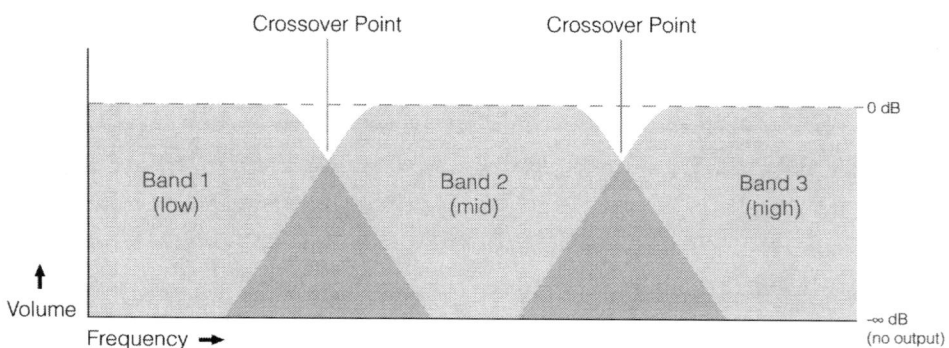

Figure 28: 3-Band Crossover

Crosstalk

Crosstalk is when signal from one channel or track bleeds into an adjoining channel or track. This is usually the result of poor wiring in a mixer or other piece of equipment. Crosstalk can sometimes occur when recording onto analog tape if poor quality tape is being used.

Cue Mix

A cue mix, or monitor mix, is a separate mix to be sent to the performer's headphones during recording. Creating a cue mix allows the engineer to continue to hear the instrument in context of the main mix while providing the performer with the mix that will be most comfortable for them and elicit the best performance.

Cycle

Sound travels by moving air particles closer together (compression) and farther apart (rarefaction) in continuing waves. A cycle is the period from the air's equilibrium point (when air pressure is the same as during silence), through its greatest points of compression and rarefaction back to equilibrium (see *Fig. 29*). The number of cycles a sound wave achieves per second is measured in hertz (Hz) and is called its frequency. Every time the frequency of a sound doubles, the pitch of the sound is raised one octave.

See also *Frequency, Appendix A: The Basics Of Sound*.

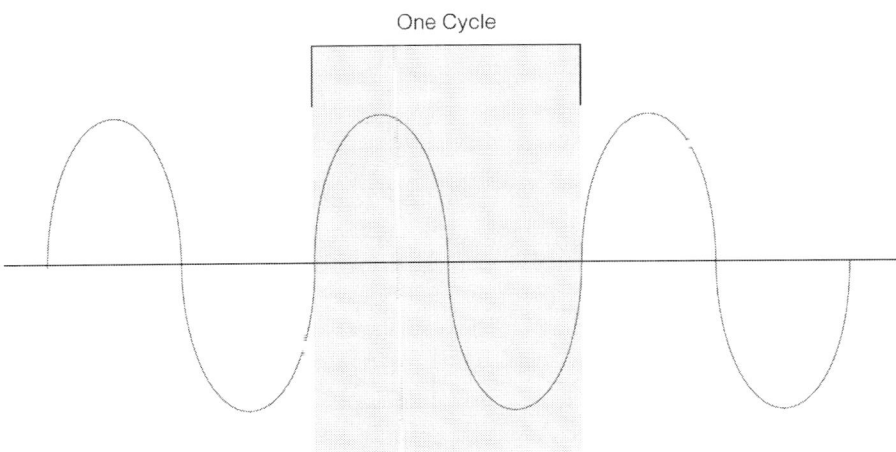

Figure 29: The Cycle of a Soundwave

D/A

See *Digital to Analog Converter*.

DAT

The DAT or Digital Audio Tape was developed by Sony in the mid-1980s. It is a compact, magnetic-tape-based stereo digital recording media that supports recording at 16-bits with sample rates of 32, 44.1, or 48 kHz. Primarily used for mastering and location recording, the DAT saw much less use once CD-R became an affordable media. It fell into relative obscurity when portable hard-disk and flash-memory based recorders started to appear on the market.

When DAT was first developed it saw significant resistance from the record industry who feared that a consumer product capable of making perfect copies of commercially recorded albums would cause a significant rise in piracy. The end result of this push back was the Serial Copy Management System, or SCMS (often referred to as "scums"). SCMS provided copy protection by allowing the manufacturer of a digital recording to assign it one of three copy statuses: copy allowed, copy prohibited, and copy once (a copy can be made, but the resulting copy will be copy prohibited).

DAW

The term DAW, or Digital Audio Workstation, describes any digital recording setup, but it is most commonly used when referring to standalone, all-in-one recording units. A basic computer-based DAW consists of a computer, recording software, and an audio interface to get sound in and out of the computer.

There are many standalone DAWs available on the market that have all the necessary pieces included in one unit. These units will generally record onto hard disk, though some smaller, more portable units record onto removable media such as compact flash cards. It has become very common for standalone DAWs to include CD burners and basic mastering capabilities, allowing the user to take the project from start to finish within the same unit.

Standalone DAWs have two main benefits. The first is portability; with everything in one box they are easy to take to any recording location. The second is stability; because their processors have only one dedicated function (unlike computer-based systems, which also perform a variety of other tasks), they virtually never crash.

Software-based recording also has advantages. If you already have a computer it can be a more affordable solution than a standalone DAW. Software based systems also allow greater flexibility for upgrading. Software plug-ins can be added to an existing setup to add functionality or to improve quality. As well, the computer and interface can be upgraded separately. With a standalone DAW, upgrading generally means trading in for a new unit.

dBm/dBu/dBv/dBV

A decibel is a measurement of sound pressure, and as such it only really has meaning in an acoustic environment. In order to allow us to translate decibels into the electrical world of signal processing, three standards of reference have been developed: dBm (1 decibel = 1 milliwatt), dBu/dBv (1 decibel = 0.775 volts), and dBV (1 decibel = 1 volt).

Decay

The term decay can be used in a couple of different contexts in recording: a segment of a sound's acoustic envelope, or a control on a reverb or delay unit. Both are covered below.

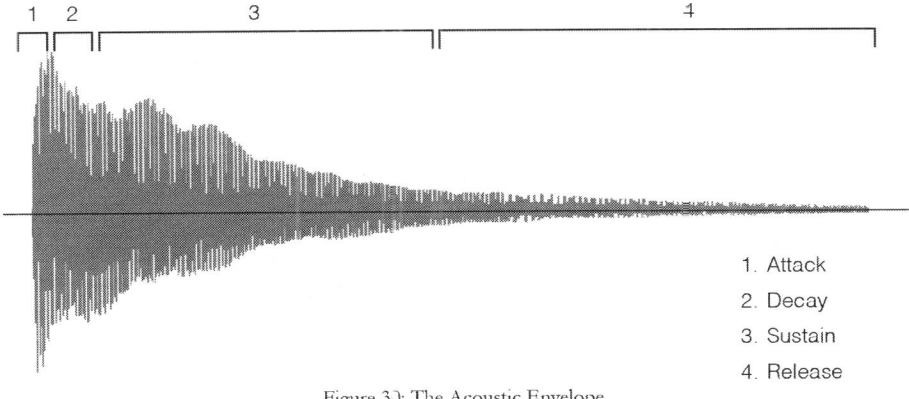

Figure 30: The Acoustic Envelope

Decay (Acoustic Envelope)

When referring to the acoustic envelope (how a sound's volume changes over time), decay refers to the quick drop in volume that occurs after the initial attack of the sound (see *Fig. 30*). After the decay, the volume level plateaus into the sustain of the sound.

See also *Acoustic Envelope*.

Decay (Reverb/Delay)

The decay control on a reverb or delay unit will affect how long the signal will reverberate or repeat before fading into silence.

See also *Delay*, *Reverberation*.

Decca Tree

The Decca Tree is a stereo recording technique used mainly for recording orchestras and was developed in the 1950s by engineers at Decca Records. The Decca Tree traditionally uses a special T-shaped mic stand suspended above the conductor's head, though the same effect can be achieved using three mic stands with booms. On the T-shaped stand are 3 cardioid microphones facing left, right, and center which are then panned to match their configuration (see *Fig. 31*).

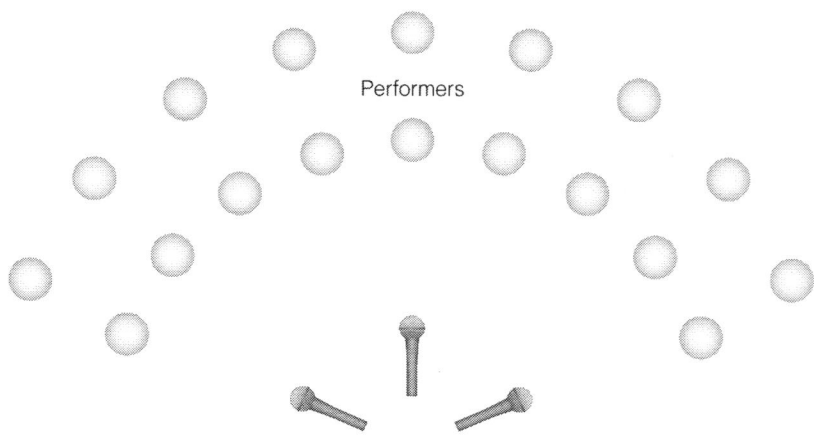

Figure 31: Decca Tree Mic Placement (Overhead View)

There are no fixed measurements for the distance between the microphones, but somewhere in the range of 5–7 feet is common. The mics are usually placed closer together for smaller orchestras and farther apart for larger ones.

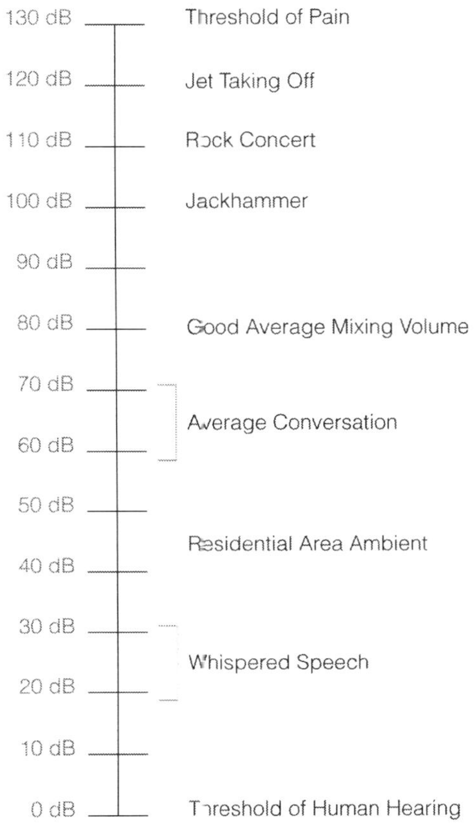

Decibel

The decibel (dB) is a unit of measurement used to measure differences in relative intensity. For our purposes here, the decibel is a measurement of sound pressure level and signal level.

Decibels can be very confusing for those new to recording because of the different ways in which they are used. Because this is a home recording book and not a physics textbook, we will be simplifying the definitions here and limiting their descriptions to their practical use in recording.

The first distinction we will make is between using decibels to measure sound pressure level and using them to measure signal level.

dB	
130 dB	Threshold of Pain
120 dB	Jet Taking Off
110 dB	Rock Concert
100 dB	Jackhammer
90 dB	
80 dB	Good Average Mixing Volume
70 dB	Average Conversation
60 dB	
50 dB	
40 dB	Residential Area Ambient
30 dB	Whispered Speech
20 dB	
10 dB	
0 dB	Threshold of Human Hearing

Figure 32: Sound Pressure Level

Decibels and Sound Pressure Level

Sound pressure level (SPL) is a measurement of the air pressure being caused by sound, which results in physical force against the eardrum (or the diaphragm of a microphone). In the acoustic environment this translates to volume. Measurements of this nature are usually expressed as dB SPL (decibels of sound pressure level).

Silence (at least as far as the human ear is concerned) is expressed as 0 dB SPL. Sound starts to become painful to our ears at approximately 130 dB SPL. Because of this, the range of human hearing is said to be roughly 130 dB.

The average rock concert is about 110 dB SPL. This is enough to cause hearing loss after only 15 minutes of exposure, so if you value your hearing, it would be wise to invest in some good ear plugs (see *Fig. 32*).

Perception of Volume

A significant factor in the way we perceive volume is the fact that the human ear does not respond equally to all frequencies at all volumes. Our ears become more sensitive to very high and very low frequencies as volume increases.

In the 1930s, Harvey Fletcher and W. A. Munson studied this effect and plotted graphs of how the ear responds at different volumes. The resulting graphs are referred to as "Fletcher-Munson curves" or "equal loudness contours". Many home and car stereo manufacturers have introduced "loudness" circuits which give the impression of louder volume by boosting frequencies according to this theory.

An important practical lesson to be learned from this information is that music mixed at loud volumes can sound quite different when played back at lower volumes. For this reason most engineers will listen to a recording at various volumes during the mixing process. 85 dB SPL is considered to be the best average volume for mixing as it tends to provide the least tonal changes.

SPL and Microphones

When recording at high sound pressure levels (such as close miking a drum or a loud guitar amp), it is worth considering maximum SPL ratings when choosing a microphone. The maximum SPL rating for a microphone indicates how much sound pressure the mic can take without causing audible distortion.

Most dynamic microphones are capable of withstanding very high SPL (often as high as 160 dB). This makes them an easy choice for high volume recording. Condenser microphones usually have lower SPL ratings than dynamic mics; however, some will have a "pad" built into them which attenuates the output of the mic capsule, increasing the maximum SPL rating. It is advisable to leave the pad off when recording at normal volumes because the mic's signal-to-noise ratio is lowered when it is engaged.

Decibels and Signal Level

When dealing with signal level as opposed to sound pressure, decibels are used a little differently. To further confuse things, there is a difference between using decibels for metering and for referring to relative signal level.

When used for metering a signal level, 0 dB is the highest signal level achievable without distortion. All signal levels below distortion are then represented as negative numbers. For example, a healthy signal level might peak around -2 dB. What can make things even more confusing is that some meters use VU (volume units) instead of decibels for metering (see *VU Meter*).

On controls and processors that affect signal level, it is necessary to use decibels to refer to relative signal levels. A volume fader may be labeled with a "0", or a "U" (for unity), part way up to mark the point at which that fader is neither boosting nor attenuating the signal. Above the unity point are positive values to indicate increased signal level, and below unity are negative values because the fader is then reducing the signal by the amount indicated. At the bottom of the fader will generally be -∞ (minus infinity) to indicate that the signal is being reduced to silence.

De-esser

A de-esser is a tool mainly used to reduce sibilant *S*s from vocal recordings. Essentially a frequency specific compressor, the user sets the de-esser to the frequency at which the problematic sound is occurring and the threshold at which

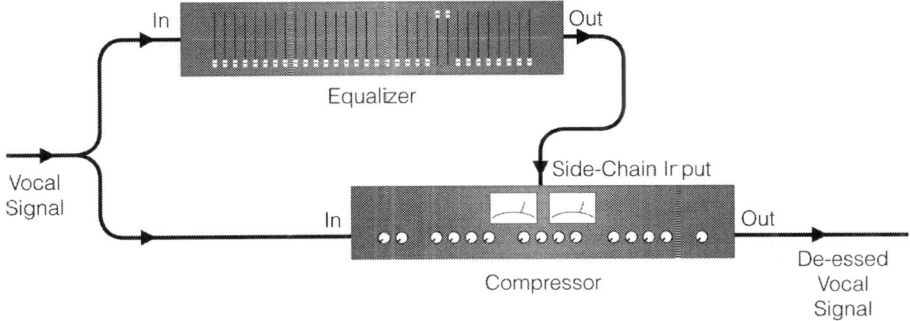

Figure 33: A Simple De-esser

it will kick in. The result is a quick burst of compression whenever a sibilant *S* occurs. Too much de-essing, however, can make a vocalist appear to have a lisp.

A simple trick can be used to find the problem frequency. First place a parametric equalizer in the signal chain and play the vocal track through it. Boost one band of the equalizer all the way, give it a high Q (narrow bandwidth) and sweep the frequency back and fourth until the sibilant 'S' is most prominent. Make a note of the frequency and use it for the de-esser.

If a de-esser is not available, a basic one can be made using an equalizer and a compressor with a side-chain input (see *Fig. 33*). First, route the vocal track so that it goes separately into the compressor and the equalizer. Then, plug the output of the equalizer into the side chain input of the compressor and set the equalizer so that the problem frequency is being boosted and all other frequencies are being cut. Finally, set the compressor to a fast attack and a fast release, then adjust the threshold until the desired amount of de-essing is achieved.

See also *Compression, Equalizer*.

Delay

Delay is an effect that repeats a signal that is fed into it. A delay may repeat only once, multiple times, or it may repeat indefinitely. Delay differs from echo in that an echo gets progressively quieter with each repeat. The repeats on delay can be quieter than the original sound, but they may also be the same volume or louder than the original.

Some delay processors allow for special delay effects such as ping-pong delay (a stereo effect where delays alternate back and forth between left and right channels), reverse delay (where the delay is backwards), or even phrase looping (the delay will replay a specified segment on a continuous loop). A variety of rhythmic options for repeats may also be included, such as triplets or dotted eighth notes.

Most modern delay processors are digital; however, analog delays are not uncommon and are often prized for their tone. One obsolete, though coveted, form of analog delay is the tape delay. A tape delay works by feeding a continuous loop of magnetic tape past a series of tape heads. A sound is recorded onto the tape by the first head and then replayed by the following heads. Parameters such as tape speed allow control over the delayed sounds.

Delay With The Beat

When using delay, the effect will be more subtle when it occurs in time with the music. Some delay units, called multi-tap delays, allow the performer to tap a pad in time to the music, setting the tempo of the delay.

When multi-tap functionality is not available, the same effect can be achieved by using a simple equation. Take the number 60,000 (which is the number of milliseconds in a minute) and divide it by the tempo of the song (in beats per minute). If the song is in 3/4 or 4/4 time, the resulting number is the number of milliseconds that make up a quarter note (if the song is in 6/8 time the result will be an eighth note, etc.). If you divide that number in two, you then have the delay required for an eighth note. You can dividing the number by two to calculate the duration of the next smaller note value (see Fig. 34).

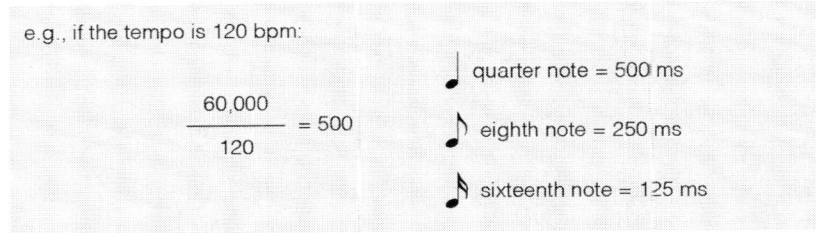

Figure 34: Calculating Delay Time

If a song feels like it is dragging, placing the delay slightly before the beat will make it feel more upbeat. If a song is feeling rushed, placing the delay slightly after the beat will help alleviate the rushed feeling.

Doubling With Delay

Delay is often used to fatten up a sound trough a technique called doubling. If a very short delay time is used, in the range of about 15–40 ms, the brain cannot perceive the two as discreet sounds, and instead we hear a fuller version of the original. Care should be used, however, as this technique can cause phase problems (see *Phase*). Careful listening (with the original and the delay both panned to center) will reveal these problems, and they can be alleviated by shifting the delay by a few milliseconds in either direction until the phase problem goes away or is reduced to an acceptable level.

Destructive Editing

The term destructive editing refers to an editing process that cannot be undone at a later point in time. This includes editing out part of a track in a way that deletes it permanently or recording over a track in a way that overwrites a previous take.

One of the greatest benefits of digital recording (with the notable exception of tape-based digital such as DAT or ADAT) is the ability to edit non-destructively. While tape-based recording is limited by a sound's physical location on the tape, hard-disk-based digital recording (and similar technologies) can store digital files anywhere on the drive and access all or part of them when necessary. This means that a segment of a recording can be moved, copied and pasted, or shortened without ever affecting the original file.

Destructive Recording

Destructive recording is a function in digital recording software where recording over a previous take will overwrite the original audio file. By default, most software will record non-destructively, which means that all previous takes are saved and can be accessed at a later time.

Recording non-destructively is one of the advantages of software-based recording because it means there is always the option to go back to a previous take. The down side of non-destructive recording is that it uses more hard drive space. With hard drives becoming cheaper and larger all the time, this is less of an issue than it once was, but in a situation where hard space is limited, destructive recording is an option.

DI Box

See *Direct Injection*.

Diffuser

A diffuser is an acoustic barrier or panel designed to break up reflections of sound waves that hit it. Diffusers help to create a more complex reverberation within a space, which generally results in a nicer-sounding room. Diffusers also reduce problems due to standing waves.

Diffusers come in a variety of shapes and sizes (see *Fig. 35*). Pre-fabricated diffusers can be purchased, but if budget is an issue, simple diffusers can be made quite easily from wood or ceiling tiles. One of the simplest and most inexpensive ways to make a diffuser is to hang egg cartons on the wall. Placing them so the egg cups face the wall gives a convex surface, scattering reflections around the room. Facing the egg cups into the room will create concave holes, reflecting sound inward and reducing overall reflections.

See also *Acoustics, Standing Wave*.

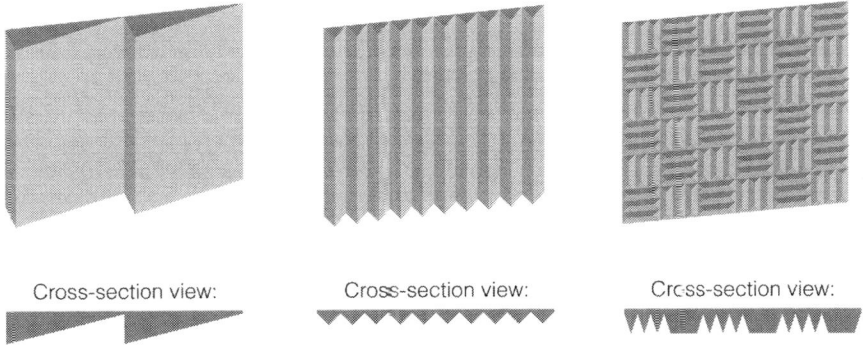

Figure 35: Examples of Different Diffuser Shapes

Digital Audio Tape

See *DAT*.

Digital Audio Workstation

See *DAW*.

Digital Delay

Digital delay is an effect that repeats a signal fed into it by use of a digital processor. Delay is much like an echo, except repeats are not necessarily quieter than the original signal.

Some digital delays, referred to as modeling effects or emulators, are designed to reproduce the tone of classic analog delays. These effects are very popular as they are much more affordable than the vintage effects they are reproducing and provide versatility in their tone.

Digital Mixing Board

A digital mixing board is a mixing board that does all of its routing digitally. Digital mixers have all the same functionality as analog mixers (see *Mixing Board*) but often have digital effects processors built into them.

Digital mixers have D/A (digital to analog) and A/D (analog to digital) converters built into them to allow them to interface with analog gear. Most digital mixers will also have digital outputs, allowing you to plug the mixer directly into a digital recording device.

Digital Signal Processing (DSP)

Digital effects are created by digital signal processors. These processors can come in either hardware or software, and the effects themselves can be either real-time (meaning the processing happens as the track plays) or non-real-time (meaning the track must be processed before playback). Real-time effects are more flexible because small adjustments can be made on the fly, while non-real-time effects have the benefit that they do not eat up processing power during playback.

Effects that require a lot of processing power, such as reverb, are often best put on an auxiliary channel with several tracks being routed to it. This allows one reverb to do all the processing for multiple tracks instead of having multiple instances of reverb hogging valuable processing speed.

Hardware Processors

Hardware signal processors may have one or more effects in a single unit. Generally speaking, units that are dedicated to a single effect tend to have more options and better quality than if the same effect was produced by a multi-effect unit.

Multi-effect processors are often an affordable option, providing a wide range of effects without buying multiple dedicated effect units. Depending on the processor, more than one effect may be able to be used at once, and in some cases routing choices are available (effect A before effect B, effect B before effect A, or parallel effects).

Software Processors

Software processors usually come in the form of plug-ins that work within your recording software. Plug-ins are usually more affordable than their hardware equivalents. Some plug-in manufacturers offer "powered plug-ins", which come with a hardware processor (usually hooked up via USB, Firewire, or PCI card) dedicated to running them. These can be a way to add more processing power to your workstation.

Many software effects are designed to emulate the sound of classic analog effects. These are far more affordable than buying their hardware equivalent. Another benefit of using software effects is that when you return to a mix they are always just as you left them when you last saved.

Different recording programs use different plug-in formats. Among the most common are VST (Virtual Studio Technology), RTAS (Real-Time AudioSuite), and AU (Audio Unit). Conversion software is often available to allow a program to use a plug-in format other than its native format; however, in some cases, conversion software can add latency (processing delay) into the track using it. This can be overcome by using delay compensation software or by moving the track ahead by the amount that it is being delayed.

See also *Plug-In, Powered Plug-Ins.*

Digital to Analog (D/A) Converter

A digital to analog converter is a device that converts a digital signal into an analog signal. All digital recording and digital playback devices (such as CD/DVD/MP3 players) have D/A converters in them in order to send a usable signal to speakers, headphones, or other audio components.

The number of D/A converters that an audio interface or DAW (digital audio workstation) has will determine how many tracks can be independently output from the device at a time. Some will have only two (for a stereo mix), while others will have many, allowing for more complex routing such as multiple mixes or sending channels to external effects.

Interfaces with D/A converters usually have A/D (analog to digital) converters as well, which are used mainly as inputs for recording. These audio interfaces are sometimes referred to as I/O (in/out) boxes or I/O modules, and in some cases they can be "piggybacked" (more than one can be used simultaneously) to allow for more inputs and outputs.

Direct Injection/Direct Input (DI)

The term DI is short for direct injection or direct input. It is a method of recording an electric instrument directly, without a microphone. A DI takes an unbalanced, high-impedance, instrument-level signal and converts it into a balanced, low-impedance, microphone-level signal. This allows it to be plugged into a standard mic preamp or mixing board.

DI boxes come in passive or active varieties. Active DIs have a preamplifier built-in, that boosts the output signal. For this reason, active DIs require a power source, provided either by battery or phantom power. An active DI may be a good solution when a passive DI is not providing enough signal level.

There are a couple of benefits to direct recording. First, by removing the amplifier and microphone from the signal chain, direct recording generally means less noise. Second, direct recording eliminates the possibility of leakage from other instruments.

Direct recording is most commonly used for bass, clean electric guitar, keyboards, and synthesizers, though some engineers prefer to amplify and mic these instruments anyway for certain types of music because of the tonal characteristics the amp adds.

One instrument that tends not to work well when recorded direct is the electric guitar with overdrive or distortion on it. This is because overdriving an electric guitar creates some harsh harmonics that are smoothed out by a guitar amp's speakers. Some DIs have a speaker emulator option that helps compensate for this problem. Using an amp emulator is another option for successfully direct recording an electric guitar.

Acoustic guitar, and other acoustic instruments will usually sound most natural if recorded with a microphone; though, if the guitar has a pleasant sounding pickup in it some engineers choose to mix the direct signal and the miked sound together in certain situations.

See also *Amp Emulator, Impedance, Speaker Emulator*.

Direct Recording

Direct recording is the act of recording an electric instrument directly into the a recording device as opposed to using a microphone. This is usually done by using a DI box, though some recording devices and interfaces have instrument level inputs that negate the necessity of a DI. The main benefits of direct recording are reduced noise and the elimination of leakage from other instruments. Amp emulators are often used in direct recording to add tonal character and to increase tonal control.

See also *Amp Emulator, Direct Injection/Direct Input (DI), Speaker Emulator*.

Directional Response

See *Pickup Pattern*.

Distortion

In recording, distortion refers to degradation of audio signal. This can result from a number of different causes, and may be intentional or unintentional.

Causes of distortion include interference from poor cabling or malfunctioning equipment, but the most common cause of distortion is clipping. Clipping occurs when a signal has more volume than the circuit or medium carrying it is capable of transmitting. The result is that the top and bottom of the waveform are clipped off (see *Fig. 36*). Clipping can generally be avoided by watching level meters and leaving enough headroom for occasional peaks to occur without distorting.

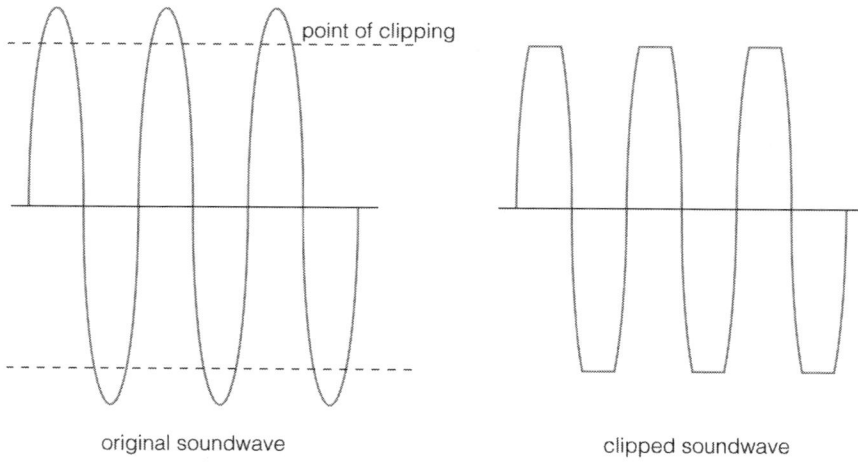

Figure 36: Distortion from Clipping

It is very common, particularly in rock music, to use a degree of intentional distortion in a recording. The most obvious instance is the use of distortion or overdrive effects for guitar or bass, but it is also used in more subtle ways to add a little "grit" or "dirt" to a recording.

Driving a tube preamp or magnetic tape a little into distortion can give a warm, gritty quality. This is referred to as "soft clipping" and is quite common for rock drums and bass. There are effect processors and software on the market that model the sound of tube or tape drive.

Distribution Amplifier

A distribution amplifier is an amplifier that takes a single input and distributes it to a number of outputs. In the recording studio, the most common use for a distribution amp is for powering headphones for multiple performers at the same time.

Dither

Dither is a small amount of white noise added to a digital audio signal when reducing it to a lower bit depth to reduce the number of errors that occur during the process. Digital converters, workstations, and processors can often sample and process at high bit depths such as 24- or 32- bits, but recordings from these machines are often converted to a lower bit-depth for reproduction. CDs, for example, are a 16-bit medium, so a recording made at 24-bit resolution would have to be converted to 16-bit before being pressed to CD.

See also *Bit Depth, Appendix A: The Basics Of Sound*

Doubling

Doubling is a technique used to fill out, or fatten up, a sound by placing together two slightly different copies of the same track. One way this can be done is to have the performer play the same passage again on a second track, resulting in two almost identical takes. If the performer has good timing, the two tracks will be so close that the listener will not perceive them as individual tracks, but rather as one thicker sounding track.

This effect can also be achieved with slightly different results using a delay. By adding a delayed version of the take approximately 15–40 ms after the original, we achieve roughly the same result. Our brains cannot differentiate between the two signals and will perceive them as one. One concern when using this effect is phase cancellation which may occur when the two tracks are panned together or played in mono. This can usually be overcome by moving the delay back or forward by a few milliseconds.

See also *Delay, Phase Cancellation*.

Dry Signal

The term dry is used to refer to a signal with no effects applied to it. Conversely, a signal with an effect on it is called wet. Running an effect through an auxiliary send provides control over the amount of wet signal that is blended with the original dry signal.

See also *Auxiliary Send, Wet Signal*.

DSP

See *Digital Signal Processing*.

Dynamic Microphone

Dynamic microphones create sound through magnetic induction. They are generally reasonably inexpensive (compared to other types of mics), very sturdy, and can withstand high sound pressure levels (SPL). These qualities make them a good choice for live use, close miking drums, or miking loud guitar amps. Dynamic mics are not as sensitive as some other microphones, so they often need to be quite close to the sound source to get a healthy signal.

Most dynamic mics are "moving coil" dynamics (see *Fig. 37*). These mics use a coil attached to a diaphragm suspended in a magnetic field. When sound hits the diaphragm the coil moves, creating magnetic flux, which is turned into the electrical signal and sent out through the cable. This is very similar to how a speaker is constructed. In fact, by wiring a speaker backwards it can be used as a microphone.

The other, less common, variety of dynamic microphone is the ribbon mic. These have a thin corrugated metal ribbon suspended in a magnetic field. Sound hitting the ribbon causes it to vibrate, creating signal. Ribbon mics are valued for

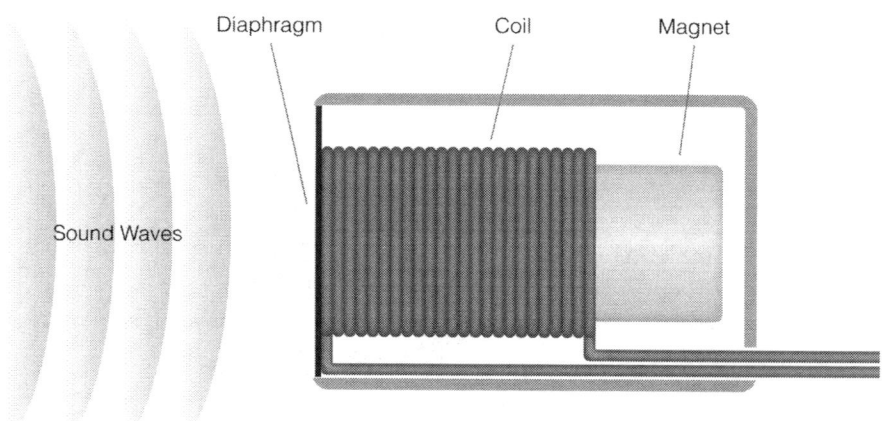

Figure 37: Capsule of a Moving-Coil Dynamic Microphone

their warm, almost vintage, tone. They are much more fragile than moving coil dynamics because the thin ribbon can be broken by heavy gusts of air. Phantom power should not be applied to ribbon mics as it can damage the microphone. Some modern ribbon microphones contain circuits to protect them from phantom power, but caution is advisable anyway.

See also *Microphones*, *Ribbon Microphone*.

Dynamic Range

Dynamic range refers to the difference between the quietest possible sound (silence) and the loudest possible sound that can be handled by a particular medium. Normal human hearing can handle a range of approximately 130 decibels (dB), however most current mediums of reproduction have lower dynamic ranges, so when mastering a recording it is important to consider what mediums the recording is likely to be reproduced on (see *Fig. 38*). CD audio, for example, has an approximate dynamic range of 96 dB, and most analog-to-digital converters have a dynamic range of around 120 dB. Compression and limiting can be used to reduce the dynamic range of a signal in order to accommodate mediums with lower dynamic ranges.

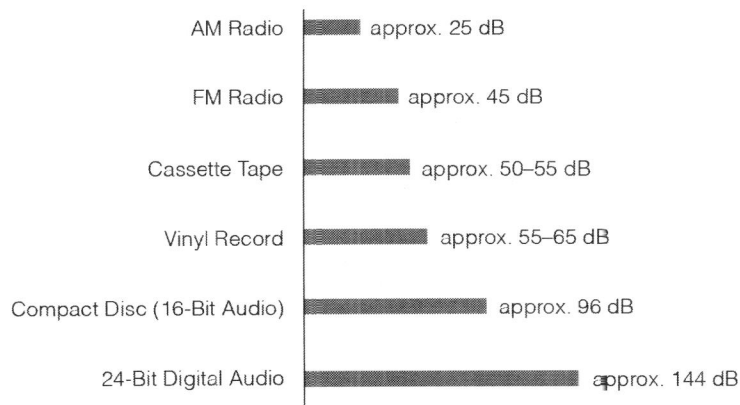

Figure 38: Dynamic Range of Various Mediums

Another consideration is that background noise in a listening environment can mask sections of a recording with lower volume, making them hard to hear. This is especially important because many people listen to music while working or driving.

Keeping the dynamic range of a song within a reasonable range will allow for listening at a comfortable level for both louder and quieter sections. The amount of dynamic range that is appropriate for a track depends on the style of music, expected listening environments, and the discretion of the engineer or producer.

While the tendency in modern music is towards heavy compression, it must be done with care because too much, or poorly executed, compression can rob a performance of its natural dynamics, leaving it dull and lifeless. The engineer and/or producer must find a balance between the dynamics of the performance and the optimal dynamic range for the song. Musical styles such as jazz and classical, where performers spend a great deal of time perfecting dynamic changes, are usually left with very little manipulation of the dynamic range.

See also *Compression, Limiting*.

Dynamics Processor

Dynamics processors are devices, such as compressors or limiters, that control the dynamic range of a signal (the variation between its loudest and quietest points). There are a variety of reasons to use dynamics processing, including stylistic choice, to boost the overall volume of a signal, or to account for limitations in a specific medium.

See also *Compression, Dynamic Range, Limiting*.

Early Reflections

The process of reverberation is broken up into three stages. These are the direct sound (sound that travels directly from the sound source to the ear or microphone), early reflections (sound that reaches the ear by reflection off of one or two surfaces), and reverberation (sound that reflects off of multiple surfaces before reaching the ear). Early reflections generally occur within 100 milliseconds of the direct sound.

The timing and amount of early reflections provide our brain with subtle clues about the size and shape of the room a recording was made in. For example: a large, empty, square room will have only a few prominent early reflections, and they will occur later in a larger room than in a smaller one. When using artificial reverb we can subtly control the listener's perception of a recording by carefully controlling variables such as the early reflections of a reverb.

See also *Acoustics, Reverberation.*

Echo

An echo is an effect in which a signal is repeated, either once or multiple times, after it has been played. An echo always gets quieter with each repeat. A related effect is delay, which differs in that repeats are not necessarily quieter, and can even be louder than the original sound. Echo and delay effects add a sense of depth to a recording but should be used sparingly to avoid making a mix feel cluttered.

See also *Delay.*

Effect Loop

Found on some amplifiers, an effect loop is essentially the same as an auxiliary send. An effect loop is used to place effects after the amplifier's preamp (its initial gain stage) rather than before. This small change in order can often result in a noticeable difference in tone.

To use an effect loop, the instrument's signal is sent out of the amplifier via the effect send and into the input of the effect. The output of the effect, or the last effect in a chain if multiple are used, is then plugged into the effect return.

See also *Auxiliary Send.*

Effect Send

See *Auxiliary Send.*

Electret-Condenser Microphone

An electret-condenser microphone differs from a standard condenser mic in that it uses a permanently charged diaphragm or plate, eliminating the need for voltage to be supplied to the capsule. Like standard condenser mics, electret-condensers still use a small preamplifier within the mic itself to boost the signal to a usable level. Therefore, an electret-condenser mic still requires electrical current, which can be supplied by phantom power or in some cases by a battery mounted within the mic. The advantage of an electret-condenser is that by eliminating the need for a charge to the capsule, the mic can operate with a lower voltage battery.

See also *Condenser Microphone*, *Microphones*.

Engineer

See *Audio Engineer*.

Envelope

See *Acoustic Envelope*.

Equal Loudness Contour

See *Fletcher-Munson Curve*.

Equalizer

Equalizers allow us to control the tonal qualities of a signal by changing the relative volume of different frequency ranges. Originally designed to compensate for frequency loss caused by inefficient cabling, equalizers are now used as a creative tool as much as a corrective one. Reasons for using an equalizer include correcting tonal problems that have occurred in the recording process, creating tonal separation between two instruments that exist in the same frequency range, and creating special tonal effects.

An equalizer affects the tone of a signal by boosting or cutting signal in different frequency ranges. This is achieved through the use of three types of filters: bell, shelf, and pass (see *Fig. 39*).

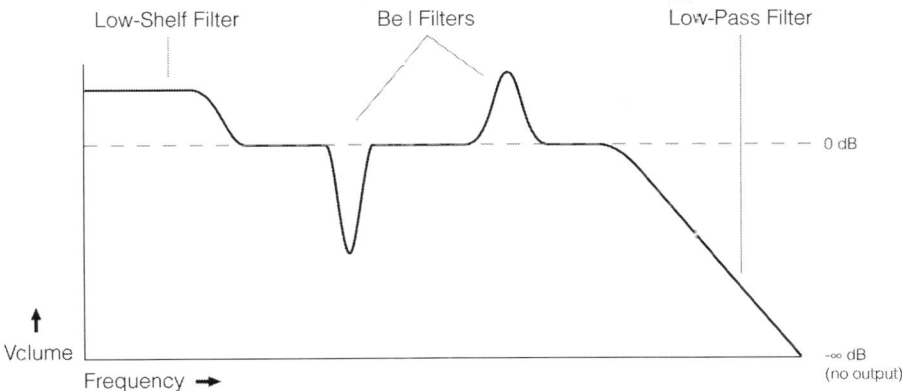

Figure 39: Bell, Shelf, and Pass Filters

Bell filters (also called peak filters) boost or cut the chosen frequency, affecting the surrounding frequencies in a bell-shaped curve. How much on either side of the target frequency is affected by the filter is controlled by the its quality factor or "Q". A high Q affects very little to either side of the target frequency, while a low Q affects a wide band of frequencies (see *Fig. 40*).

Shelf filters work at either end of the frequency spectrum. A high-shelf slopes up or down to the desired amount of boost or cut, then shelfs off to boost or cut all frequencies above by the same amount (see *Fig. 39*). A low-shelf does the same, only affecting all frequencies below. For example, a high-shelf set to boost 2 dB at 7 kHz will increase the volume of all frequencies above 7 kHz by 2 dB. A low-shelf set to -3 dB at 80 Hz will attenuate all frequencies below 80 Hz by 3 dB.

Pass filters can only cut signal. Like shelving filters, pass filters occur at either end of the spectrum, but rather than shelving off, the cut continues on the same slope until signal is completely removed (see *Fig. 39*). The target frequency is the point on the slope where the volume of the signal has been reduced by 3 dB. A high-pass filter cuts all sound below the target frequency completely, allowing only the higher frequencies to pass while a low-pass filter cuts everything higher than the target frequency, with all lower frequencies allowed to pass though unaffected. When both a high-pass and a low-pass filter are used together, it is called a band-pass filter. A band-pass filter leaves a band of frequencies, with everything above and below being cut.

The effect of an equalizer is often represented with an "EQ curve", a graphic depiction of what is happening to a signal (see *Fig. 41*). The dashed horizontal

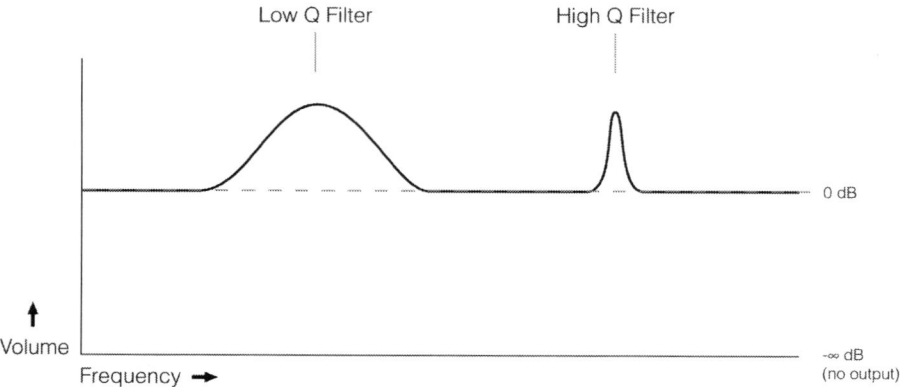

Figure 40: High Q and Low Q Filters

line represents the signal coming into the EQ, and the black line represents the signal coming out. When the black line is above the dashed line, the signal is being boosted, when it is below, the signal is being cut, and when the dark line is even to the dashed line, there is no cut or boost. The curve being shown in *Fig. 41* shows that the signal is being cut with a shelf filter at 100 Hz and boosted with a bell filter at 2.5 kHz. All other frequencies are unaffected.

Types Of Equalizers

There are two basic types of equalizers: parametric and graphic (see *Fig. 42*). Parametric equalizers vary in the number of bands they have (essentially, the

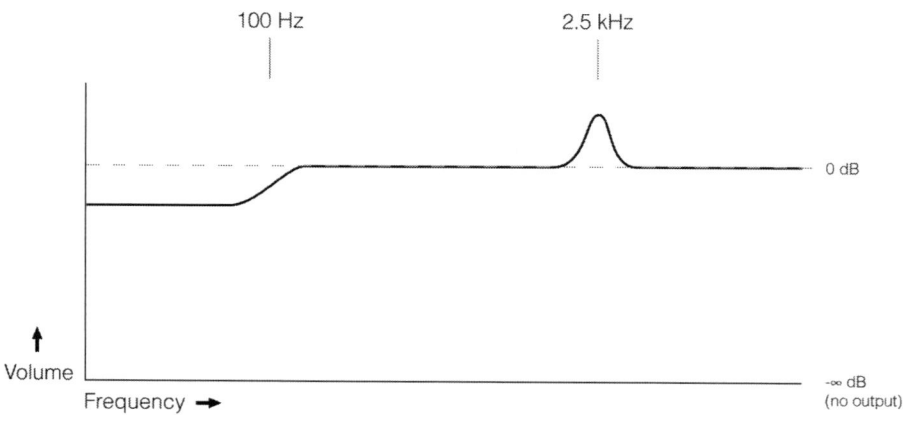

Figure 41: An EQ Curve

number of frequencies that can be affected at the same time), generally ranging from 3 to 7. The highest and lowest bands are shelf filters (unless labelled otherwise), with the bands in between being bell filters. On a parametric EQ, each band has controls to set the target frequency and the amount of boost or cut that is to be applied to that frequency. If a band uses a bell filter, it will also have a control for the filter's Q. An equalizer that works in this manner but has less fewer (for example on a mixing board) is called a semi-parametric equalizer. Parametric equalizers are favored in recording because they can be used to hone in on precise frequencies.

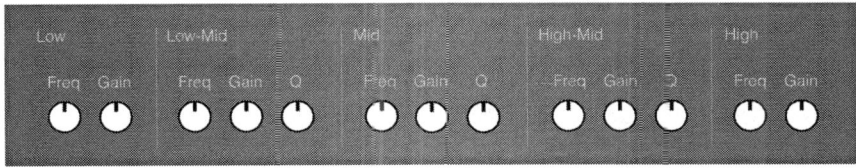
Parametric Equalizer

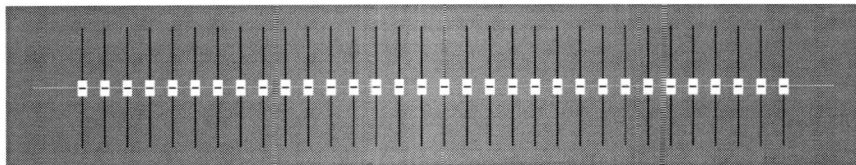
Graphic Equalizer

Figure 42: Parametric and Graphic Equalizers

Graphic equalizers use a series of set-frequency, set-Q faders to control frequency balance. They are called graphic equalizers because the positions of the faders provide a graphic representation of the equalization curve they are producing (see *Fig. 43*). Like parametric equalizers, graphic equalizers have a shelf filter at either end of the spectrum with bell filters in between. The number of bands a graphic EQ has varies, though 15- and 31-band are among the most common. Graphic EQs are less precise than parametric EQs, but they can be used more quickly, making them preferable for use in live sound reinforcement.

Finding Frequencies

Equalizers are usually used with the goal of boosting or cutting a specific portion of a signal, such as the crack of a snare drum, the pick hitting the strings

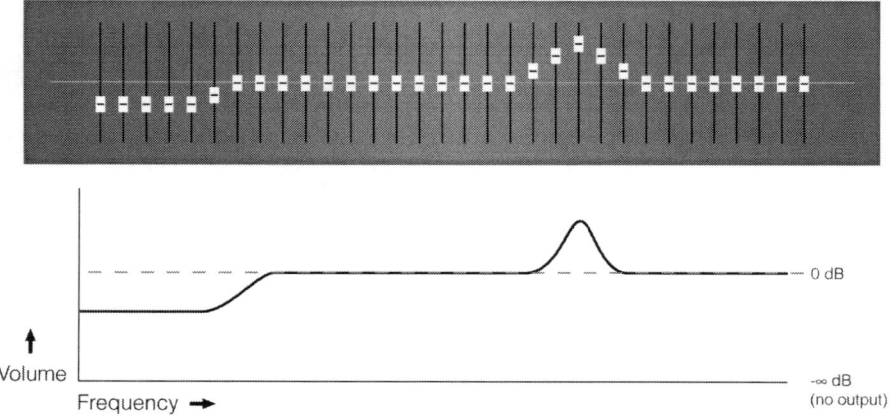

Figure 43: Graphic Equalizers

on an acoustic guitar, or the scratch of the bow on a fiddle track. Using a parametric EQ, there is a quick and easy way to find the frequency of a specific quality you want to affect within the signal.

On one band of the equalizer, turn the Q up quite high and boost the band all the way. Then, play the sound and slowly sweep the frequency back and forth until you find the point where the tone you are looking to focus on is loudest. Make a note of the frequency and put the EQ back to zero. You now know the frequency where your target tone occurs, and you can cut or boost appropriately.

General Equalizer Tips

Don't "fix it in the mix". Try changing the sound by other means first, such as using a different microphone or mic placement. Heavy EQ often sounds manipulated and can lead to phasing issues (see *Phase*).

It is usually better to cut than to boost. Boosting in EQ makes the instrument take up more space in the mix, which can contribute to muddy or unintelligible mixes. Also, the phase problems mentioned above are more common with boosting than with cutting.

An instrument only needs to sound good on its own if it is heard on its own at some point in the song. Otherwise all that matters is how it sounds in the mix.

Don't be a low-mid junky. When an instrument has a lot happening in the low-mid range (120–250 Hz), it sounds big, but this range tends to get crowded very quickly resulting in a muddy or muffled mix. Avoid allowing too much to happen in this frequency range.

Make space. Every instrument needs its own place in the mix in order for it to be heard clearly. Try cutting a bit of volume from the less important frequency ranges of each instrument to make room for other instruments in that range.

If two instruments exist in the same basic frequency range (for example bass and kick drum) try interlocking their EQ curves. This means that any frequency boosted on one should be cut in the other and vice-versa. In the example of a bass and kick drum, if you boost the bass at 100 Hz to give it more thump, then cut from the kick drum at 100 Hz.

Cut narrow, boost wide. As a rule of thumb, equalization tends to be less obvious when a narrow band (high Q) is used to cut frequencies and a wide band (low Q) is used for boosting frequencies.

Expansion

As the name implies, expansion is the opposite of compression. An expander increases the dynamic range of a signal. Expanders are often used, along with a compressor, to reduce noise in wireless systems through a process called compansion.

See also *Compansion, Compression, Dynamic Range*.

Fade

A fade is a gradual change in volume beginning with silence (called a fade-in) or ending with it (a fade-out). When one signal is faded-out while another signal is faded-in to take its place, it is referred to as a crossfade.

When splicing together segments from two different takes, or different segments of the same take, it is good practice to put a subtle cross-fade at the splicing point to eliminate any clicks or other unwanted sounds that may occur as one segment ends and the other begins. Most recording software will have tools to automatically create cross-fades, fade-ins, and fade-outs.

See also *Crossfade*.

Fader

A fader is a potentiometer (variable resistor) used to control the volume of a signal. The term fader generally implies a control that moves along a linear track rather than a rotating knob, though they are functionally the same.

See also *Channel Strip*.

Far-Field Monitors

Far-field monitors are large loudspeakers designed to provide accurate reference for studio recording. They are called far-field because they are designed to be mounted on the wall several feet from mix position.

Far-field monitors were very popular until the late 1970s and early 1980s when near-field monitors started to become the norm. Many large studios have both near- and far-field monitors, though most engineers choose to primarily mix on near-fields, occasionally switching to the far-field monitors to check the low end of the frequency spectrum. This is because mixes tend to "translate" better when mixed on near-field monitors. That is to say, it is easier to make a mix sound good in a wide range of listening environments when mixing with near-field monitors.

For home studios, far-field monitors are impractical because they tend to be very expensive and very large. The greater distance between monitor and listener also poses a problem in the home studio environment, as the sound of the room itself has a greater impact on the mix than it does with near-field monitors. This is an issue because the average home or project studio owner does not have a large budget to acoustically treat their mixing room the way major studios do.

Feedback Loop

A feedback loop occurs when an amplified sound gets into a microphone that is feeding into the amplifier that originally produced it. The sound is then amplified again and again, resulting in a loud howling or screeching noise. In the recording studio, feedback is a less common problem than in live sound reinforcement; however, a studio engineer needs to be careful to mute monitors and other speakers whenever live microphones are in the room.

Figure-8 Microphone

See *Bi-Directional Pickup Pattern*.

File Compression

File compression is a process that encodes digital information to achieve a smaller file size. File compression can be either lossless, meaning all information can be retrieved without any degradation of quality, or lossy, meaning some information is irreversibly discarded. Generally, lossy forms of compression achieve a greater reduction in file size at the expense of a loss in audio quality.

MP3s are a popular form of lossy compression for use online and in portable devices because of their small file size. Greater amounts of MP3 compression result in smaller file sizes but also greater quality loss, so when compressing files to post online, an acceptable trade-off must be made between file size and audio quality.

Some older muti-track recording devices, notably those that recorded to mini-disc, compressed all files as they were recorded to increase recording time per disc. Most current digital workstations no longer use file compression, as file storage has become more affordable to produce.

Flanging

Flanging is a time-based effect created by combining a signal with a slightly delayed version of itself. The amount of delay is continually varied, resulting in a constant change in the sound's tonal quality or timbre. The effect is called flanging because the delayed signal was originally varied by pressing on the tape flange of a reel-to-reel tape deck.

Fletcher-Munson Curve

In the early 1930s, scientists Harvey Fletcher and W. A. Munson conducted a series of experiments on how we hear. They determined from their findings that the human ear responds differently to different frequencies at different volumes. Most notably, the ear becomes more sensitive to very high and very low frequencies as volume increases. They created a series of charts plotting these changes in sensitivity, which are referred to as Fletcher-Munson Curves. More recent studies have refined these curves, resulting in what are referred to as Equal Loudness Contours.

Home stereo manufacturers often include a "loudness" circuit, which uses these curves to make music seem louder than it actually is.

The lesson that engineers have learned from these discoveries is that a mix will sound different at different volumes. For this reason, most engineers check their mixes at a variety of volumes during the mixing process. Optimal average mixing volume is considered to be 80 dB SPL, as this yields a mix that will vary the least at common listening volumes.

Foley

Foley is the process of creating and altering sound effects for film, television, radio, or other mediums. Foley artists use a variety of props to create realistic or exaggerated sound effects.

Frequency

Frequency refers to the number of cycles a sound wave completes per second, and is measured in hertz (Hz). A sound wave with a frequency of 70 Hz, for example, completes 70 cycles per second, while a 20 kHz (kilohertz) sound wave completes 20,000. Frequency corresponds directly to pitch, so a 70 Hz sound wave is a much lower pitch than one at 20 kHz. The frequency of a signal doubles for every octave it is raised.

See also *Amplitude, Cycle, Appendix A: The Basics Of Sound.*

Frequency Response

Frequency response refers to the ability of a piece of studio equipment, particularly microphones and speakers, to accurately reproduce sound at different frequencies. The frequency response of a piece of equipment can be charted on a graph, called a frequency response curve, which provides a visual reference for the effect the equipment will have on the tone of a signal that is run through it.

Most equipment is, to some extent, more sensitive to some frequency ranges than others. Equipment that reproduces all frequencies equally is referred to as having a "flat" response. This is because when its frequency response is charted on a frequency response curve, it will produce a flat line.

See also *Frequency Response Curve, Microphones, Monitors, Spectrum Analyzer*.

Frequency Response Curve

A frequency response curve is a chart used to visually represent a piece of equipment's ability to accurately reproduce sound (see *Fig. 44*). Frequency response curves are often included with microphones to show what frequency ranges they are more, or less, sensitive in. Frequency response curves are similar to EQ curves, as they represent tonal changes that will occur in a signal when it passes through the equipment in question.

See also *Frequency Response, Microphones, Monitors, Spectrum Analyzer*.

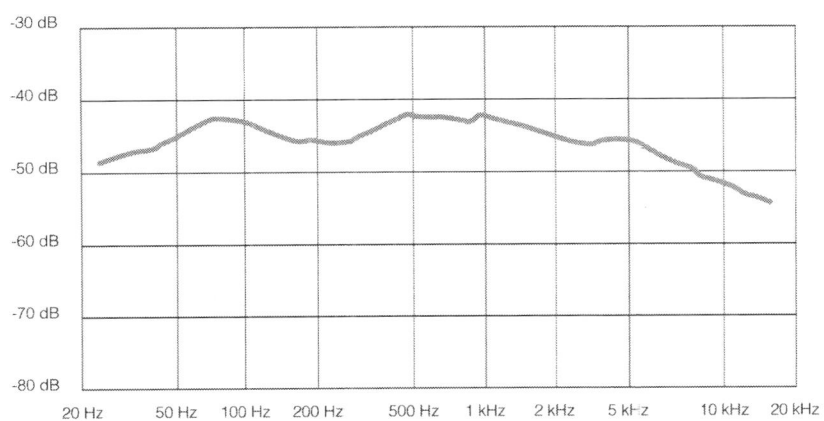

Figure 44: A Frequency Response Curve

Front of House

The term front of house refers to the part of a sound system directed at the audience. Most often this refers to the main speakers of the system or the mix that is being played through them, but it can refer to all equipment being used to mix and process the signal as well. The term is used to differentiate signals and equipment that are part of the main mix from those that are part of the stage monitor mix or a feed for live recording or broadcast.

Fundamental Tone

The speed at which a sound-producing object vibrates determines the pitch it will create. The A string of a guitar, for example, vibrates at a rate of 440 Hz (in North American tuning). 440 Hz is both the most prominent and the lowest pitch it creates; this is called its fundamental tone. While the string is vibrating, it also creates other, higher pitches at mathematical intervals. These are called harmonics or overtones, and they occur at multiples of the fundamental frequency. The relative volume of these tones creates the tonal character of a specific instrument, called its timbre, which is why two different instruments playing the same note will sound different.

See also *Frequency, Timbre, Appendix A: The Fundamentals of Sound.*

Gain

The term gain simply refers to amplification of a signal. Common places for controls to be labelled as gain include a preamplifier, where the gain boosts the entire signal; makeup gain on a compressor, where it boosts the signal to compensate for the subtractive nature of compression; and on an equalizer, where it controls the volume of a specific frequency band.

Gate

A gate is essentially a volume triggered mute switch. When the signal being fed into the gate exceeds a user-determined level, called a threshold, the gate is opened, allowing all signal to pass through. When the signal falls below the threshold, the gate is closed, cutting all signal completely.

Similar to compressors, gates sometimes have attack and release controls. The attack controls how quickly, once the threshold has been passed, the gate opens. The release controls how quickly it closes again once the signal has fallen below the threshold. This allows the user to determine whether fleeting changes in volume will trigger the gate or not. Due to the similarity in function, gates and compressors are sometimes included in the same device.

See also *Compression*.

General MIDI

General MIDI (GM) is a specification standard for MIDI devices that ensures a certain level of compatibility. GM took the existing MIDI standard a step farther by imposing a minimum feature set for General MIDI compatibility and setting instrument sounds to specific program numbers.

See also *MIDI*.

Graphic Equalizer

A graphic equalizer controls the relative volume of a series of preset frequency bands by way of a bank of faders (see *Fig. 45*). They are called graphic equalizers because the positions of the faders provide a graphic representation of the equalization curve they are producing. This quick visual reference makes them common for use in live sound reinforcement.

See also *Equalizer*.

Hard-Disk Recorder

A hard-disk recorder is a recording device that records onto an internal hard disk or hard drive. Some hard-disk recorders are meant to be used with a mixing board and outboard equipment, while others are complete standalone workstations. Hard-disk recording has become very common in recent years as the cost of hard

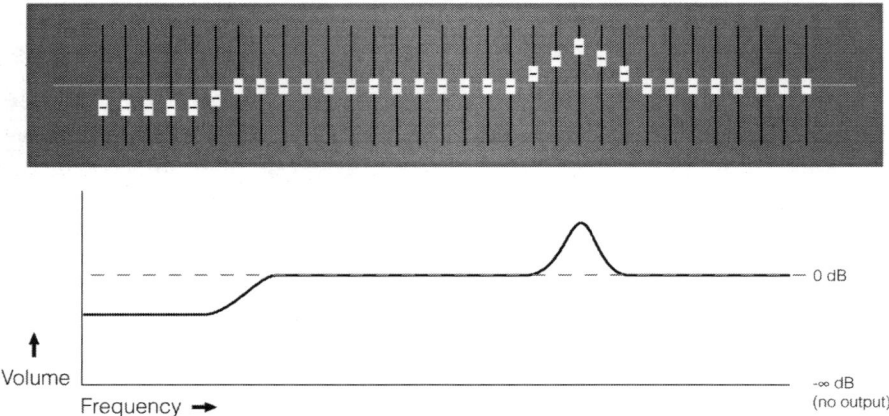

Figure 45: Graphic Equalizer and Resulting EQ Curve

drives has come down significantly, and removable backup media, such as CD/DVD burners, have become more common.

Random-access editing is a distinct advantage that hard-disk recorders, and many other digital media, have over older technologies such as tape, DAT, and ADAT. Random-access editing means that sections of audio can be copied and pasted, moved, and stretched regardless of the data's physical location on the disk.

See also *DAW*, *Random Access Editing*.

Harmonics

See *Overtones*.

Harmonic Content

See *Timbre*.

Harmonic Distortion

Harmonic distortion is when additional harmonics (overtones) are created that did not exist in the original signal. This can happen either in the human ear or in a piece of audio equipment and is generally the result of excessive volume.

See also *Timbre, Appendix A: The Basics of Sound.*

Headphones

Headphones are essential in almost all studios, regardless of size. Their main use in the studio is during the tracking process to allow performers to hear themselves, other performers, and any previously recorded tracks without risk of the sound feeding back into the microphone.

While mixing, the engineer will usually check how the mix sounds on headphones; however, it is inadvisable to use headphones as the main monitoring source because the proximity of the speakers to the ear can affect perception of space and frequency response.

Headphones come in a wide range of styles and quality. The main considerations when selecting headphones for the studio are frequency response, comfort, impedance, and whether they are closed or open backed.

Frequency Response

As with studio monitors, choosing a pair of headphones that has a reasonably flat frequency response (meaning their focus is on accurate reproduction rather than sounding good) will provide the best frame of reference for decisions during the recording process. This is especially true for those who are recording themselves or are recording while in the same room as the performer (as is often the case in the home studio) because headphones will be the only way to monitor the signal coming from the microphone.

Comfort

While comfort is a self-explanatory consideration, its importance should not be underestimated. It is not uncommon in the studio for the performer and/or engineer to wear headphones for hours on end. If they are uncomfortable, it can affect the performance and the longevity of the studio session.

Impedance

The impedance of a pair of headphones will directly affect how much power is required to drive them. A pair of low-impedance headphones will sound much louder that a high-impedance pair when fed the same amount of power. That being said, high-impedance headphones generally are more robust, resulting in a longer life span. When it seems impossible to get enough volume out of a headphone feed, switching to lower-impedance headphones can often be the solution.

Closed- and Open-Back Headphones

Headphones are either open or closed back. This refers to whether the casing behind the speakers is sealed or not. They each have their advantages, so the choice ultimately comes down to their intended use. Open-back headphones generally have a more accurate frequency response than closed-backed ones, making them better for critical listening. Closed-back headphones provide more acoustic isolation, however, which results in less bleed from the headphones into the microphone when tracking.

See also *Mixing, Monitors*.

Headphone Amplifier

A headphone amplifier is a low-power distribution amplifier used to route a single audio signal to multiple pairs of headphones, providing individual volume control for each output.

Headroom

Headroom is a specification for audio devices that indicates the difference between the average operating signal level and the maximum level the signal can reach before distortion. This information allows us to know how well the device will handle transient volume peaks; devices with more headroom will be able to handle louder peaks without distorting.

See also *Clipping, Dynamic Range*.

Hearing

See *Appendix A: The Basics Of Sound*.

Hertz

Hertz (Hz) is a measurement of frequency in cycles per second. A 200 Hz frequency, for example, repeats its cycle 200 times every second. When frequencies get into the thousands, kilohertz (kHz) are often used, which refer to thousands of cycles per second. The average range of adult human hearing is approximately 20 Hz–20 kHz (20 cycles per second to 20,000 cycles per second).

See also *Frequency, Pitch, Sample Rate, Appendix A: The Basics Of Sound*.

High-Pass Filter

A high-pass filter cuts all frequencies below a specified target or cutoff frequency, allowing all higher frequencies to pass. Pass filters cut in a continuous slope until the signal is cut entirely (see *Fig. 46*). The slope of a pass filter is measured in decibels per octave, and the target frequency is the point on the slope where the signal has reached 3 dB of attenuation.

See also *Band-Pass Filter, Equalizer, Low-Pass Filter*.

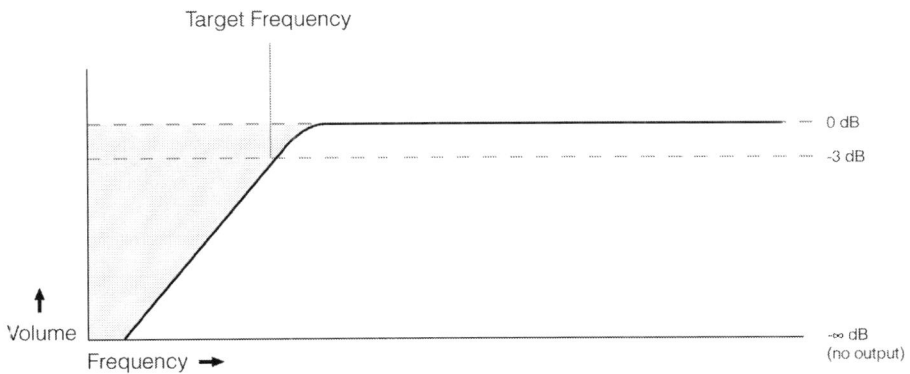

Figure 46: A High-Pass Filter

Hyper-Cardioid Pickup Pattern

Hyper-Cardioid is a microphone pickup pattern. Like the heart-shaped cardioid pattern, it is most sensitive from directly in front; however, the hyper-cardioid pattern provides more rejection from the sides than the cardioid pattern (see *Fig. 47*). The hyper-cardioid pattern also has a lobe of sensitivity at the back, making its angle of most rejection approximately 45° off of the back of the microphone. Any sounds that are specifically being avoided should be placed at this angle.

See also *Cardioid Pickup Pattern, Microphones, Pickup Pattern*.

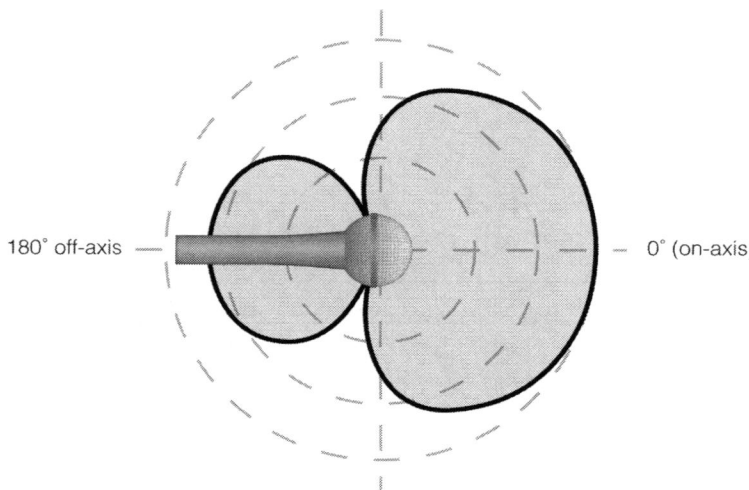

Figure 47: Hyper-Cardioid Pickup Pattern

Impedance

Impedance is an extensive topic with subtleties best left to physics text books, so for our purposes here we will use a definition of impedance that is narrower than that used in the realm of physics. For practical use in the recording studio, impedance refers to resistance to an electrical current. The word impedance is often represented with the letter Z, and is measured in ohms (Ω). For a recording engineer, the main uses of impedance are for matching the inputs and outputs of instruments, microphones, and devices, and for matching speakers to amplifiers.

Impedance For Microphones, Instruments, and Devices

All audio device outputs are rated with an output impedance that should be matched to the impedance of the input it is hooked up to. The most common impedance ranges are high-impedance (generally around 20–50kΩ), which is used for most instruments, and low-impedance (around 150–250Ω), which is most common for microphones, mixers, and processors. Most of the time, impedance matching in these situations is as simple as plugging high-impedance devices into high-impedance inputs and low-impedance devices into low-impedance inputs.

In situations where you want to plug a high-impedance output into a low-impedance input (such as direct recording an instrument), a DI (direct injection) box should be used. A DI box converts the low-impedance signal to a high-impedance one and balances the signal (see *Balanced Cabling*). It can then be plugged into a high-impedance input such as a mic preamp.

In some cases, usually for special effect purposes, it may be necessary to plug a low-impedance device, such as a microphone, into a high impedance input, such as an amp or effect processor designed for a guitar or other instrument. In these cases, a step-down, or impedance-matching, transformer should be used. This will take signal from a balanced XLR cable and convert it to an unbalanced high-impedance output (usually a ¼" jack).

Impedance For Speakers And Amplifiers

When matching speakers to amplifiers, impedance needs to be approached a little differently. Amplifiers are labelled with a minimum impedance rating, which is generally located next to the speaker outputs. This is usually in the realm of 4Ω, 8Ω, or 16Ω. Optimal output comes from matching this load exactly (i.e., plugging an 8Ω speaker into an amp with a min. 8Ω rating). Putting a higher load (such as a 16Ω speaker with a min. 8Ω amp) will result in slightly less volume but is otherwise not problematic. Placing a lower load than the minimum impedance rating puts unnecessary strain on the amplifier and can ultimately damage it.

Matching amps and speakers gets a little more difficult when multiple speakers are hooked up to the same output. In this case, the manner in which they are wired will affect the total load they represent to the amplifier. The three configurations for wiring multiple speakers are series, parallel, and series/parallel (see *Fig. 48*).

Speakers are connected in series when the positive lead of the amplifier is hooked to the positive lead of the first speaker, the negative lead of that speaker is then connected to the positive lead of the next speaker, and so on until the negative lead of the last speaker is connected to the negative lead of the amplifier. When speakers are connected in this manner, the total load is the sum of all the individual speakers' impedances. For example, three 8Ω speakers in series would represent a total load of 24Ω (8Ω + 8Ω+ 8Ω = 24Ω).

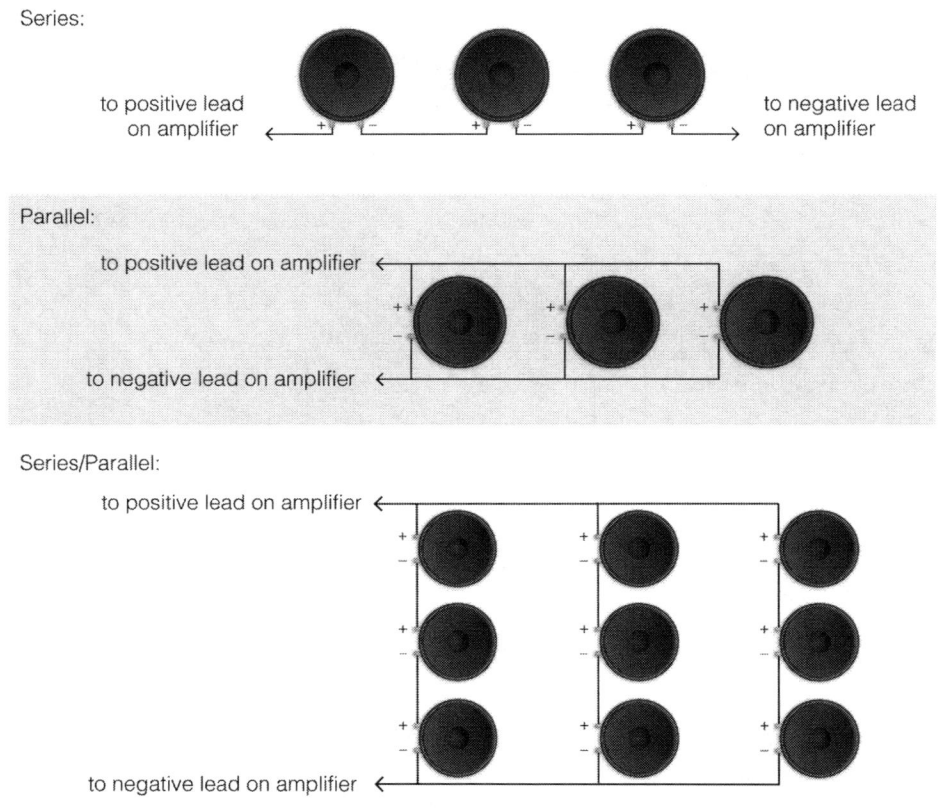

Figure 48: Series, Parallel, and Series/Parallel Speaker Configurations

Speakers are connected in parallel when all speakers' positive leads are connected to the positive lead on the amplifier and all negative leads are connected to the negative in the amplifier. When connected in parallel, the math is more complicated. The total load of a set of parallel-connected speakers can be calculated using the equation in *Fig. 49*. The good news is that when all speakers in a parallel circuit are the same impedance, the math is as simple as dividing the impedance of one speaker by the total number of speakers. So, in the case of three 8Ω speakers, the total load would be 2.67Ω (8Ω ÷ 3 = 2.67Ω).

$$\text{Total Load} = \frac{1}{\frac{1}{A} + \frac{1}{B} + \frac{1}{C}}$$

Figure 49: Calculating Total Load of Parallel-Connected Speakers

The third manner of connecting multiple speakers is called series/parallel. This consists of the parallel connection of series-connected arms. In this situation, the total load is calculated by adding up the total impedance of each arm using the math for a series connection and then calculating the total impedance of the circuit using the equation for a parallel connection as if each arm was an individual speaker. So, if a series/parallel connection consists of three arms, each with three 4Ω speakers, the total impedance would be 4Ω (4Ω + 4Ω + 4Ω = 12Ω, and 12Ω ÷ 3 = 4Ω).

I/O

I/O is a common abbreviation for inputs and outputs. This expression is often used when referring to the specifications of a piece of audio equipment, for example "This workstation has 24 channels of I/O," means that is has 24 inputs and 24 outputs.

Input and Output Module

See *Audio Interface*.

Insert

An insert is a point on a channel strip where the signal can be routed to another device then returned to the channel. Unlike an auxiliary send, which is used to blend the dry (unprocessed) signal with the wet (processed) sound, an insert sends the entire signal out of the channel and then returns the processed signal to the channel strip. An insert, then, is best for effects that require the entire signal to be processed, such as a compressor or equalizer, and an aux send is better for blended effects such as reverb or delay.

Inserts send and receive the signal via a single jack by use of an insert cable, also called a send/return cable. A standard insert cable has one ¼" TRS jack at one end and spits to two unbalanced ¼" jacks which are labelled either "send" and "return", or "tip" and "ring" (see *Fig. 50*). The TRS jack is plugged into the channel strip's insert jack, the send or tip jack is connected to the input of the processor, and the return or ring into the output of the processor.

See also *Auxiliary Send, Channel Strip*.

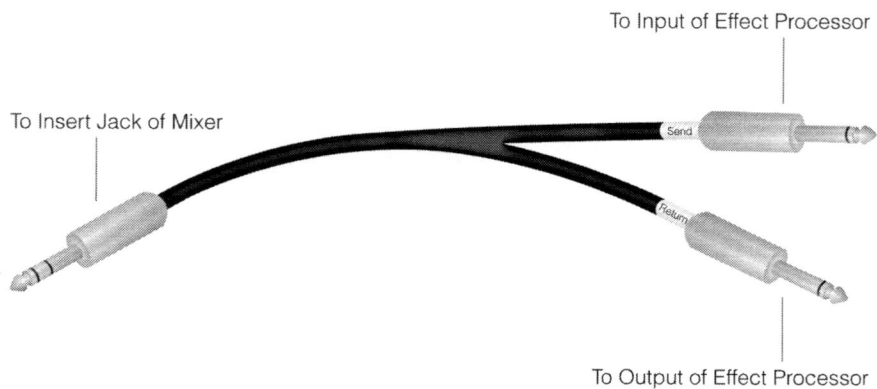

Isolation Room

An isolation room, or isolation booth, is an acoustically isolated room generally off of the control room or main live room. It is used to acoustically separate an instrument from others being recorded at the same time, eliminating bleed between microphones.

Kilohertz

Frequency is measured in hertz (Hz), a unit of cycles per second. When the number of cycles per second gets into the thousands, it is common to instead use kilohertz (kHz), meaning thousand cycles per second. For example, 2 kHz is equal to 2,000 Hz, and a CD's sample rate of 44.1 kHz means it has 44,100 samples for every second of recording.

See also *Frequency, Pitch, Sample Rate, Appendix A: The Basics Of Sound.*

Latency

Latency is a short lag (usually only milliseconds long) in a digital signal that occurs during the recording process. This is the result of the time it takes for the processor to receive the signal, process it, and reproduce it. When a recording system has significant amounts of latency, it can affect the performers' musical timing and can be disconcerting for performers listening on headphones, because what they hear feels disjointed from their performance. While latency is unavoidable in digital workstations, careful setup of the recording system can minimize it to the point that it is virtually unnoticeable.

Some digital audio interfaces offer "latency-free" monitoring. This works by feeding a signal back to the headphones that has not gone through the processor. While this is effective for recording an individual track, it does not allow for effects to be applied during tracking and is problematic when recording to pre-recorded tracks.

See also *DAW*.

Loop

A loop is a segment of audio that is played repeatedly. Some engineers/producers create their own loops; however, they can also be purchased from a variety of commercial suppliers. These usually come in the form of 1-, 2-, or 4-bar segments of an individual instrument. These segments can be looped and layered to create entire songs or backing tracks for vocals and acoustic instruments.

Initially made popular in electronic music, loops are now common in many styles of music. Drum loops are probably the most common, particularly amongst solo songwriters, as multiple drum loops of the same tempo can be used together to built the drum part for an entire song.

When using loops that you have not created yourself, it is advisable to check any copyright information associated with it to ensure that you have the right to use it for the application. This is especially important when using loops for commercial projects.

Loop Record

Some recording workstations offer a "loop record" feature. This allows a segment to be recorded multiple times in quick succession. The workstation may use "virtual tracks" or non-destructive recording, leaving a selection of takes to choose from. For example, if a 4-bar segment of a track needs to be recorded, the loop record feature allows the performer to record the segment several times without stopping in between and then go back and choose the best take from amongst them.

Lossless

Lossless is a term used to describe types of file compression that do not result in any loss of quality. Lossless file types for audio include AIFF and WAV files. Forms of file compression that discard information to create smaller files (such as MP3) are called "lossy" compression.

See also *AIFF, File Compression, WAV File*.

Lossy

Forms of file compression that achieve small file sizes by discarding information are referred to as "lossy". Lossy formats always result in reduced quality, but the degree of quality loss depends on the amount of file compression used. A file that has been saved in a lossy format cannot be restored to its original quality.

The most widely used lossy format for audio is MP3. Lossy formats are used for the superior level of comperssion they achieve, which is important when transferring the file over the internet or storing them on portable mass storage such as portable MP3 players.

See also *File Compression, MP3*.

Loudness

See *Fletcher-Munson Curve*.

Low-Pass Filter

A low-pass filter cuts all frequencies above a specified target or cutoff frequency, allowing all lower frequencies to pass through unaffected. The filter cuts in a continuous slope, increasing the amount of attenuation as the frequency gets higher until the signal is cut completely (see *Fig. 51*). The slope or rate at which this cut increases is measured in decibels per octave. The target frequency is the point on the slope where it has reached 3 dB of attenuation.

See also *Band-Pass Filter, Equalizer, High-Pass Filter*.

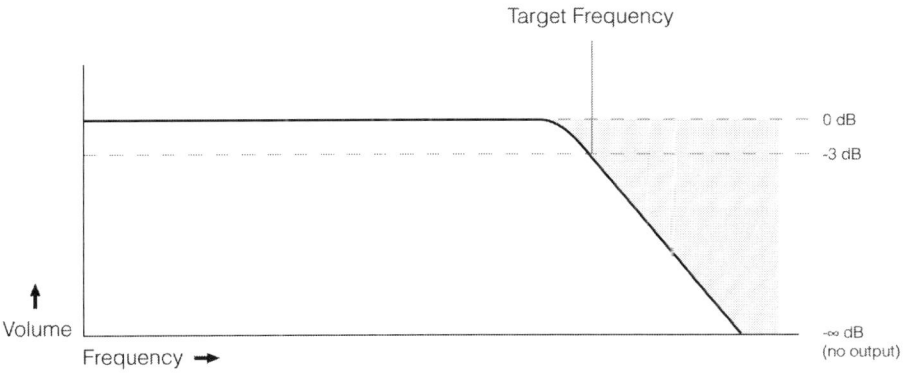

Figure 51: A Low-Pass Filter

Lightpipe

See *ADAT Optical Interface*.

Limiting

Limiting is compression that uses a compression ratio of 10:1 or higher. Because of this high ratio, a limiter can be thought of as a "brick wall" for signal level – volume will never get much above the threshold. For this reason, limiters are often used to protect against clipping during the tracking and mixing stages of a recording.

See also *Compression, Dynamic Range*.

Line Level

Line level is the standard operating level for most audio devices. Because this signal level is standard, plugging a line-level output into a line-level input (such as a CD player into a mixer, or a mixer into a video recorder) will always provide acceptable levels. Notable exceptions are microphones, power amplifiers (output), and speakers. A microphone, for example, must be plugged into a preamplifier to raise its signal to line level, and the output of the preamp can then be plugged into a line-level input.

See also *Impedance*.

Live Room

Most professional studios make use of at least two environments: a live room for the performance and a control room where the engineer controls the recording equipment. Some studios will have more than one live room as well as isolation booths to separate specific instruments. In the home studio, the live room and the control room are often combined due to space constraints.

See also *Control Room, Isolation Room*.

Masking

Masking is when a sound is made inaudible by another louder sound in the same frequency range. Examples of this include a bass masking the kick drum in a mix, or a keyboard being masked by an electric guitar.

Some ways to overcome the masking phenomenon include changing the arrangement so the instruments are no longer playing in the same frequency range, panning one instrument to the left and the other to the right (though this only works when the mix is played back in stereo), and using an equalizer to make the instruments prominent in different parts of the frequency range.

Master Buss

The master buss is the signal path on a mixing board that routes individual channels to the master outputs. Some mixing boards have inserts on the master buss, allowing a processor, such as a compressor, to affect the entire mix.

See also *Buss, Channel Strip, Mixing Board.*

Mastering

Mastering is the process of preparing an album for duplication. The mastering engineer takes the finished stereo tracks provided by the studio and creates a completed master recording that can be sent to the duplication plant. During this process, the tracks are brought to a consistent volume and tone, gaps between songs are set, and a final "polish" is put on the recordings. This is mainly achieved through careful use of compression (often multi-band compression) and equalization.

The mastering process is often under-valued by home studio users; however, a skilled mastering engineer can significantly improve the final recording. Sending tracks to be mastered by another engineer is also an opportunity to have a fresh, unbiased pair of ears listen to a recording before reproduction.

Microphones

Microphones convert acoustic energy into electrical energy. The quality of sound produced by a microphone will depend on factors such as the type of microphone, the manufacturing quality of the microphone, its placement in relation to the instrument, and its placement within the room.

Choosing the right microphone for a particular application is a matter of personal taste. Every instrument, room, performer, and microphone are different, and because of this, the results of a recording change along with these variables. The ideal situation is to have a variety of microphones available for a session and to try a few of them, each in several placements, before settling on a decision for the instrument at hand. As with all things in recording, there are no hard-and-fast rules, only suggestions for best practice; often the best results come from breaking the rules of traditional usage.

Dynamic Microphones

There are two main types of microphones that are in common usage in the studio: dynamic and condenser. These use different methods to convert acoustic energy and yield different results.

Dynamic microphones work through the process of magnetic induction. They are usually comparatively inexpensive, rugged, and they can withstand large amounts of sound pressure, making them very popular for use in live sound reinforcement. In the studio, these characteristics make dynamic mics a good choice for high sound pressure placements, such as close miking drums or loud guitar amplifiers.

Most dynamic mics create electrical current by using a coil attached to a diaphragm suspended in a magnetic field (see *Fig. 52*). When sound hits the

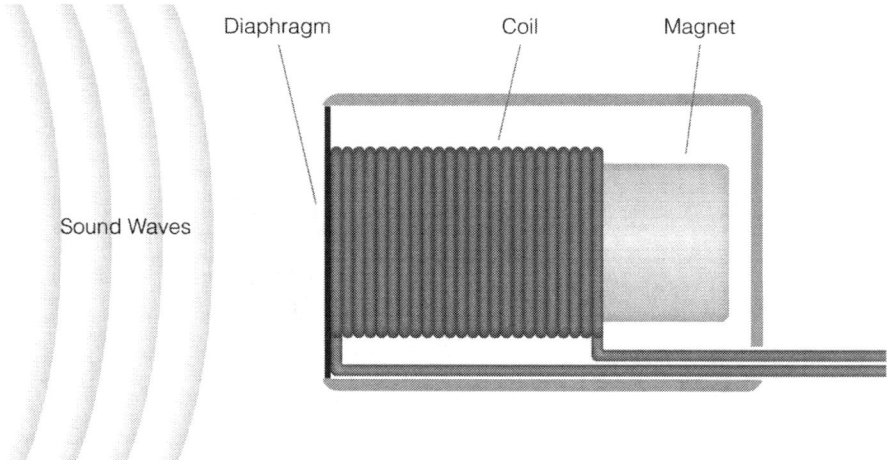

Figure 52: Capsule of a Moving-Coil Dynamic Microphone

diaphragm, the coil moves, creating magnetic flux, which is turned into electrical signal and sent out the cable. These are called "moving coil" dynamics, and their construction is very similar to a speaker. In fact, by wiring a speaker backwards, it can be used as a microphone.

There is another type of dynamic microphone that is commonly used in the studio, and that is the ribbon microphone. Ribbon mics work in a similar manner to moving coil dynamics, but instead of the diaphragm and coil, they use a thin ribbon of corrugated metal (see *Fig. 53*). These mics are coveted for their warm, vintage-style tone.

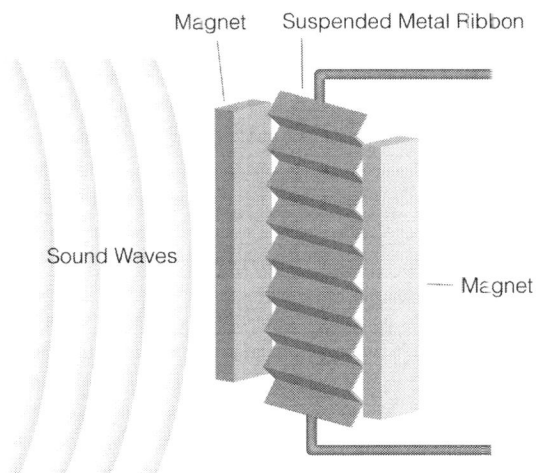

Figure 53: Capsule of a Ribbon Microphone

Ribbon mics are, however, more fragile than moving-coil microphones. The thin metal ribbon can be damaged by sharp gusts of air, so placement should be done carefully with some instruments (such as trumpet or trombone). Ribbon mics also cannot receive phantom power (a voltage supplied through the cable that is necessary for condenser mics). Some modern designs have circuits to protect them from phantom power, but caution is still advisable.

Condenser Microphones

Condenser microphones reproduce sound by use of electrical induction. The capsule of a condenser mic is made up of a positively-charged, fixed plate and a negatively-charged, movable diaphragm. As sound pressure hits the diaphragm, it moves closer and farther from the plate and creates electrical flux, which makes up the microphone's output (see *Fig. 54*).

Condenser mics are usually more sensitive than dynamics, allowing them to be placed farther away from the instrument, and they generally pick up more of the tone of the room. This results in a more natural sound but also means that environmental noises (such as heating, ventilation, and computer fans) can be problematic. Because they are usually not as rugged as most dynamic mics, placing condenser mics on instruments that create high sound pressure levels should be done with care. Condensers are usually a good choice for acoustic instruments, vocals, drum overheads, and ambient mics.

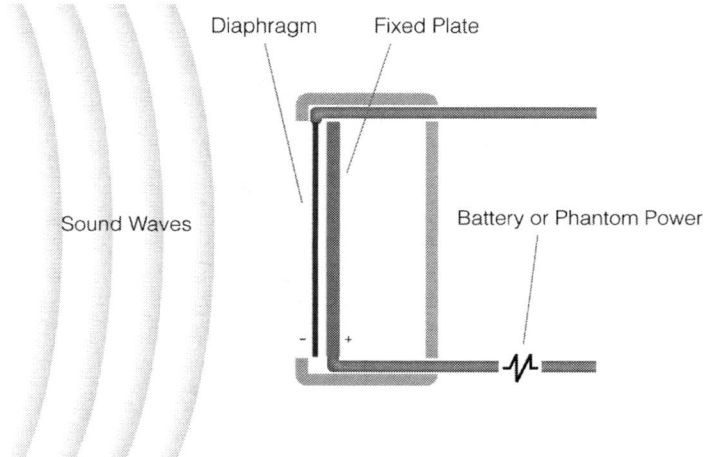

Figure 54: Capsule of a Typical Condenser Microphone

Because the signal generated by the capsule of a condenser mic is quite low, they have a small preamplifier built into them to boost the signal to standard mic level. This preamplifier requires electrical current to function. In some cases this can be supplied by a battery mounted within the mic itself, but most rely on the use of phantom power: a current that is supplied through the cable from the preamp or mixer. If phantom power is not available on the mixer or preamp being used, a phantom power supply can be placed between the microphone and the mic input.

As mentioned above, phantom power should not be used when a ribbon mic is connected. Other dynamic microphones, however, are not affected by phantom power as long as a proper XLR cable is used.

Pickup Patterns

A microphone's pickup pattern (also called directional response or polar pattern) describes from what directions it is sensitive to sound energy (see *Fig. 55*). The most common pickup patterns are omnidirectional, bi-directional (also called figure-8), cardioid, and hyper-cardioid.

As the name implies, the omnidirectional patten picks up equally from all sides.

The bi-directional pattern results in equal sensitivity from the front and the back, while rejecting information from the side. It should be noted that the signal from the rear of a bi-directional mic is 180° out of phase from the front (see *Phase*).

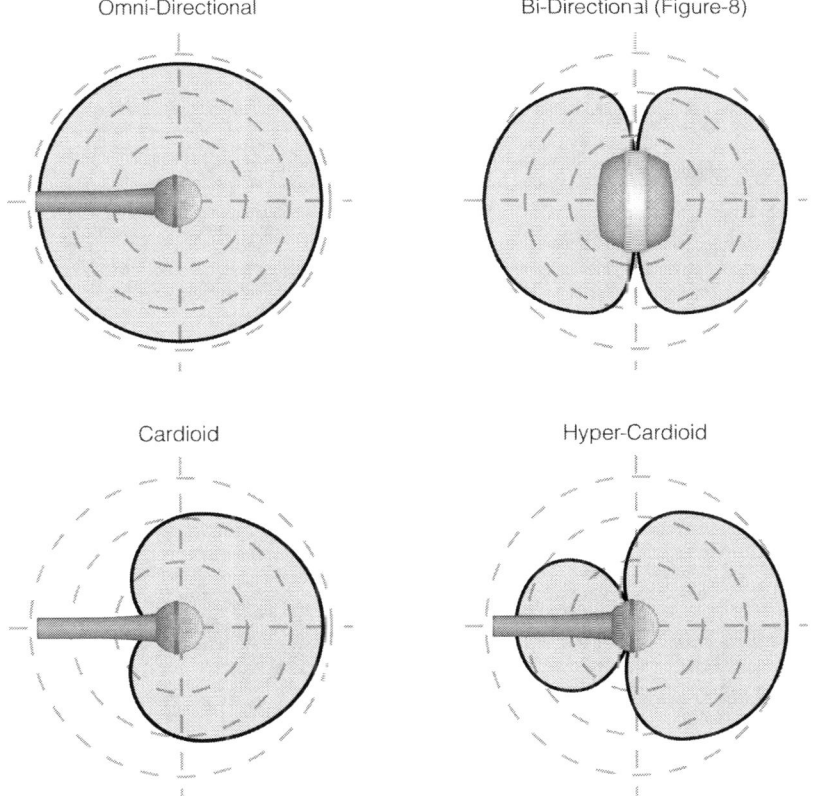

Figure 55: Pickup Patterns

The Encyclopedia of Home Recording

The cardioid pattern, named for its heart-like shape, is most sensitive directly in front and has the strongest rejection from directly behind.

Closely related to the cardioid pattern is the hyper-cardioid pattern, which is less sensitive from its sides than a cardioid mic. As you will notice in the diagram, the hyper-cardioid pattern has a small lobe of sensitivity from directly behind. This means the angle of most rejection is approximately 45° off of the rear of the mic.

As a uni-directional mic, such as a cardioid pattern, is placed closer to a sound source, its sensitivity to bass frequencies increases. This is called proximity effect and is common to all uni-directional mics.

Many microphones allow the pickup pattern to be changed, either by a switch or with a cap that is placed over the capsule.

Frequency Response

Sensitivity in different frequency ranges varies greatly from one mic to another. These variations give each mic its own character and tone. Frequency response charts are available for most microphones, either packaged with the mic or online. These charts show what ranges the mic is most and least sensitive in.

While a frequency response chart will give you a place to start when choosing a mic for a particular application, the only way to know how a mic will sound is to try it out. Variations in placement will affect a mic's tonal characteristics, and its response can often change greatly as the mic is rotated away from the sound source. When choosing a mic and placement for a task, it is usually best to try many variations to find the best solution for the task at hand.

Maximum SPL Rating

The maximum SPL (sound pressure level) rating of a microphone tells us how much sound pressure (volume) a microphone can pickup without distorting. This is expressed in decibels (for example, "Max SPL: 160 dB"). The sound pressure from an instrument decreases with distance, so microphones with lower SPL ratings can still be used on a loud instruments if they are placed at a greater distance. When close miking a loud instrument, such as a drum or loud amplifier, it is best to use a microphone with a high max SPL rating.

See also *Appendix C: Microphone Placement Guide*

Microphone Preamplifier

See *Preamplifier*.

Microphone Snake

A microphone snake is a single conduit-style cable that contains multiple individual mic cables, used to cleanly run multiple mic signals over a distance. Mic snakes are most commonly used in live sound reproduction between the stage and the mixing board.

Mic snakes come in many configurations, but most commonly they have a box at one end with a number of female XLR plugs for microphones to be plugged in to and at the other end have an equal number of male XLR jacks that are plugged into the mixing board. Often mic snakes will have a pair of jacks for returning the stereo output of the mixer to the stage where they are plugged into the amplifiers for the front-of-house speakers.

Mid-Side Technique

Mid-side (or M-S) is a stereo miking technique that uses one cardioid microphone and one bi-directional microphone. The cardioid mic is placed facing the sound source and the bi-directional mic is placed perpendicular to the cardioid mic so it is picking up the sides of the room (see *Fig. 56*). They are each recorded onto one track.

The track with the bidirectional microphone is then copied to a third track, and the phase is inverted on the copy. The two bi-directional tracks are then panned hard left and right while the cardioid mic is panned center. By adjusting the relative volume if the cardioid mic we can control how close or far away the recorded

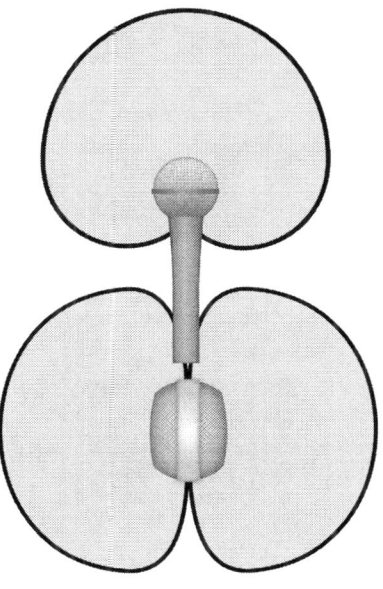

Figure 56: Mid-Side Microphone Technique

instrument sounds. It is important to note that this technique only works in stereo. If this is played back in mono, the two tracks from the bi-directional mic will cancel each other out completely, leaving only the signal from the cardioid mic.

MIDI

MIDI is an acronym for Musical Instrument Digital Interface. It allows multiple devices, including computers and digital instruments, to communicate with each other. MIDI can be used in live performance to trigger sounds in one device from another or to control certain MIDI-compatible devices such as lighting. A software or hardware sequencer can be used to record and playback MIDI performances with highly flexible editing capabilities.

Many people struggle with the idea that MIDI signals contain no audio. A MIDI signal contains only event information such as the note being played, how long it was held for, and how hard the note was played. A typical MIDI setup may involve a MIDI-compatible keyboard hooked into a computer with sequencing software. When the keyboard is played, it sends information about the performance to the sequencer, which records this information. When the sequenced performance is played back, the sequencer sends the information back to the keyboard, triggering the appropriate sounds to recreate the performance.

One of the greatest advantages of MIDI is the flexible nature of its editing:

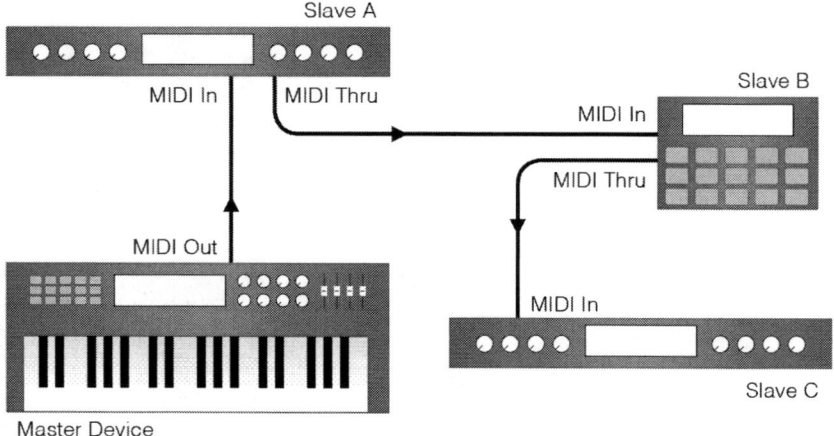

Figure 57: Daisy Chained MIDI Devices

mistakes can be corrected, timing made perfect, and instruments changed. Every detail about a performance is fully editable at any time.

A MIDI signal can transmit up to 16 channels of information, meaning that multiple devices can be "daisy-chained" together to allow one sequencer to trigger up to 16 different MIDI devices (see *Fig. 57*). Similarly, a controller device, such as a keyboard, can be split to allow different keys to control different devices.

MIDI Machine Control

Some devices, including some multitrack recorders, can be controlled using MIDI Machine Control (MMC), allowing some of their functions to be triggered by MIDI. One example of this would be having a recorder begin recording when play is hit on a sequencer.

MIDI Module

A MIDI module, or sound module, is a device that contains sets of digital samples to be triggered by an external MIDI controller such as a keyboard, drum machine, or sequencer. MIDI modules often have samples to recreate a variety of instruments, though some, more specialized, modules focus on a single instrument. In effect, a MIDI module can be thought of as a synthesizer without keys.

MIDI Interface

A MIDI interface is used to connect MIDI devices to a computer, allowing for software sequencing, control of software synthesizers, or control of events in MIDI-compatible software. Some newer MIDI keyboards come with USB outputs, allowing them to act as a MIDI interface as well.

Mix Automation

See *Automation*.

Mixdown

See *Mixing*.

Mixing

Mixing, or mixdown, is the act of taking multiple discrete tracks and turning them into one stereo, mono, or surround-sound track. The resulting track is then ready for mastering and/or reproduction.

Mixing is a very important part of the recording process because many irreversible decisions need to be made. Some engineers will pass their recordings on to be mixed by another engineer who specializes in mixing. This can be of particular benefit for those who record their own music, as it brings a fresh, objective set of ears to the project.

There are four basic areas which must be considered when mixing: spatial, tonal, dynamic, and attentional characteristics. A successful mix takes advantage of all four of these aspects.

Spatial Characteristics

A good mix provides a feeling of space, both in the stereo field (left to right) and depth (front to back). Instruments should feel as if they are originating from different places, some closer, some farther away, and in a variety of locations within the stereo field. The primary tools for manipulating spatial perception during mixing are the pan knob, reverb, and compression.

If the goal of the mix is to recreate a natural listening environment, such as a live performance, then spatial decisions should reflect that goal. Instruments should be placed in logical positions and reverb should reflect natural environments. Alternatively, recording is often used as a venue to create listening situations that could never exist in a live performance. With this approach the engineer has great creative freedom and can create fantastical or "larger than life" mixes.

Tonal Characteristics

The tonal range and balance of a mix affects its intelligibility and its fullness. A great mix feels like the entire range of the audible spectrum is being represented somewhat evenly. This is mainly controlled with arrangement, choice of instruments/microphones, and equalization.

There are two problems in the area of tone that should be avoided: gaps and buildup. Gaps occur when part of the frequency spectrum is not being used. When gaps occur, the engineer needs to asses why and whether it is acceptable. In some cases, gaps are necessary and expected due to the content. A children's choir, for example, will be only in the upper part of the frequency spectrum. In some traditional musical styles, gaps are also common and expected. Awareness of cultural and traditional expectations of the musical style's tone is important in these situations.

Buildup is a more common problem in modern music. Buildup occurs when too much is happening in a given frequency range, usually because more than one instrument is fighting for attention. The most problematic area for buildup is in the low-mid range where multiple instruments' ranges overlap.

To avoid frequency buildup it is best to plan what instrument needs to be most prominent in each frequency range and to cut that range in other instruments that overlap it. For example, if the thump of the bass guitar needs to be prominent, the kick drum should be cut in that range. The slap of the beater hitting the skin on the kick can, in turn, be made more prominent, while cutting the bass in that range to make room.

Dynamic Characteristics

The term dynamics is mainly used in recording to refer to changes in volume, but other dynamic variations are important as well. Because people are naturally drawn to contrast, dynamic changes make songs more engaging and keep them from becoming monotonous. Changes in volume, tone, key, tempo, and instrumentation are examples of the ways a mix can be made more dynamic.

Attentional Characteristics

A great mix not only sounds good but draws the attention of the listener and pulls it through the song. When a song has a strong melodic hook, getting attention is much easier. A dynamic change, unique tonality, or distinct effect can draw attention to this hook. An example of this is the warble of over-done pitch correction in Cher's "Believe".

The mix should also draw the listener through the song as it progresses. When the lead instrument (often the vocals) pauses, something needs to take the listener's attention in the interim. This may mean bringing in another instrument or bringing the focus to one that was previously in the background. It may be helpful to think of the mix as the stage of a TV show or play. When the focal characters leave the stage, others need to enter right away. Even a few moments without a focal point would cause the pace of the show to seem slow and cause the viewer to lose interest. The same is true in music. Carefully guiding the listener's attention through the song results in an interesting and engaging mix.

Studio Monitors

Ideally, mixing should be done using studio reference monitors. These are speakers that are designed to reproduce the sound accurately, with as little tonal coloration as possible. Studio monitors are said to have a "flat" frequency response, meaning they don't boost or cut in any frequency range. An important distinction here is that while home stereo speakers are designed to sound good, studio monitors are designed to sound accurate.

Near-field monitors are by far the most common speakers for mixing. These are reasonably small, accurate speakers that are designed for a close listening distance (usually about 3–6') at moderate volumes. There are many different brands and models of near-field monitors available, and the prices vary greatly. It is advisable to buy the best quality monitors your budget will allow because all decisions about your mix will be based on their reproduction. The most important thing, however, is to know the monitors you have. It is a good idea to frequently listen to well produced music though your monitors to know how a good mix sounds through them.

In addition to near-field monitors, most studios will have at least two other listening devices, usually a pair of large speakers with good bass response and a small, cheap stereo. While the engineer will spend most of the time mixing on the near-field monitors, he or she will check the mix on the alternate speakers periodically during the mix. The mix should also be checked on headphones, but it is inadvisable to use headphones as a primary monitoring source because the proximity of the speaker to the ear strongly affects perception of tonal and spatial characteristics.

Mix Position

The ideal mix position creates an equilateral triangle, with the engineer's head and the two monitors making up the three points (see Fig. 58). Vertically, the engineer's ears should be even with the midpoint between the woofer and the tweeter of the monitors.

Because the human ear responds differently to frequencies at different volumes, a mix can sound quite different when the volume is changed. The ideal mixing volume is said to be 80 dB SPL, as this is a common listening level and will yield the least change as the volume is raised or lowered. Most engineers will check their mixes at different volumes throughout the mixing process to ensure that the mix does not change drastically as the volume changes.

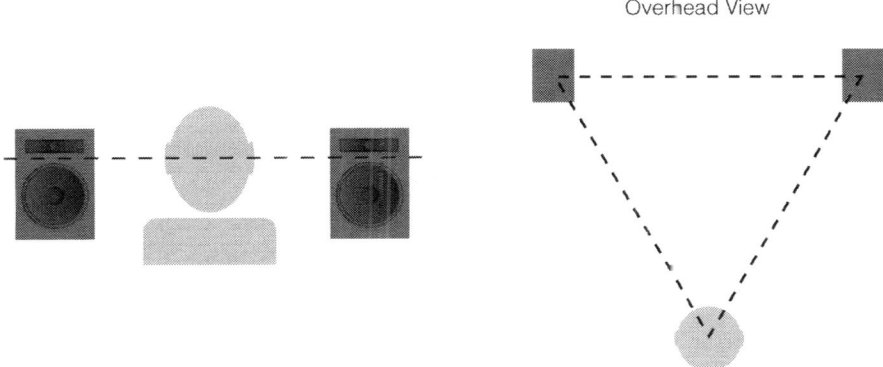

Figure 58: Mix Position

The room that mixing takes place in should also be considered when optimizing the mixing environment. Care should be taken to control the amount of reflected sound within the room. The amount of reflections being created in the room will affect decisions when adding reverb and EQ to elements of a mix. A highly reflective room will sway decisions towards less reverb and less brightness in a mix, while a very dead room will often result in adding too much reverb and too much brightness. An appropriate balance must be found that fits the specific room. Much like knowing your monitors, being highly familiar with how your room sounds will improve the quality of your mixes.

Once a mix has been completed, it is generally advisable to listen to it on a variety of sound systems before sending it for reproduction. This will help ensure that there will be no surprises in the final product. One of the most important places to check the mix is the car. The car is a very unique listening environment and can strongly color the tone of the mix. The car is also one of the places where people listen to music the most, making it an important consideration.

Mixing Board

A mixing board, also called a mixing desk or mixing console, is a device used to control the routing, tone, panoramic positioning, and relative volume of multiple audio signals. Mixing boards come in a wide variety of sizes, and the number of channels, busses, and mic preamps are among the variables from one model to the next.

The mixing board can, for the most part, be thought of in terms of its two main components: channels, which control the individual audio sources; and busses, which combine them and route them to various outputs.

Channels

Channels are the initial signal path for each audio source. Each input has its own channel, allowing it to be manipulated independently, without affecting other signals. Each channel can be controlled by use of its channel strip, a vertical column of controls used to manipulate the signal.

In a channel strip, signal travels from top to bottom, and all controls (with the exception of the aux send as noted below) are placed in the order in which they sit in the signal path (see *Fig. 59*). Adjusting a control on the channel strip will effect all controls below it and none above (e.g., the equalizer does not affect the preamp, but the gain, at the top of the strip, affects everything else).

The elements of the channel strip (as shown in *Fig. 59*) are listed and described below:

1. Gain/Trim: This provides control over the preamp. It is a means of controlling how "hot" your signal is. It

Figure 59: A Channel Strip

is best to get as much signal at this stage as possible without the signal clipping (distorting). Some channel strips will have a "clip light" to indicate when the signal is beginning to distort. See *Preamplifier*.

2. Insert Point: This allows you to send the entire signal to an external device (such as a compressor or equalizer) and return it to the channel on the same cable (called an insert cable or a send/return cable). See *Insert*.

3. Aux Sends: These knobs control how much signal is sent to an auxiliary output. An auxiliary send is used for parallel effects (effects where the processed signal is blended with the original, dry signal), or for creating separate monitor mixes. When using an aux send for effects, the aux output is plugged into the input of the effect unit and the output of the effect is plugged into the auxiliary return. See *Auxiliary Send*.

4. Pre-fader Select: This button controls whether the sends are "pre-fader" or "post-fader". If sends are "pre-fader", then the master fader will not affect the output of the send (better for creating monitor mixes). If a send is "post-fader", then the output of the send will go up or down with the master fader (better for effects). See *Auxiliary Send*.

5. Equalizer: Like the equalizer on your stereo, these knobs control the tonal qualities of your signal. Each knob will cut or boost the frequency range specified. See *Equalizer*.

6. Pan: The pan, or panorama, control allows you to place the signal anywhere in the stereo field by adjusting the amount of signal that goes to either speaker. Turning this knob all the way to one side will send the signal only to one speaker. See *Stereo Mixing*.

7. Mute: As the name suggests, this removes the channel from the mix and from any post-fader sends. This will not affect pre-fader sends.

8. Buss Assignment: These allow you to choose where you send your signal. Busses are most frequently used to select outputs but can allow for more complex routing as well, such as sub mixes. See *Buss*.

9. Fader: This controls the volume for the channel going into its assigned buss.

Busses

If channels are visualized as moving vertically across the mixing board, busses can be thought of as a horizontal route across the mixer (see *Fig. 60*). Busses are

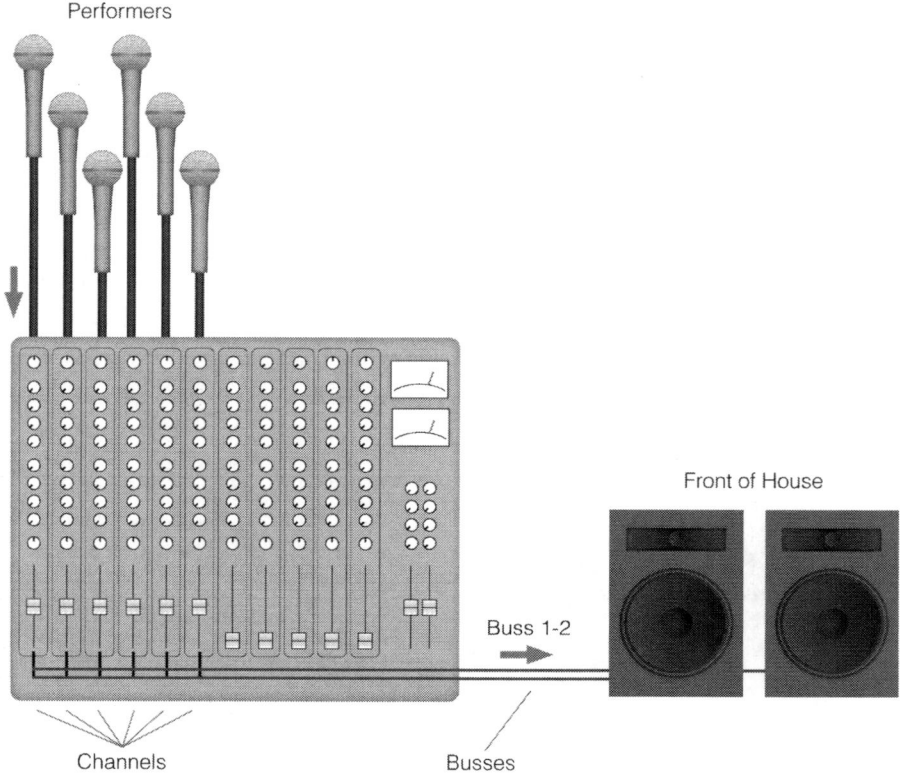

Figure 60: Channels and Busses

paths used to combine multiple channels and send them to a common destination. The most obvious example is the master buss: a stereo buss, or pair of busses, which combines all channels assigned to it and sends them to the master outputs of the mixer. On a basic 2-buss mixer, all un-muted channels are automatically assigned to the master buss.

Larger mixers have multiple busses, allowing for more complex routing possibilities. For example, channels 1-8 may be set to the master buss, sending them to the main outputs, while channels 9-16 are set to buss 3-4, sending them to entirely different outputs. In this example, the one mixer is creating two completely different mixes, effectively working as two mixers.

Another use for busses is for sub-mixing. For example, all drum tracks could be assigned to buss 3-4, which is then sent to a stereo channel assigned to the master buss. This stereo channel would then control all drum tracks simultaneously, allowing for faster volume changes or for a compressor or other processor to be placed on all drum tracks at once.

See also *Auxiliary Send, Equalizer, Insert, Preamplifier.*

Mix Position

See *Mixing.*

MMC

See *MIDI Machine Control.*

Modular Digital Multitrack Recorder

Modular digital multitrack recorders are recording devices that can be synchronized and used together to increase the number of tracks that can recorded at once. These originated with 8-track recorders such as ADAT and similar tape-based digital recorders, though current modular recorders tend to be hard disk recorders and may offer 24 or more tracks per unit.

See also *Multitrack Recording.*

Monitor Mix

See *Cue Mix.*

Monitors

Monitors, also called reference or studio monitors, are speakers designed for use in critical listening situations such as recording. Studio monitors are designed to have a "flat" frequency response, which is to say that they are designed to reproduce the sound exactly as it is recorded, with minimal tonal "coloration" of the sound. Studio monitors differ from home stereo speakers in that they are designed to accurately reproduce sound, while home stereo speakers are designed to produce a pleasant sound.

Traditionally, engineers relied mostly on far-field monitors. These large, often wall-mounted speakers have good bass response and are designed for a listening distance of several feet. In the late 70s and early 80s, smaller, near-field monitors became the norm for mixing. Near-field monitors are meant for a closer placement (3–6′) and are generally considered to "translate" better, meaning they are conducive to mixes that are consistent in a variety of listening environments. Large studios will often have far-field monitors as well, but these days they are generally used only to occasionally check the low end of the mix.

The proper setup for studio monitors is to form an equilateral triangle, with the points being formed by the engineer's head and the two monitors. Vertically, the engineer's ears should be centered between the woofer and the tweeter of the monitors (see *Fig. 61*).

In the home studio, near-field monitors are usually the best route as they are both more space efficient and more affordable. There are many brands and models of monitors on the market offering a range of pricing and quality. It is a good idea to buy the best quality monitors that are available within your budget because decisions about the recording will be made based on their ability to reproduce sound accurately. The most important thing, however, is to know well the monitors you have. Listening to well-produced music on your studio monitors will give you a good idea of what a good mix should sound like on them.

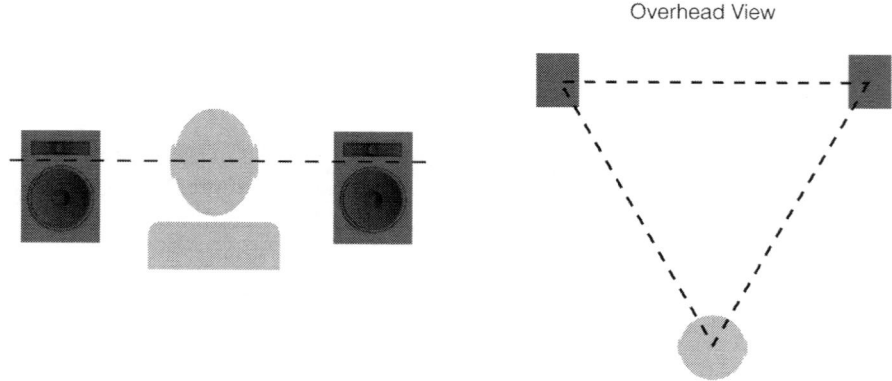

Figure 61: Mix Position

It is also common to keep two or three other sets of speakers in the studio and to check the mix on them periodically. A large set with good bass response, a small inexpensive pair, and headphones are the most common choices.

See also *Mixing*.

Mono

The term mono is short for monophonic, meaning "one sound". The term mono is usually used to refer to a mix that is reproduced with all instruments mixed to a single channel. This is opposed to a stereo recording, which uses two channels (one for the left speaker and one for the right), or surround sound, which uses five or more.

See also *Mixing*.

Monophonic

The term monophonic can refer to either a monophonic recording or mix (a mix that has all instruments run to a single channel) or a synthesizer that is only capable of producing one note at a time.

See also *Mono, Polyphony*.

Motorized Faders

Motorized faders are used on some mixing boards, software control surfaces, and digital audio workstations. When mix automation is being used, or when a previously saved mix is being recalled, the motorized faders will automatically move to the appropriate locations to represent what is happening in the mix. They are also handy in situations where the faders on a control surface or digital workstation are used to control more than one track each. In this situation, when the control is switched to a different set of tracks, the faders move to the appropriate locations for the tracks they are now representing, eliminating potential confusion over track volume.

See also *Control Surface, DAW, Mixing Board*.

Moving-Coil Microphone

Moving-coil microphones are the most common type of dynamic microphone. They are built very much like a speaker. In fact, wired correctly, a speaker will work as a microphone. A moving coil microphone has a diaphragm attached to a coil, suspended in a magnetic field. Sound pressure hits the diaphragm, moving the coil, which creates flux in the magnetic field. This flux is turned into electric signal and sent out though the mic cable.

See also *Dynamic Microphone, Microphone*.

MP3

MP3 is a common audio file type. MP3 uses "lossy" compression, meaning that some data is irrevocably thrown away to reduce file size. MP3s are the most common audio format for online distribution and for portable digital music players because of their small file size.

When an MP3 is encoded, options for bit rate and quality can be set. Smaller bit rates and lower quality settings will result in smaller file sizes but at the expense of sound quality. When creating an MP3, a balance must be found between size and audio quality that is appropriate for the situation.

See also *File Compression*.

Multi-Band Compression

Multi-band compression allows different frequency bands to be compressed separately. The signal is broken into multiple frequency ranges that are then fed into individual compression circuits. The benefit of this is that dynamic changes in one band will not affect compression in another.

Multi-band compression is most often used for mastering when individual instruments can no longer be controlled separately. For example, an over-active kick drum can be controlled without causing higher frequencies to pump, which can happen with standard compression.

Multi-band compression also acts a little like an equalizer. A frequency range can be compressed and its volume raised to make it more prominent without its volume peaks being any louder.

See also *Compression*, *Equalizer*.

Multitimbral

When a synthesizer or sampler has the ability to reproduce more than one instrument or set of samples at the same time, it is said to be multitimbral. This may mean that a keyboard can be split to have part of it sound like one instrument while the other part plays a second, or multiple sounds may be triggered simultaneously by the same key.

See also *Timbre*.

Multitrack Recording

Multitrack recording allows instruments to be recorded onto independent tracks that are played back alongside each other. Each track can be re-recorded and manipulated independently without affecting the others.

To best understand how multitrack recording works, it may be best to think of the beginnings of home multitrack recording. The first home multitrack recorders were cassette-based. A cassette tape has four tracks: side A left, side A right, side B left, and side B right. Cassette-based multitrack recorders used these four simultaneously, allowing the user to record, and re-record, onto the four tracks independently (see *Fig. 62*).

Before the invention of multitrack recording, all instruments were recorded simultaneously and mixed to a mono, and later stereo, recording device. The song was performed over and over until the entire band got it perfect at the same time. All mixing was done, and effects added, as the recording was being made, and no changes could be made afterward. When multitrack recording came on the scene in the 1940s and 50s, it completely changed the way we record. Suddenly, individual instruments could be manipulated or re-recorded after the initial recording session, and no longer was it necessary for the entire band to have a perfect take at once.

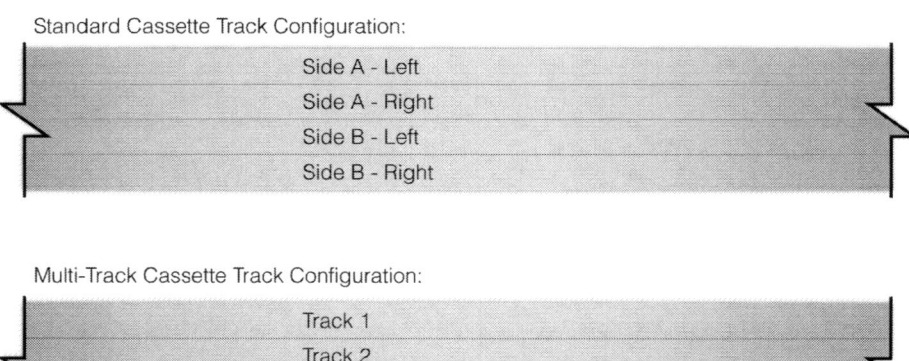

Figure 62: Cassette Used for Multi-Tracking

There are two basic approaches that tend to be taken in multitrack recording. Depending on the band and the situation, some engineers will record the whole band together, then re-record tracks in isolation as needed to improve the performance or recording quality. In other situations, the engineer may record the rhythm section on their own, then record the other tracks overtop (called overdubbing). Variations in between the two are also used.

The number of tracks that are available on a multitrack recorder can be increased by using a technique called bouncing or ping-ponging. In bouncing, multiple tracks are mixed together and recorded onto an empty track, making the original tracks available to be recorded on. For example, if a four-track recording device has guitar, bass, and percussion each on a track, those three tracks can be recorded together onto the last available track. This would leave one track with guitar, bass, and percussion on it and three tracks that are now available to be recorded on again (see *Fig. 63*). This can then be repeated, recording two more tracks and bouncing them to the third available track, then recording onto the two tracks that are now available. This effectively allows seven tracks to be recorded onto a four-track recorder. The danger of bouncing tracks is that they can no longer be controlled independently. In the example above, the guitar, bass, and tambourine are now on the same track, and any effects or processing will affect all three together. In analog recordings, bouncing also results in some quality loss from the reproduction. Digital recording does not suffer from this problem because the resulting track will theoretically be a perfect copy of the originals.

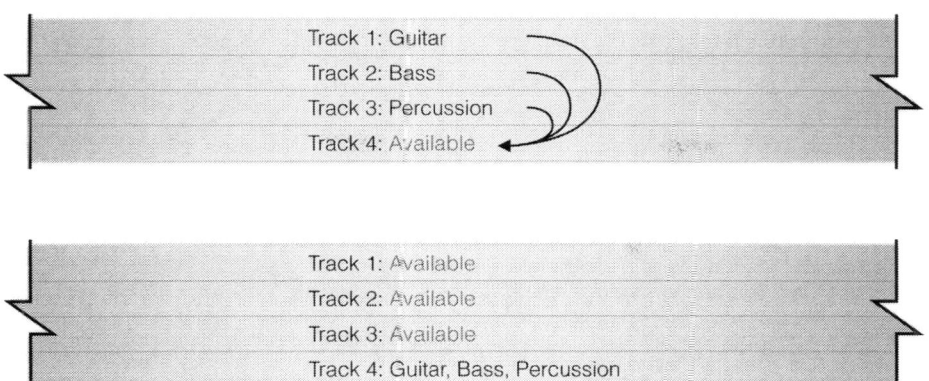

Figure 63: Bouncing Tracks on a 4-Track Recording

Mute

Most mixing boards have a mute button on every channel. This button will silence the channel, removing it from the mix. Some mixers have the mute switch do double duty; when the channel is muted, the signal is removed from the main mix but sent to an alternate buss, allowing it to be routed elsewhere.

See also *Channel Strip, Mixing Board*.

Near-Field Monitors

Near-field monitors are speakers designed for reference use in the recording studio. They are called near-field monitors because they are designed to be used at a reasonably close distance (about 3–6').

While larger far-field monitors were more common until the early 1980s, near-field monitors are now the norm in most studios. Large studios will often have far-field monitors as well, and mixes will be checked on them periodically to hear bass response, but the bulk of the mixing is done on near-field monitors.

Near-field monitors are far more practical in the home studio environment because they are more affordable, and their smaller size makes them easier to accommodate in small studios. The close listening distance with near-field monitors means that the acoustics of the mixing environment has a lesser effect on the mix than it does with far-field monitors.

See also *Far-Field Monitors, Monitors*.

Noise Gate

See *Gate*.

Noise Reduction

Noise reduction is the process of eliminating extraneous noise from a signal. This is of greater concern in tape-based recording than in digital recording, since tape has an inherent self-noise. Various manufactures have created noise-reduction systems over the years, the most widely known being the Dolby Noise Reduction System. While digital recording has made use of noise reduction less common, some manufacturers produce software with noise removal in mind. Uses for such software can include cleaning up digital conversions of analog recordings and removing extraneous acoustic noises such as computer fans or hum caused by fluorescent lighting.

Non-Destructive Editing

Non-destructive editing is one of the major benefits of modern digital recording. Non-destructive editing means that the original recording is not affected in any way and can be retrieved as it was originally recorded at any time.

With hard-disk recorders and other similar technologies, edits made to a track do not affect the original audio file, only how and when it is accessed. For example, if a portion of a track is edited out, the recorder stops accessing that part of the file but the data remains intact. At any point, that edit can be undone, restoring the edited portion of the track.

See also *Destructive Editing*.

Non-Destructive Recording

Most current digital audio workstations allow multiple takes to be recorded on the same track without erasing previous takes. This is called non-destructive recording. On some workstations this is done by entering a non-destructive recording mode that will record as many new takes as required, building a library of audio files that can be retrieved at any time, while other workstations do this by using "virtual tracks", which usually must be explicitly selected and may be limited in quantity.

Non-destructive recording has the obvious benefit that no take is ever lost, and the decision to try another take does not mean losing the existing one as it does in analog recording. The trade-off of non-destructive recording is in storage space. Non-destructive recording takes up much more space on the hard drive or whatever storage medium is being used. If space is not an issue, it is always safer to record non-destructively.

See also *Destructive Recording*.

Non-Linear Editing

See *Random Access Editing*.

Normalizing

Normalizing is a process available in most digital audio workstations that increases or decreases the overall volume of a selected audio segment so that

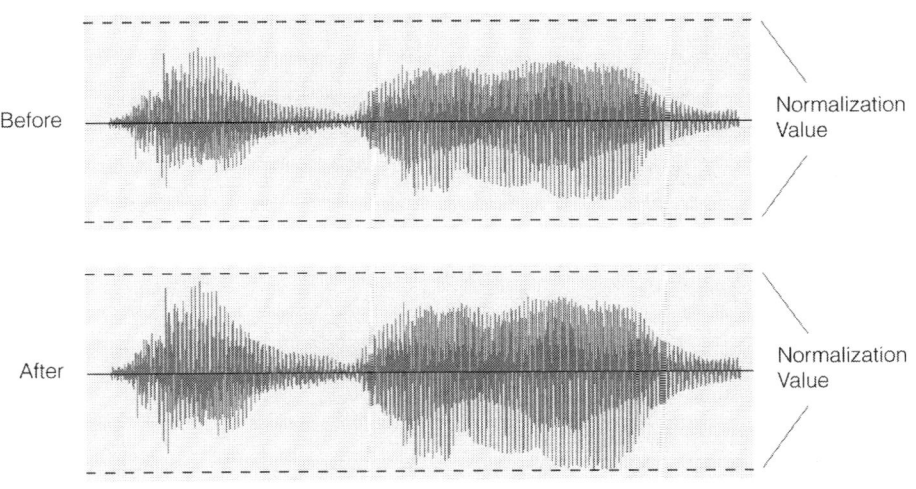

Figure 64: Normaliation

the highest volume peak is at specified level. For example, if an audio segment has its loudest peak at -1 dB, and it was normalized to 0 dB, the volume of the entire segment would be increased by 1 dB (see *Fig. 64*). Unlike the process of compression, normalizing does not affect the dynamic range of the audio segment.

Notch Filter

An EQ cut with a very narrow bandwidth (high-Q) is referred to as a notch filter (see *Fig. 65*). Notch filters are usually used in an attempt to remove a specific unwanted noise, such as hum from poor cabling, the sound of the pick against a guitar's strings, or ringing from a poorly tuned drum.

See also *Equalizer*.

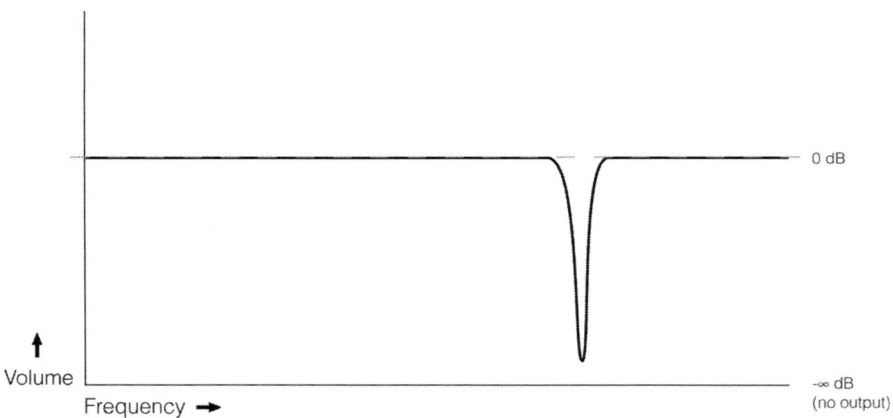

Figure 65: A Notch Filter

Null Point

See *Angle of Most Rejection*.

Nyquist Theorem

The Nyquist theorem relates to the conversion of analog signal to digital information. It states that in order for an analog signal to be properly converted to digital, the sample rate must be at least double the highest frequency being recorded (see *Fig. 66*). If a frequency of greater that one-half of the sample rate is introduced into an analog-to-digital converter, inharmonic "ghost" or "alias" frequencies will occur in the resulting digital signal.

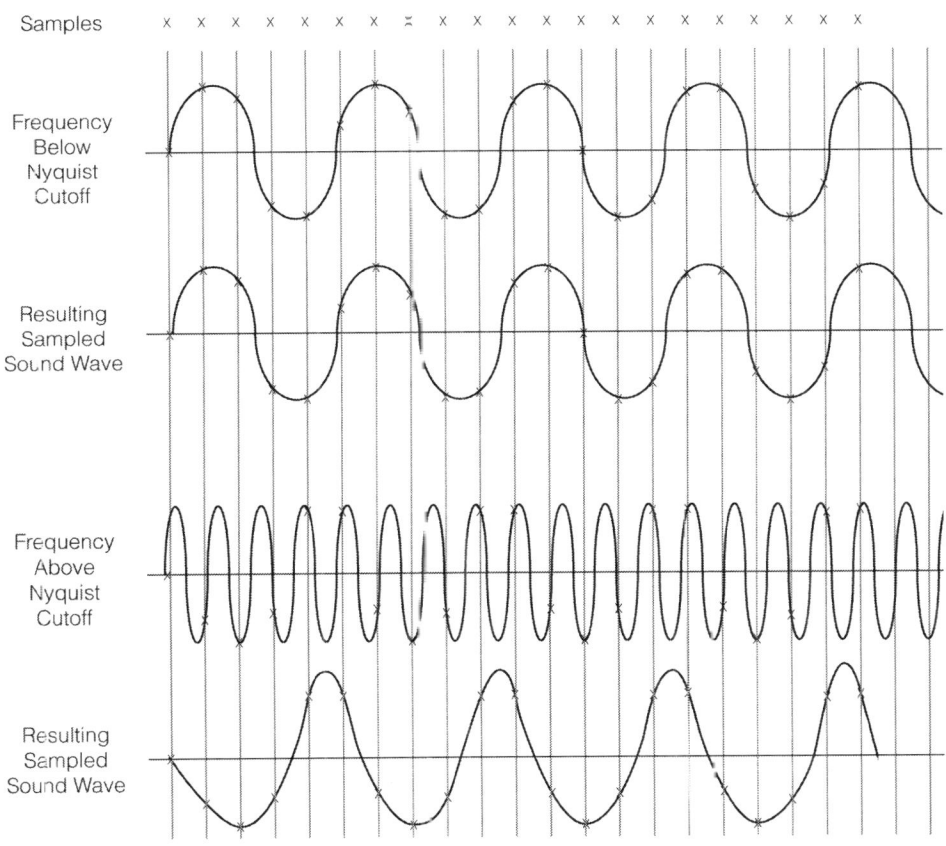

Figure 66: Results of Sampling Frequencies Above and Below Nyquist Cutoff

The upper range of human hearing is approximately 20 kHz. According to the Nyquist theorem, to properly record this entire range, a sample rate of at least 40 kHz must be used.

Because of this effect, digital-to-analog converters use a filter to block any frequencies above their Nyquist cutoff points. Because no filter can cut at a precise frequency, the filter is placed a little below one-half of the sample rate. For example, a converter that samples at 44.1 kHz (the sample rate of a CD) will have a filter cutting at approximately 20 kHz.

See also *Frequency, Sample Rate, Appendix A: The Basics Of Sound.*

Off-Axis Mic Placement

When a microphone is placed so that an instrument it is picking up is not in the area of greatest sensitivity for its pickup pattern, it is said to be off-axis (see *Fig. 67*). With many microphones, rotating the mic off-axis can yield a significantly different tone than when it is placed on-axis. When choosing mic placement, it is advisable to experiment with both on- and off-axis placements.

See also *Microphones, Pickup Pattern, Appendix C: Microphone Placement Guide.*

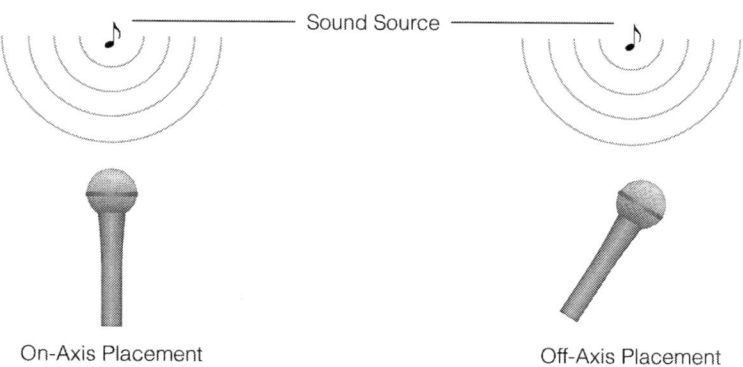

Figure 67: On- and Off-Axis Microphone Placement

Ohm

Ohms are a measurement of electrical resistance and are represented by the character Ω. In the world of professional audio, we use ohms to measure impedance. For the recording engineer, a basic understanding of impedance is important for matching outputs to inputs and matching speakers to amplifiers.

See also *Impedance.*

Omnidirectional Pickup Pattern

An omnidirectional microphone picks up signal from all sides equally (see *Fig. 68*). They are useful in situations where all sound in a room needs to be picked up equally, such as a performance in an acoustically pleasing venue. Because this pickup pattern does not reject signal from any direction, it is important that the room being recorded in has reasonable acoustics and that any sources of undesirable noise are removed.

See also *Microphones, Pickup Pattern, Appendix C: Microphone Placement Guide*.

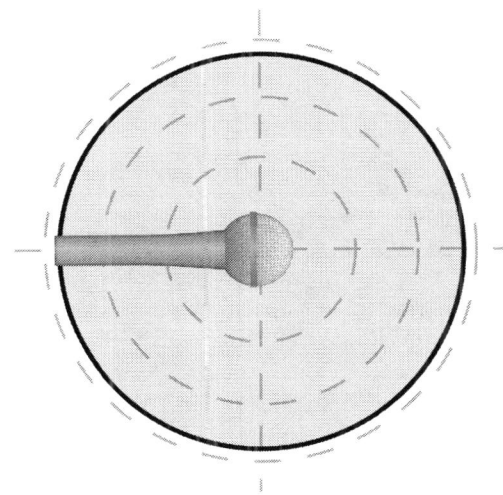

Figure 68: Omnidirectional Pickup Pattern

Orange Book

The Orange Book is the specifications guide for CD-R (recordable CD) and CD-RW (re-writeable CD) discs. The Orange Book is part of a series of specification manuals called the Rainbow Books that set standards for the various CD formats. These manuals also include the Red Book (CD audio) and the Yellow Book (CD-ROM), among others. By adhering to these standards, the recording industry can ensure that a CD-R will play on all CD-R compatible players.

ORTF Mic Technique

ORTF is a stereo miking technique named after the French television and radio commission that developed it (Office de Radiodiffusion-Télévision Française). ORTF is a binaural mic technique, which means it is meant to approximate the response of a listener's two ears. In the ORTF techniquem two cardioid mics are placed at an angle of 110° with the heads 17cm (7") apart (see *Fig. 69*). This technique not only provides excellent stereo imaging, but choosing a mic placement to start from can be as simple as moving around the room until it sounds good and then placing the mics where your head was.

See also *Microphones, Pickup Pattern, Stereo Miking, Appendix C: Microphone Placement Guide*.

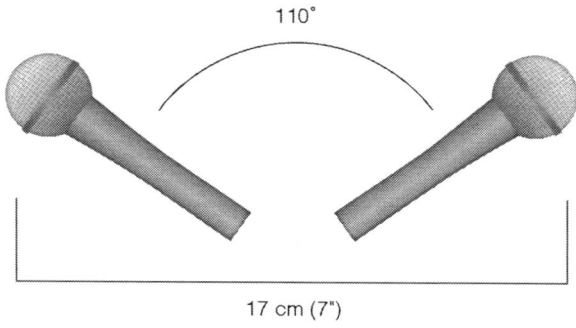

Figure 69: ORTF Stereo Miking Technique

Outboard Equipment

The term outboard equipment refers to any equipment or processors that are not contained within a mixing board or digital audio workstation.

Overdubbing

Overdubbing is the process of recording additional tracks to previously recorded audio. A common practice for multitrack recording is to record "bed tracks", usually the rhythm section, then to overdub the rest of the band. In this situation, the performers will listen and play along to the previously recorded tracks as if they were being performed live. Another common approach is to record "scratch tracks" (tracks that are meant to be thrown away) of the entire band playing, then to overdub each instrument individually to the scratch tracks.

See also *Multitrack Recording*.

Overhead Microphones

Overhead microphones, or overheads, are mics suspended above an instrument. This technique is most often used for miking drum kits. A single overhead mic or a stereo pair can be used. When a pair is used, all the standard stereo miking techniques apply.

See also *Stereo Miking, Appendix C: Microphone Placement Guide*.

Overtones

All naturally created notes contain not only their fundamental frequency (which the note is named for – e.g., A 440 Hz), but also a series of overtones, or harmonics, that occur at mathematical intervals related to the fundamental frequency. The difference in relative volume of these overtones between different instruments is why two instruments playing the same note will sound different. This is called the instrument's timbre.

See also *Fundamental Tone, Timbre, Appendix A: The Basics of Sound*.

Pad

In purely musical terms, pad refers to a droning background note or chord. In recording, however, it also refers to a circuit that reduces signal level by a set amount. Pads are often found on microphones or mic preamps. When a loud instrument is being miked, the pad will reduce the signal, keeping it from overloading the preamp and clipping (distorting).

See also *Preamplifier*.

Pan

Pan, short for panorama, controls where in the stereo field a signal will be placed, meaning how much of the signal will be sent to each of the speakers. Originally, pan was controlled with switches that had three positions: left, right, and center. A signal could only be placed entirely in the left speaker, entirely in the right speaker, or in both speakers equally. Modern mixers have a knob rather than a switch, so signals can be placed at any point from left to right.

When the pan knob is placed in the center, the signal will be sent to both speakers equally. As the knob is turned to the left of the center, the signal is sent more to the left speaker than to the right, giving the illusion that the instrument is to the listener's left. The further left the knob is placed, the more the signal is weighted in the left speaker, and when it is entirely to the left the signal comes only out of the left speaker. The effect works exactly the same when the knob is turned to the right, only the volume is increased in the right speaker and decreased in the left.

See also *Channel Strip*.

Parallel Effect

Parallel effects work by blending the wet (processed) signal with the dry (unprocessed) signal. Examples of effects that are usually used in parallel are reverb and delay. The term parallel refers to the two signals heading to the same destination (see *Fig. 70*).

The most common way to set up a parallel effect is to use an auxiliary send on a mixing board. The auxiliary send will route a copy of the signal to an output that can be connected to the effect processor, while the original signal continues down the channel strip into the main mix. The output of the effect processor (the "wet" signal) is then connected to the auxiliary return of the mixing board, which routes it to the main mix. Using the auxiliary send knob on the channel strip, the amount of signal that is sent to the effect processor can be raised or lowered. This will control how much effect is mixed with the signal.

Some effects processors will have a mix or blend knob that allows the processor to be placed in series, with the blending of the wet and dry signal being controlled within the processor.

See also *Auxiliary Send, Channel Strip, Serial Effect*.

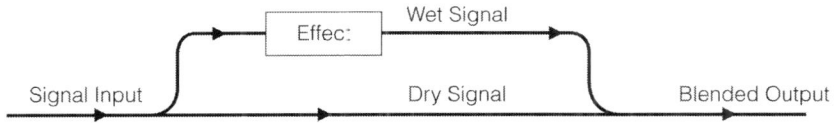

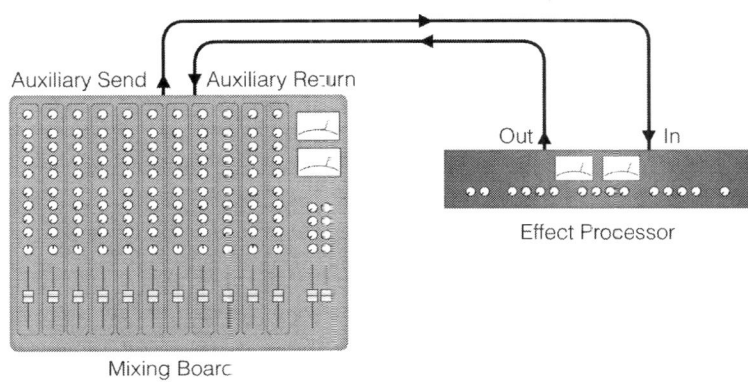

Figure 70: Signal Path and Hook-Up of a Parallel Effect

Parametric Equalizer

Parametric equalizers control the frequency balance of a signal by use of a number of frequency bands, each of which has definable parameters. Each band has control over the target frequency and the amount of boost or cut. Additionally, all but the highest and lowest bands have a Q control (explained below). The number of bands varies from one unit to the next, but 3–5 bands is most common.

Parametric EQs use bell filters for all bands except the highest and lowest. Bell filters boost or cut in a bell shape around the target frequency. The amount on either side of the target frequency that is affected is set by the Q (quality factor) control. A high Q affects a narrow band of frequencies, while a low Q affects a wide band (see *Fig. 71*).

The highest and lowest bands use shelving filters, which slope to the desired amount of boost or cut at the target frequency then shelf off to affect all frequencies above (on a high-shelf) or below (on a low-shelf) by the same amount (see *Fig. 71*). For example, if a high-shelf is set to +2 dB at 5 kHz, all frequencies above 5 kHz will be boosted by 2 dB.

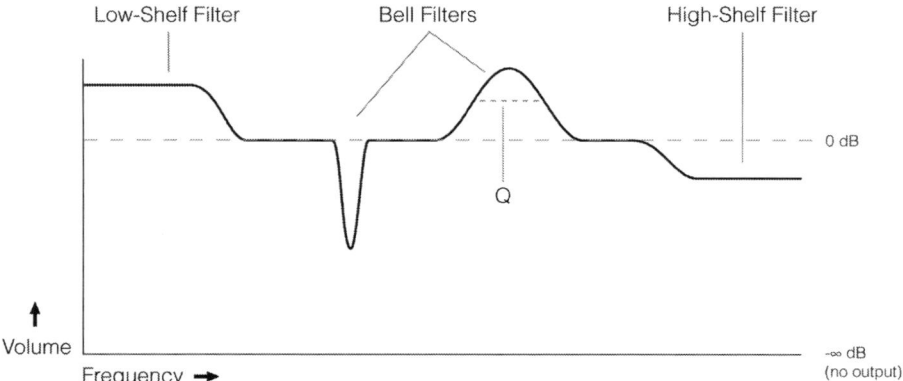

Figure 71: Bell Filters, Shelf Filters, and Q

Parametric EQs are preferred for studio use because they are more accurate than graphic equalizers. An equalizer that functions in this manner, but does not have all the above controls (frequency, gain, and Q), is called a semi-parametric equalizer.

See also *Equalizer, Frequency, Graphic Equalizer, Q*.

Pass Filter

A pass filter cuts the high or low end of the frequency spectrum by sloping down to the target frequency, then continuing on the same slope until the signal is completely cut (see *Fig. 72*). The target frequency is the point on the slope where the signal has been cut by 3 dB. A high-pass filter cuts all sound below the target frequency, completely allowing only the higher frequencies to pass, while a low-pass cuts everything higher than the target frequency, allowing all lower frequencies to pass.

Using both a high-pass and a low-pass filter together creates what is called a band-pass filter. A band-pass leaves a band of frequencies, while cutting all frequencies above and below.

See also *Equalizer*.

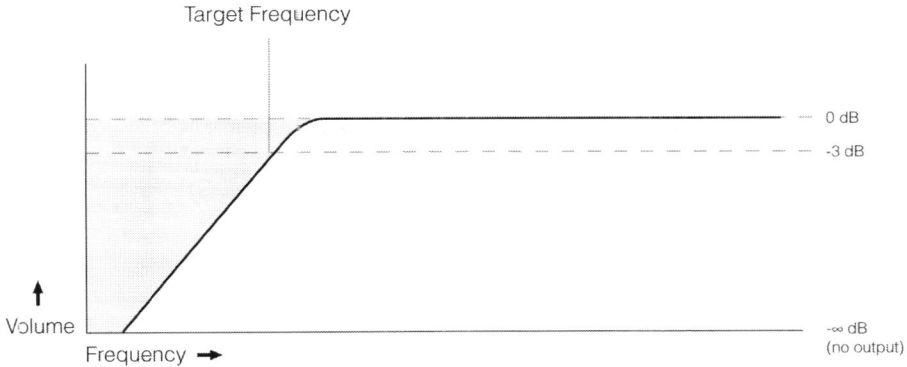

Figure 72: A High-Pass Filter

Patch Bay

A patch bay is a panel with a series of jacks on its front and back used to make routing and connecting equipment flexible, easy, and accessible. The jacks on the back of the patch bay are connected to the inputs and outputs of the mixer and other pieces of studio equipment. The jacks on the front are labeled to describe what is connected to the corresponding jack. Short cables are used to connect the jacks at the front, making connections from one piece of equipment to another.

Peak Meter

A peak meter is used to display the highest volume peaks of an audio signal. In hardware, peak meters are often made up of colored LEDs, and in software they come in many visual styes. Most peak meters follow the same color code: green for regular signal, yellow for signal that is approaching overload, and red for a signal that has overloaded, or clipped.

Signal levels should be set to give as much signal as possible without the signal overloading at any point. Enough headroom should be left above the highest peak to allow unexpected volume peaks to pass by without overloading and ruining an otherwise good take.

See also *VU Meter*.

Pencil Condenser

Small diaphragm condenser microphones are often referred to as "pencil condensers" because of their skinny, cylindrical shape. Because their diaphragms are light-weight, they usually have a fast transient response, making them a good choice for capturing detail.

See also *Condenser Microphone, Microphones.*

PFL

See *Pre-Fader Listen.*

Phantom Power

Phantom power is an electrical current supplied through a microphone cable by a mic preamp, mixer, or phantom power supply. Phantom power is used to power condenser microphones and active DI boxes.

The voltage of phantom power can vary from one device to the next, though the most common is 48 volts. If a device supplies less than 48 V of phantom power, it is advisable to check how much voltage is required by the microphone being used to ensure that the supplied voltage will be sufficient. On many devices, phantom power is merely labelled as "48 V".

While phantom power is only of use to condenser mics, active DIs, and the occasional other device, it will not harm other microphones as long as proper balanced cabling is being used. The exception to this rule is ribbon microphones, which can be damaged by the introduction of phantom power. When introducing phantom power with devices other than microphones, user manuals for these devices should be consulted to ensure that the device will not be harmed. When in doubt, it is usually best to err on the side of caution.

While some mixing boards have individual switches for implementing phantom power on each channel independently, most have "global" phantom power, meaning that when it is turned on phantom power is supplied to all channels. This can be a problem when using a condenser mic and a ribbon mic at the same time. In this case a phantom power supply can be used to power the condenser mic.

To avoid damage to the microphone, phantom power should be turned off and given a moment to completely power down before any microphones are connected or disconnected.

See also *Condenser Microphone, Direct Injection, Mixing Board.*

Phase

The word phase is used to refer to points along the progression of the cycle of a sound wave (see *Fig. 73*). Points along this progression are designated in degrees, just as if the sound wave was a circle. The point where the sound wave is furthest into positive amplitude is 90°, where it reaches the center line again is 180°, the point furthest into negative amplitude is 270°, and so on.

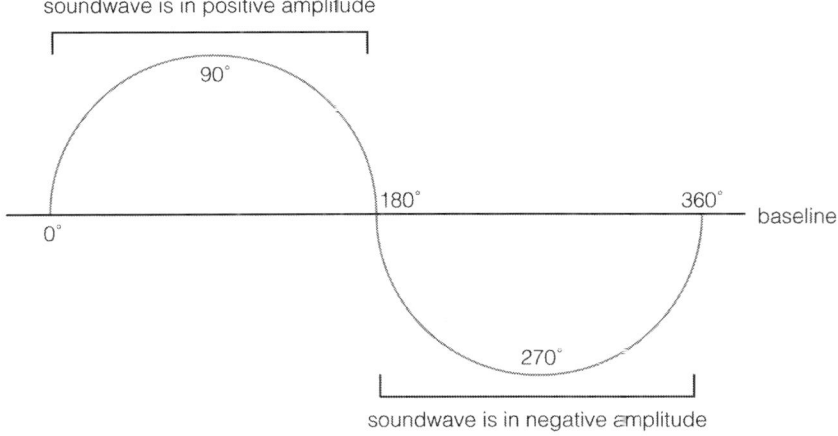

Figure 73: Phase

When two identical signals are not perfectly aligned, they are said to be "out-of-phase". When out-of-phase signals are combined, they will begin to cancel each other out in areas where one is in positive amplitude and the other is in negative amplitude and boost each other when they are both in positive or both in negative amplitude (see *Fig. 73*), resulting in a washy modulated sound. When two identical signals are 180° out-of-phase (a vertical mirror image) they will cancel each other out completely, resulting in silence.

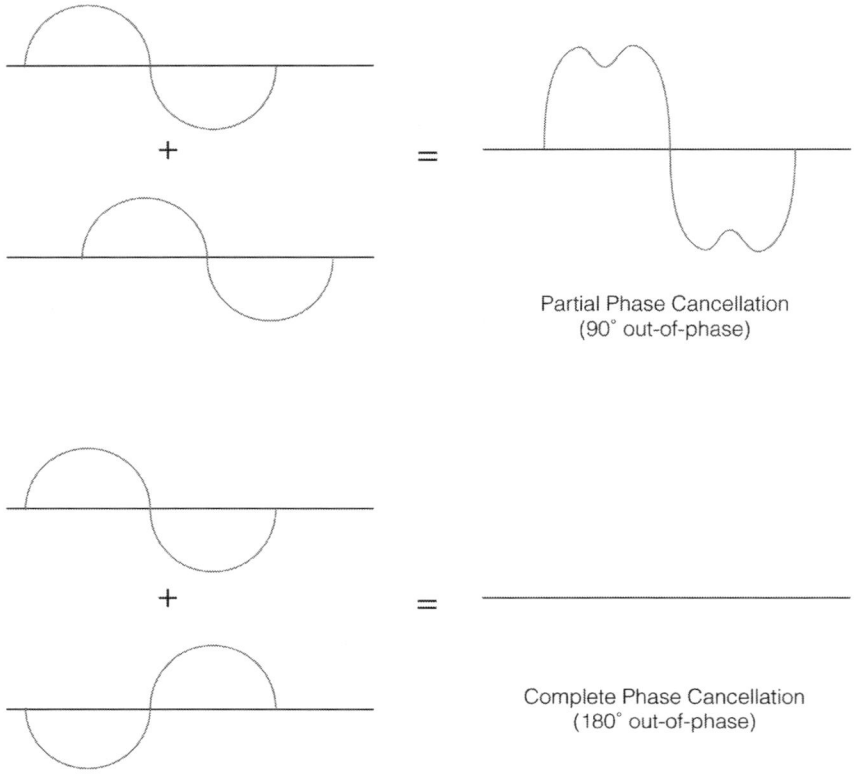

Figure 74: Phase Cancellation

Most problems with out-of-phase signals come from delay effects or from poor stereo mic placement. When phase problems result from delay effects, the solution is usually as simple as adjusting the delay time until the phasing stops. Phase issues from mic placement can be avoided by using coincident pairs (mics placed with the capsules together) or by following the 3:1 rule (mics should be three times as far from each other as they are from the instrument). Because phase problems only show up when the two signals are being played through the same speaker, it is very important to always check mixes in mono.

When two mics are used on the same instrument from different sides, for example miking the top and bottom of a snare drum, the resulting signals will usually be 180° out-of-phase from each other. This can be fixed by reversing the phase on one of the signals. Many devices have phase reversal circuits, which are usually labelled with the "Ø" symbol. If a phase reversal circuit is not available, a mic cable can be made to reverse the phase by swapping its hot and cold leads at one end. This is usually a last resort, as it makes the cable unusable for any other application and creates the possibility of accidental phase reversal by inadvertently using the modified cable.

See also *Stereo Miking, Appendix A: The Basics Of Sound*.

Phase Cancellation

When two versions of the same sound are combined with a slight difference in timing, they can partially or completely cancel each other out (*Fig. 74*). This is called phase cancellation. This is most often the result of poorly placed stereo microphones or from the use of delay effects.

See also *Phase, Appendix A: The Basics Of Sound*.

Phase Reversal

Phase reversal is the act of inverting the phase of a sound wave so that the sound wave goes into negative amplitude when it would previously have gone into positive amplitude and vice-versa (see *Fig. 75*). Many devices have phase reversal circuits, which are usually labelled with the "Ø" symbol. If it is necessary to invert the phase of a signal, but a phase reversal circuit is not available, an ordinary

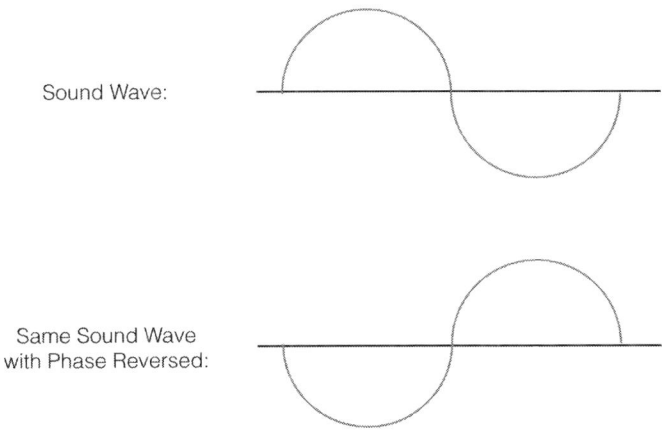

Figure 75: Phase Reversal

The Encyclopedia of Home Recording

mic cable can be made to reverse the phase by swapping the hot and cold leads on one end of the cable. This will, however, leave the cable unusable for other applications.

See also *Phase, Appendix A: The Basics Of Sound*.

Phaser

A phaser is an effect processor, similar to a flanger, that combines two out-of-phase signals, modulating the phase on one, to create a sweeping, washy sound effect.

Phono Preamp

In the early days of record production, manufacturers ran into the problem that recording a loud, low sound onto a record meant cutting a deep, wide groove. This often resulted in the record lathe cutting right through the disc or breaking the wall to the next pass of the groove. To prevent this problem, a slanted frequency response is applied to records before they are cut, meaning the lower the frequency, the quieter it is. A phono preamp applies an EQ with an opposite frequency response to return the signal to its original state.

To connect a turntable to the line-level input of a mixer or other device, a phono preamp is needed. The phono preamp grounds the signal to prevent hum, returns the frequency response to normal, and provides a line-level output that can be accepted by other devices. Devices that are meant for use with turntables, such as DJ mixers, have built-in phono preamps, but most audio devices require a separate phono preamp to be used.

See also *Preamplifier*.

Phrase Looping

Phrase looping is a feature that allows a performer to record a segment of audio on the fly then have it repeat in a continuous loop. Other segments of audio can be then layered overtop, allowing a performer to create an entire arrangement solo. Phrase loopers, or phrase samplers, are becoming quite common in live performance, particularly with performers who usually record their albums alone.

See also *Loop*.

Pickup Pattern

A microphone's pickup pattern (also called its polar pattern or directional response) describes from what direction it is most and least sensitive. When the microphone is placed so that the sound is directly in front of it, it is said to be on-axis. If the mic, is rotated so that the sound source is at an angle to the front of the mic it is referred to as off-axis (see *Fig. 76*). Depending on the mic and its pickup pattern, an off-axis placement can significantly affect both the signal level and the tone produced. The direction from which the microphone is least sensitive is called its angle of most rejection, or null point.

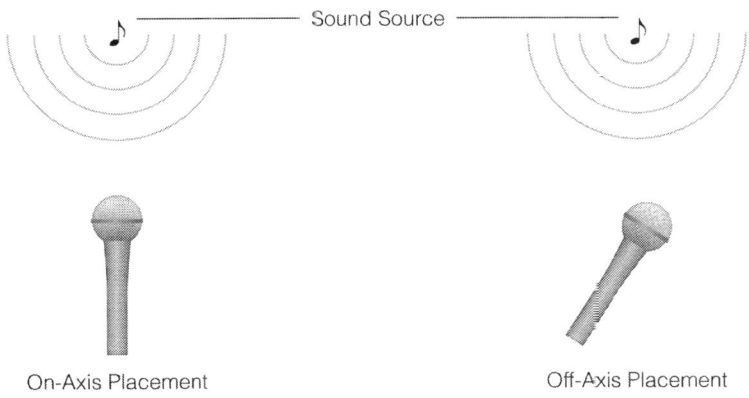

Figure 76: On- and Off-Axis Microphone Placement

The most common pickup patterns are cardioid, hyper-cardioid, omnidirectional, and bi-directional (also called figure-8) (see *Fig. 77*). Some microphones can provide more than one pickup pattern by way of a selector switch or a physical adaptor that is placed over the mic capsule.

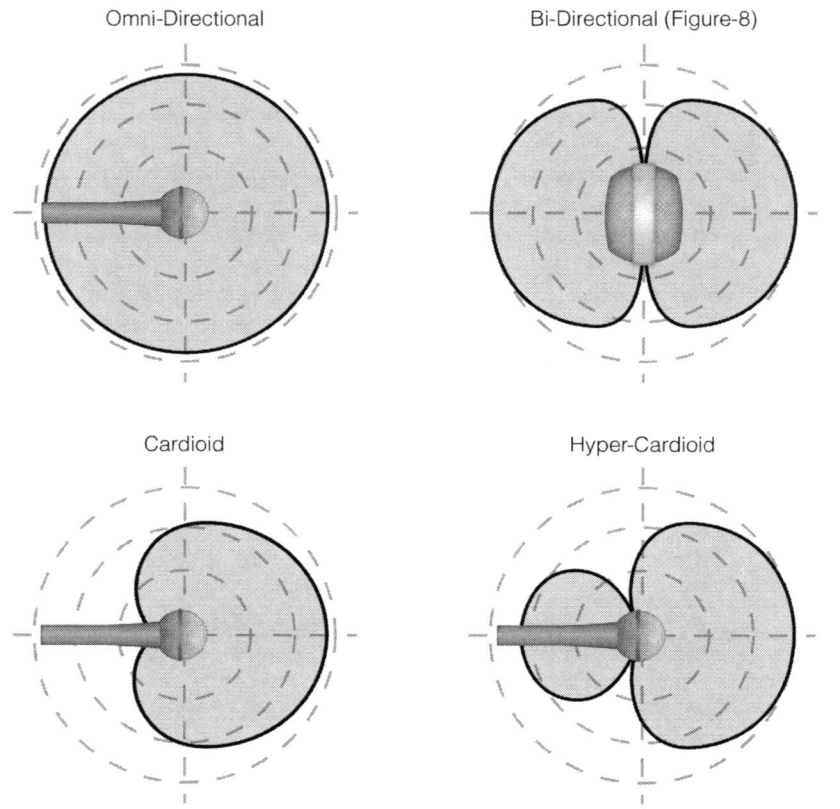

Figure 77: Pickup Patterns

The Cardioid Pattern

The cardioid pickup pattern is named for its heart-shaped response. Cardioid mics are most sensitive from the front, with the angle of most rejection being directly behind it (180° off-axis).

The Hyper-Cardioid Pattern

The hyper-cardioid pattern very is similar to the cardioid. Hyper-cardioid mics, however, are less sensitive from the sides than cardioid and have a small lobe of pickup from directly behind. This makes the hyper-cardioid's null point approximately 45° from the rear of the microphone (135° off-axis).

The Omnidirectional Pattern

As its name implies, the omnidirectional pattern picks up equally from all sides. Some omnidirectional mics may provide a slight tonal change with an off-axis placement, but when this occurs, it is usually very minimal. There is no null point on an omnidirectional pattern.

The Bi-Directional Pattern

The bi-directional, or figure-8, pattern picks up equally from the front and the back but rejects heavily from its sides. This means its null point is at 90° off-axis. With most figure-8 mics, the front of the microphone will produce a slightly brighter response (more high frequencies) than the back, and it should also be noted that the signal from the back of the microphone will be 180° out-of-phase compared to signal from the front.

Proximity Effect

All unidirectional microphones (such as cardioid and hyper-cardioid) will yield increased bass response as the mic is placed closer to the sound source. This phenomenon is called proximity effect, and it should be taken into account when choosing a placement for a unidirectional mic.

Ping-Pong Delay

Ping-pong delay is an effect where a signal is repeated multiple times, with the repeats alternating between the left and right speakers.

See also *Delay*.

Ping Ponging

See *Bouncing*.

Pink Noise

Pink noise is an artificially generated sound that is equal volume at all frequencies. It is used to test the frequency response of equipment or acoustic spaces.

In high-budget studios, it is common to test the frequency response of the mixing environment. To do this, pink noise is played through the studio monitors, and a flat-response microphone (one that picks up equally at all frequencies) is placed in mix position. The signal from the microphone is fed into a spectrum analyzer that compares the resulting signal to the original pink noise, showing which frequencies have been boosted or cut by the room. The room can then be acoustically treated to reduce its tonal effects.

While analyzing a room in this way is not necessarily a costly procedure itself, acoustically treating a room based on the results can be both expensive and time consuming. For the home or project studio budget, the "ignorance is bliss" approach may be advisable.

Pitch

We use the term pitch to describe our perception of a sound's frequency. Sounds with low frequencies we describe as being low pitched and high-frequency sounds we call high pitched.

While frequency is usually measured mathematically, such as 440 Hz, pitch is usually measured by the note it represents, such as A above middle C. Mathematical changes in frequency directly relate to the intervals of pitch. For example, when the frequency of a sound is doubled, its pitch is increased by one octave.

See also *Frequency, Timbre*.

Pitch Control

A pitch control changes the speed of the transport on a tape deck, the speed of rotation on a turntable, or the playback sample rate on a digital device. The practical result of this change in speed is a change in the pitch of the sound being played back.

Pitch Correction

Pitch correction is the process of fixing the pitch of any off-key notes in a performance without affecting the performance's timing. Automatic pitch correctors work by setting the key and scale of the performance and a threshold of error that should be allowed to pass through uncorrected. Any notes that are not on-key for the selected scale and are not within the allowed threshold of error are shifted to the nearest on-key note. While pitch correction is extremely common in modern music, it should be used carefully because it can also remove intentional dissonance and vibrato from a performance.

Pitch Shifting

Pitch shifting is the process of changing the pitch of a signal without affecting its speed. This change in pitch can be used to create harmonies in a performance, as a special effect, or to fill out the tone of an instrument. Some engineers will use pitch shifting to add thump to a bass or kick drum by subtly adding a copy of the sound that has been shifted down one octave.

Plate Reverb

Plate reverb is a form of artificial reverb. Plate reverberators create artificial reverb by playing the signal through a transducer attached to a large plate of sheet metal. A pickup, or multiple pickups, then capture the vibrations from the plate, which are combined with the original signal to give the illusion of natural reverberation.

While plate reverberators are no longer common, many digital reverb processors have a "plate" setting that emulates the tonal characteristics of plate reverb.

See also *Reverberation*.

Plosive

Plosives are quick gusts of air created by certain vocal sounds such as the letters *P* and *T*. These sounds can easily overload the capsule of a microphone, causing distortion. A trained vocalist can reduce or eliminate these issues though technique, but it is also common practice to use a pop filter when recording vocals to help prevent distorted plosives from ruining an otherwise good take.

See also *Pop Filter*.

Plug-In

A plug-in is a piece of software that works within a host application. It allows the manufacturer, as well as third-party developers, to add new features and capabilities to an existing program. For digital audio workstations, plug-ins are usually used to add effects and software instruments.

The format used for plug-ins varies depending on the software it is interfacing with. Common audio plug-in formats include VST (Virtual Studio Technology), TDM (Time-Division Multiplexing), RTAS (Real-Time AudioSuite), and AU (Audio Units). These formats are not directly interchangeable, so it is important to check what format your system uses before purchasing new plug-ins. Software is available that will work as an adapter to allow some formats to be used with a host that do not normally support them; however, these can sometimes add latency (time delay) to the effect.

See also *DAW*, *Latency*.

Polar Pattern

See *Pickup Pattern*.

Polyphonic

See *Polyphony*.

Polyphony

Polyphony refers to the number of notes that can be produced at the same time by a synthesizer or other digital instrument. Instruments that can produce multiple notes simultaneously are called polyphonic, while monophonic instruments can only produce one sound at a time.

Pop Filter

A pop filter, or pop shield, is a screen placed between a vocalist and a microphone to reduce blasts of air (called plosives) that can overload the microphone and causing distortion. Pop filters have the secondary benefit of preventing saliva from getting on the microphone capsule.

The most common pop filter design consists of nylon stretched across a hoop at the end of a goose neck (see *Fig. 78*), though some designs use a specially shaped metal screen instead of nylon. A basic pop filter can be made at home from a pair of pantyhose stretched over a shaped clothes hanger or embroidery hoop.

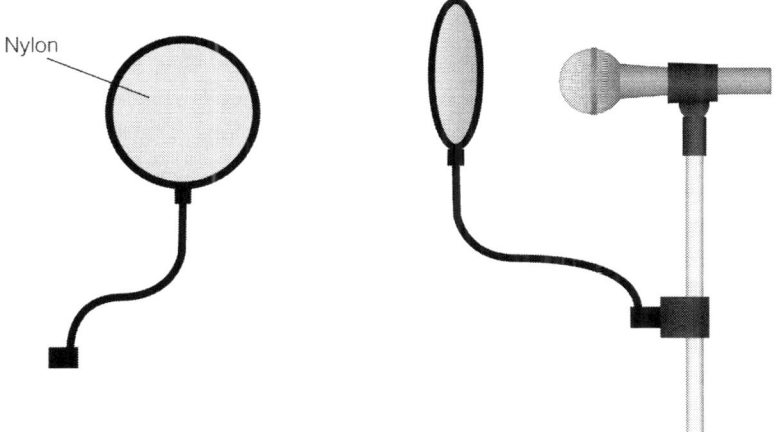

Figure 78: A Pop Filter and its Usage

One drawback of pop filters is that they can slightly shroud high frequencies from the performance. Despite this, most engineers choose to use them to prevent errant gusts of breath from ruining a good take. It should be noted that mic placement and the vocalist's mic technique can go a long way towards eliminating the effect of plosives, but a pop filter provides an added layer of protection.

See also *Plosive*.

Post-Fader Send

A post-fader send is an auxiliary send that routes the signal to the auxiliary output after the channel's master fader. This means that a change in the volume of the channel will affect the output of the auxiliary send. Post-fader sends are usually the best choice for effects because changing the volume of the dry signal (without effect) will also change the volume of the wet signal (with effect), keeping the amount of effect consistent.

See also *Auxiliary Send, Channel Strip, Pre-Fader Send*.

Pot

See *Potentiometer*.

Potentiometer

A potentiometer, or "pot" for short, is a variable-value resistor. It is the functional component behind all knobs and faders on audio equipment. It is not uncommon for recording engineers to use refer to these controls as "pots"; for example, "pan pot" and "volume pot" are common expressions.

See also *Mixing Board*.

Powered Plug-Ins

Powered plug-ins are software/hardware packages consisting of plug-in effects for recording software and a dedicated processing unit to run them. Because these plug-ins have their own processor, complex effects can be run with next to no additional load on the computer's CPU. Powered plug-in processors are often on a PCI card or a USB/Firewire device, which can be easily added to an existing computer-based recording system, effectively increasing its capabilities.

See also *DAW*, *Plug-in*.

Pre-Delay

In reverberation, pre-delay is the amount of time between the original (dry) signal and the first reflections of the reverberation. Reverb can be broken up into three sections: direct sound (directly from the sound source to the listener's ear), early reflections (reflected off of a surface), and reverberation (reflected off of multiple surfaces). The pre-delay is the difference in time between the direct sound and the first early reflections.

When using artificial reverb, adjusting the pre-delay can affect the clarity of the sound. The length of pre-delay also affects the listener's perception of the size of the space the performance was in. The ideal pre-delay time will vary depending on the style of music, the acoustic space being simulated, and the complexity of the arrangement.

See also *Reverberation*.

Pre-Fader Listen

Pre-fader listen (PFL) is a function common on many mixing boards and digital audio workstations. It allows a channel to be monitored without the volume fader applied, allowing the engineer to check the signal quality and level. On most mixers, when PFL is selected, the unit's level meters will display the channel's level before the fader. PFL differs from the "solo" function in that soloing is done post-fader.

See also *Channel Strip*.

Pre-Fader Send

A pre-fader send is an auxiliary send that routes the signal to the auxiliary output before the channel's master fader. When a send is set pre-fader, changes in the volume of the channel will not affect the output of the auxiliary send. Pre-fader sends are often used for creating separate mixes, such as separate monitor mixes for different performers, because changes in the main mix will not affect the auxiliary mixes.

See also *Auxiliary Send, Channel Strip, Post-Fader Send.*

Preamplifier

A preamplifier, or preamp, is a device for boosting the level of a signal. Specialized preamps exist for a number of purposes, such as a guitar preamp or a phono preamp, but the most common for recording purposes is the mic preamp.

The preamp can significantly affect the tone of a signal. Much like microphones, many studios have a variety of preamps on hand to allow them to create the right tone for the application. The quality of the preamp's construction and components, as well as whether it works on transistors or vacuum tubes, are among the factors that will affect its tone. Tube preamps are often used in digital recording to help "warm up" the tone of the signal.

Often preamplifiers are packaged with an equalizer and a compressor in the same unit. This combination is referred to as a channel strip.

Preamplifier Controls

Preamplifiers often have only one control, gain, which controls the amount of signal boost provided. This should be set at the highest level possible without the signal distorting in order to provide a healthy signal to the rest of the signal chain.

Most preamps have the ability to provide phantom power. Phantom power is a current supplied through the microphone cable to power condenser mics, active DIs, and some other devices. If a preamp has phantom power capabilities it will have a switch, usually labeled "phantom" or "48V".

Many preamps also have a pad feature. Turning on the pad will reduce the signal at the input by a specified amount (usually labelled on the pad switch). This is handy in situations where too much signal is coming from the microphone.

A low-cut is also common on preamps. This will place a high-pass filter on the signal, cutting all signal below a set frequency. The cut frequency varies from one preamp to the next, but the switch will almost always be labeled with it. A low-cut can be used when recording an instrument that does not generate any frequencies in the range being cut. This will reduce unwanted low-frequency rumble that can make its way into the recording through the mic stand.

Phono Preamps

Phono preamps are used to connect a turntable to a mixer or other device.

In the early days of record production, manufacturers ran into the problem that creating a loud, low sound required a deep, wide groove to be cut in the record. This often resulted in the record lathe cutting right through the disc, or breaking the wall to the next pass of the groove. To solve this problem, records are recorded with a slanted frequency response, meaning the lower the frequency, the quieter it is.

A phono preamp takes the signal from a turntable, grounds it to prevent hum, restores the original frequency response, and provides a line-level output that can be accepted by other devices.

See also *Channel Strip, Microphones, Mixing Board, Phantom Power*.

Pressure Zone Microphone

See *Boundary Mic*.

Pro Tools

Pro Tools is digital recording and production software manufactured by Digidesign. It is the industry standard in large studios. At the time of writing, Digidesign offers three levels of Pro Tools: Pro Tools HD, Pro Tools LE, and Pro Tools M-Powered. The LE and M-Powered versions of Pro Tools are geared towards home and project studios and are not fundamentally different from recording software offered by their competitors.

The significant difference in Digidesign's professional-level product, Pro Tools HD, is in the hardware that accompanies it. Pro Tools HD runs on a series of dedicated processing cards, meaning the host computer is doing very little work. The result is a more stable system with next to no latency. Because of the hardware required to run them, HD systems have a hefty price tag, and as a result are generally only seen in high-end studios.

See also *DAW*.

Producer

In a recording project, the producer makes the final decisions about production, song choices, and arrangement. It is the producer's responsibility to ensure that the final recording will be a successful and marketable product.

In the early days of recording, the producer was hired by the record company. It was his or her job to work closely with the artist(s), representing the record company's interests. As a representative of the label, the producer controlled the money and therefore had the final say in all decisions.

The role of the producer has changed significantly over the years, and it is now quite common for producers to also act as audio engineer on a project. Additionally, some record contracts allow the artist to hire a producer of their choice, and some artists even choose to produce their own albums.

Project Studio

A project studio is a small recording studio used for hobby or semi-professional recording projects. With recording equipment becoming more and more affordable, project studios have become very common.

Proximity Effect

All unidirectional microphones (e.g., cardioid, hyper-cardioid) produce greater bass response as they are placed closer to the sound source. This is called proximity effect, and it should be considered when choosing mic placements, as the difference in tone can be significant.

See also *Microphones, Pickup Pattern*.

Psychoacoustics

Psychoacoustics is the study of how we perceive sound. Some aspects of psychoacoustics include the effects of frequencies above the threshold of human hearing and our perception of loudness and volume.

Punch-In/Punch-Out

Punching-in is the process of re-recording a small section of an existing take. The engineer determines a punch-in point (where recording will begin) and a punch-out point (where the recording will end). The performer will be able to listen to and play along with the original recording. When the punch-in point is reached, the new performance is recorded over the existing section of the take. When done properly, this can be a very effective way of fixing small mistakes in an otherwise good take. Most digital recorders allow for non-destructive punch-in, meaning the original take is preserved and can be restored at any time.

Punch Point

See *Punch-In/Punch-Out*.

PZM

See *Boundary Microphone*.

Q

The term Q is short for quality factor and describes the bandwidth of a bell filter on an equalizer. Bell filters (also called peak filters) boost or cut the chosen frequency, affecting the surrounding frequencies in a bell-shaped curve. The range of frequencies affected on either side of the target frequency is controlled by the filter's Q. A high Q affects very little to either side of the target frequency, while a low Q affects a wide band (see *Fig. 79*).

See also *Equalizer*.

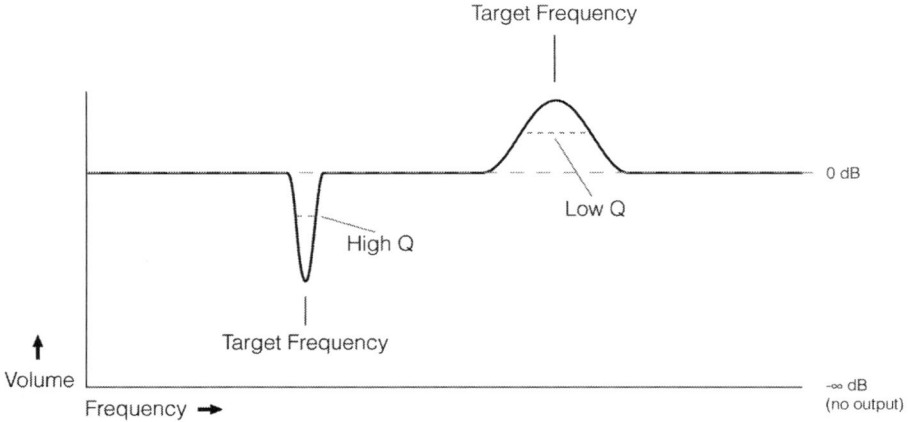

Figure 79: High- and Low-Q Bell Filters

Quantization

Quantization is a mathematical term that means taking a set of values along a continuum and restricting them to a set of discrete intervals. In audio and music production, it can refer to one of two things.

Quantization In MIDI Production

When working with MIDI, quantization is the process of taking the performed notes and moving them to exact beats. This will make the timing of the performance technically perfect but can also make it feel lifeless by removing the human element. Most MIDI sequencers will allow you to set a margin of error when quantizing to prevent this de-humanizing effect.

See also *MIDI*.

Quantization In Digital Recording

In analog-to-digital signal conversion, quantization refers to the measurement of the amplitude of the signal. In order to document the amplitude level for a given sample, the amplitude must be broken into discrete steps (see *Fig. 80*). The number of steps this value is broken into dictates how precise the measurement is and is dictated by the bit-depth of the signal. A 16-bit (CD quality) sample, for example, can record 1,048,576 possible degrees of amplitude, while a 24-bit sample can record 16,777,216.

See also *Appendix A: The Basics of Sound*.

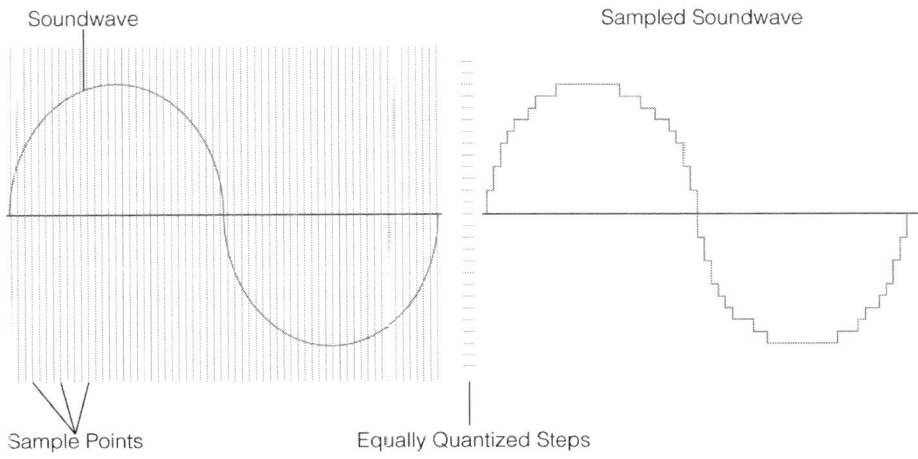

Figure 80: Digital Sampling of a Sound Wave

Random Access Editing

One of the greatest benefits of workstations that record to hard disk or similar technologies is random access editing (also called non-linear editing). With tape-based recording, timing of playback is completely governed by the recorded segment's physical location on the tape. This is not the case with random access editing.

Digital recording devices (except for tape-based digital such as DAT) place an audio file on an available segment of the recording drive. When the track is played back, timing is based on when the workstation accesses the file, not on its location. This means that any segment can be shifted back or forth in the timeline of the recording, trimmed shorter, stretched, copied and pasted, or moved.

Random access editing allows for great flexibility that was previously unavailable. As a result of this technology, it is common for an engineer to fix timing mistakes, use a segment of a take to replace another segment from the same take, or even build an entire song building-block style from a few short audio samples.

See also *Hard-Disk Recorder*.

Ratio

See *Compression Ratio*.

Real-Time AudioSuite

Real-Time AudioSuite (RTAS) is a software plug-in format developed by Digidesign and used in user-grade versions of Pro Tools, such as Pro Tools LE and Pro Tools M-Powered.

See also *Plug-In*.

Real-Time Effect

An effect that is processed as the track is playing or being recorded is called a real-time effect. Adjustments can usually be made on the fly with instant results. The original sound file is never affected. Real-time effects are, therefore, very flexible because they can be changed at any time.

Non-real-time effects are processed once, writing a separate sound file to the recorder's drive with the effect applied. These effects are less flexible because changing a parameter on the effect means reprocessing and will create an additional sound file. While they are more work to change, non-real-time effects have the benefit of not presenting an ongoing load on the processor, leaving processing power available for other effects.

See also *Digital Signal Processing, Plug-In, Powered Plug-Ins*.

Real-Time Spectrum Analyzer

See *Spectrum Analyzer*.

Recording Console

See *Mixing Board*.

Recording Engineer

See *Audio Engineer*.

Recording Studio

A recording studio is a facility for the recording, mixing, and production of audio recordings. Ideally, studio space is soundproofed to prevent outside sounds from leaking into recordings and is treated with acoustic paneling to reduce excessive reflections and to minimize frequency dips and boosts that can occur as a result of standing waves.

Recording studios can vary greatly in size from small, one-room home or project studios to large, multi-studio production facilities. Ideally, a studio has a minimum of two rooms: a live room where the performance takes place, and a control room where the engineer can work. Acoustic isolation (soundproofing) between the live room and the control room is very important so that the recorded signal can be heard without any acoustic leakage mixing with it.

Larger studios may have additional isolation rooms that are acoustically separated from the main live room and control room. These can be used to place amplifiers in, to track vocals in, or for separating performers to prevent other sounds from bleeding into the microphones. Ideally, all rooms should be connected by windows and provide clear line of sight between the different performers and the engineer.

With the increased affordability of recording equipment and the drastic changes in the industry from technology and web-based distribution, large studios are becoming less common, and small studios are taking their place. This has greatly changed the dynamic of the recording industry and turned many recording engineers into small business owners.

See also *Acoustics, Soundproofing, Standing Wave*.

Red Book

The Red Book is the specifications guide for the CD audio format. The Red Book is part of a series of specification manuals called the Rainbow Books that set standards for the various CD formats, including the Yellow Book (CD-ROM) and the Orange Book (CD-R and CD-RW) among others. By adhering to Red Book standards, the recording industry can ensure that a CD will play on all CD players.

Release

The term release can refer to either a control on a compressor or the final segment of a sound's acoustic envelope. Both are covered below.

Release (compressor)

On a compressor, the release control sets how quickly, once the signal level has fallen below the threshold, the compressor stops compressing. A fast release means that the compression will stop promptly, whereas the compressor will take longer to disengage if a longer release time is set. By carefully setting the release time and the attack time the engineer can control which part of the acoustic envelope is being compressed

See also *Compression*.

Release (acoustic envelope)

In the context of the acoustic envelope, which represents the volume of a sound over time, the term release refers to the final drop in volume as the sustain of the sound dies out (see *Fig. 81*).

See also *Acoustic Envelope*.

Return

See *Auxiliary Return*.

Reverberation

Reverberation, or reverb, is a series of acoustic reflections that occur within a space when sound is created. The timing, frequency, and volume of the reflections

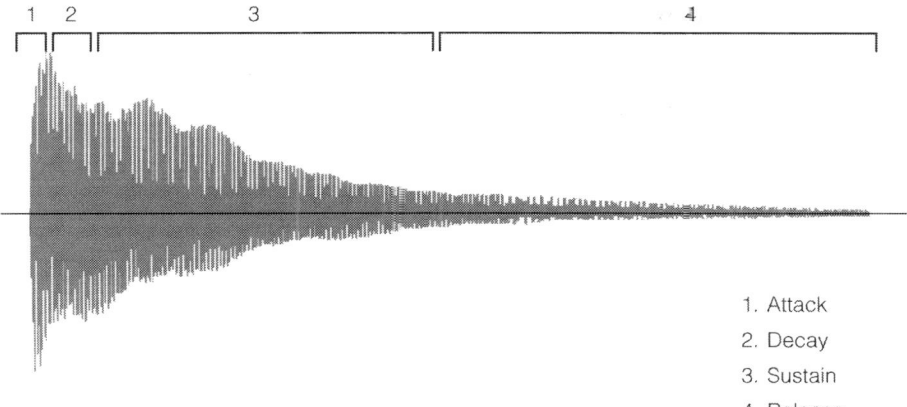

Figure 81: The Acoustic Envelope

will vary depending on the size, shape, and contents of the space. Whether natural or artificial, reverberation provides depth to a recording and provides the listener with subconscious clues about the environment where the performance took place, or is being represented as taking place. Reverb should be used carefully, however, because excessive reverb can result in muddy or unintelligible recordings.

The Three Stages Of Reverberation

Reverb can be broken down into three basic stages: direct sound, early reflections, and reverberation (see *Fig. 82*). The direct signal is sound that travels directly from the sound source to the microphone or listener's ear.

Early reflections reach the microphone or ear by reflecting off of surrounding surfaces. Because of the added distance these reflections travel, they can reach the ear or microphone up to 100 milliseconds (ms) after the direct sound. The number of these early reflections, their volume, and their tonal content all provide subconscious clues to the listener about the size of room and the materials in it.

In the final stage, reverberation, sound reflects off of multiple surfaces in the space before finally reaching the listener or microphone. In large, complex spaces such as cathedrals, reverberation can be seconds long. The listener's brain subconsciously interprets the volume, tone, and duration of the reverberation to form an idea of the performance space.

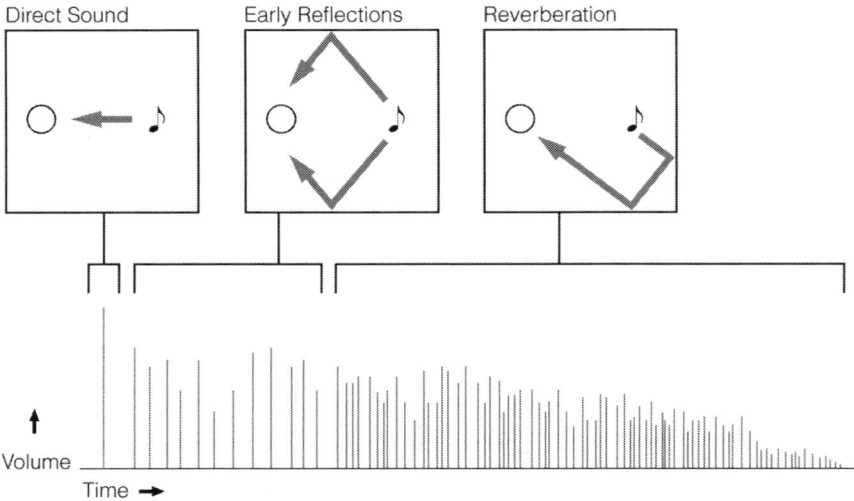

Figure 82: Elements of Reveberation

Types Of Reverb

In addition to natural, acoustic reverberation, many forms of artificial reverb exist. The most common of these by far is now digital reverb, but an understanding of other forms of artificial reverb is important as they are emulated by many digital reverb units.

Chamber reverb uses a speaker to reproduce the signal in a highly reflective room (often tiled). Microphones placed in various locations around the room, and facing different directions, pick up the reflections within the room. Les Paul created a famous design for a reverb chamber that consists of multiple trapezoid-shaped rooms, each with a microphone and a speaker placed in a different configuration.

Spring reverb uses a transducer to convert the signal to mechanical energy that vibrates through suspended springs. A pickup at the other end of the springs collects these vibrations, converting them to electrical signal, which is then combined with the original sound to give the illusion of reverb. Spring reverb is still commonly found on guitar amplifiers.

Plate reverb works in a similar fashion to spring reverb. A transducer is attached to a large plate of sheet metal and a signal played through it. A pickup, or multiple pickups, then capture the vibrations from the plate, which are then combined with the original signal.

Analog reverb units use analog circuits to create a series of delayed signals, which are combined to mimic reverberation.

Digital reverb uses complex algorithms to simulate reverb. Some digital reverb units use digital modeling technology to convincingly replicate the tone of vintage reverb equipment. Some reverb software even allows a virtual environment to be created with control of size, shape, and materials the room is made from.

Convolution reverbs are digital reproductions of the acoustic qualities of actual acoustic environments. To create them, a controlled impulse is played in the acoustic space and its reverberation is recorded. The difference between the initial impulse and the recorded signal is analyzed and this acoustic behavior is then applied to other audio signals.

Common Reverb Controls

Reverb time, also called decay time, controls the total duration of the reverb. Specifically, reverb time is measured from the initial sound to the point where the reverb volume decreases to 60 dB below its initial level. Long reverb times tend to reduce the intelligibility of a performance because the reverb from one note overlaps the next. Generally speaking, the faster the song is, the shorter the reverb time should be to maintain intelligibility.

Pre-delay is the time between the direct sound and the first early reflections. The length of the pre-delay is a key component in the listener's perception of the size of the performance space. The ideal pre-delay time will vary depending on the style of music, the acoustic space being simulated, and the complexity of the arrangement.

Size is a common control on digital reverbs. As the name implies, this control will affect the size of the simulated environment. This control usually affects the total reverb time as well as the amount and volume of reflections.

Reverb type is usually only found on digital reverbs. This allows the user to select a style of reverb to be used. Common options are spaces such as room, hall, or cathedral, and classic artificial reverb types such as spring, plate, or chamber.

An **early reflections** control affects the volume of early reflections. This option provides control over how subtle or bold the initial stage of reverb is.

See also *Acoustics*.

Reverb Time

Reverb time, or decay time, sets the duration of an artificial reverb. Reverb time is measured from the initial, direct signal until the point where the reverb volume has decreased to 60 dB below its initial level. The reverb time acts as a subconscious clue to the size and complexity of the space being simulated.

The length of reverb used depends of the style of music, the speed of the music, and the personal tastes of the engineer. A performance's intelligibility can be compromised by excessively long reverb times, however, because the reverb continues to sustain while new notes are beginning to reverberate. This overlap can result in muddiness. As a general rule of thumb, faster songs need shorter reverb times to maintain intelligibility.

See also *Reverberation*.

Reverse Delay

Reverse delay is an effect that comes in two forms. One type of reverse delay is created by reversing an audio track, placing a delay effect on it, and recording the track with the effect onto an empty track. The resulting recording is then reversed to make the original sound forwards again. The result is that the delay that was recorded onto the track while it was backwards occurs before the original sound rather than after.

Live effect processors often have an effect called reverse delay as well. Because this effect is created on the fly, it would be impossible for the delay to come before the original sound as it does above. With these effects, the signal is repeated in reverse directly after the original.

See also *Delay, Reverse Reverb*.

Reverse Reverb

A reverse reverb is an effect where the reverb on a track occurs in reverse, before the sound that created it. To create reverse reverb, a recorded track is reversed so that it is playing backwards. Reverb is then applied to the backward recording, and the sound with the reverb is recorded onto an empty track. The new track is then reversed again, making the original recording play forwards again. Because the reverb was added when the track was in reverse, it will now be backwards, starting from silence and building to a crescendo of the original sound (see *Fig. 83*).

See also *Reverb, Reverse Delay*.

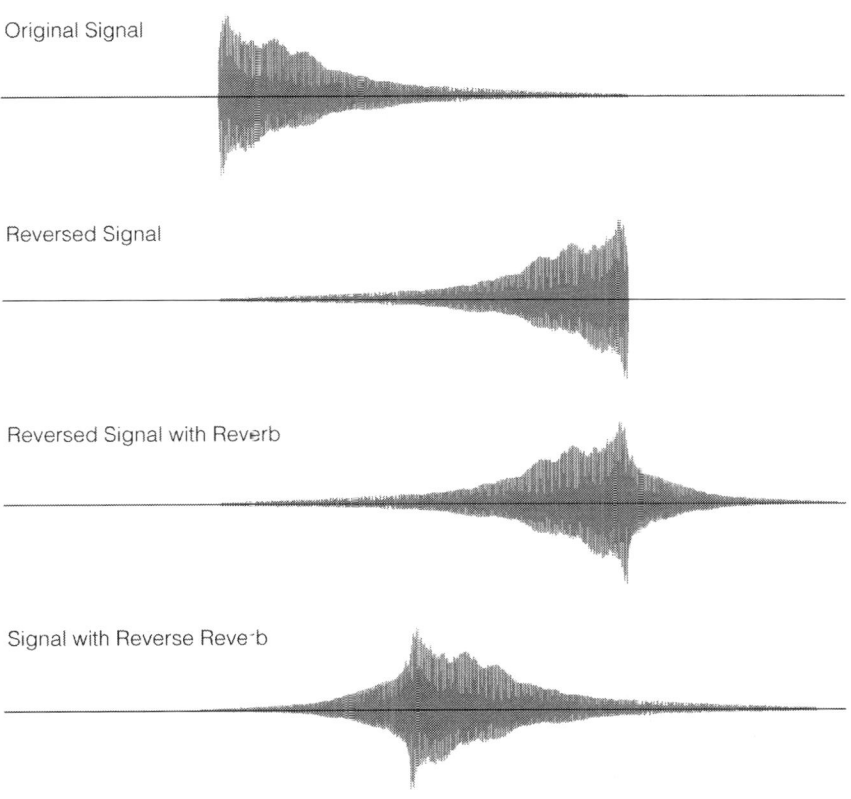

Figure 83: Reverse Reverb

Reverse Tracking

Reverse tracking is a technique where an instrument or other track is recorded in reverse. Reportedly, it originated as the result of an accident in the 1960s when a session tape was loaded backwards in to the recording deck. In digital recording, reverse tracking can be achieved by simply reversing a track digitally with a workstation's "reverse" feature.

Ribbon Microphone

Ribbon microphones are a type of dynamic mic that use a thin piece of corrugated metal suspended in a magnetic field. As sound waves vibrate the ribbon, it creates flux in the magnetic field that is turned into an electrical pulse. Ribbon mics produce a warm, often vintage-sounding, tone and have recently regained popularity. While ribbon mics are traditionally quite pricey, some more affordable, mass-produced ribbon mics have come on the market in recent years.

Ribbon mics are less durable than the more common, moving-coil dynamic mics. While newer designs have improved resilience over classic ribbon mics, the thin metal ribbon can still be damaged by blasts of high sound pressure. For this reason care should be taken when using a ribbon mic on high sound pressure instruments such as horns or drums.

Ribbon mics should never be exposed to phantom power because this can cause damage to the mic. Some newer ribbon mics incorporate phantom power protection circuits, but caution is still advisable.

See also *Dynamic Microphone*, *Microphones*.

RMS

RMS is an acronym for root mean square. It is a form of mathematical averaging used to express the level of a signal. It is calculated by taking periodic voltages from along the sound wave, squaring them, finding the average of the squared values, then calculating the square root of that average. RMS is used to rate amplitude and amplifier power because it provides an average that approximates auditory perception of the signal.

RTAS

See *Real-Time AudioSuite*.

Sample

A sample is a piece of digital information that records the amplitude of a sound wave at a specific point in time. Much like the way video uses a series of static pictures to give the illusion of movement, digital audio recordings use a series of static samples of a sound wave to recreate it digitally (see *Fig. 84*). The sample rate (number of samples per second) affects the accuracy of the reproduction as well as the overall frequency range that can be recorded.

See also *Sample Rate, Appendix A: The Basics of Sound*.

Sample Rate

The sample rate of a digital audio signal refers to how many digital samples make up each second of audio. Much like video uses a series of static pictures to give the illusion of movement, digital audio recordings use a series of samples of a sound wave to recreate it digitally (see *Fig. 84*). A CD, for example, uses a sample rate of 44.1 kHz, meaning the recording is made up of 44,100 samples for every second of audio. The sample rate used will affect how realistic the reproduction sounds as well as the frequency range that can be recorded.

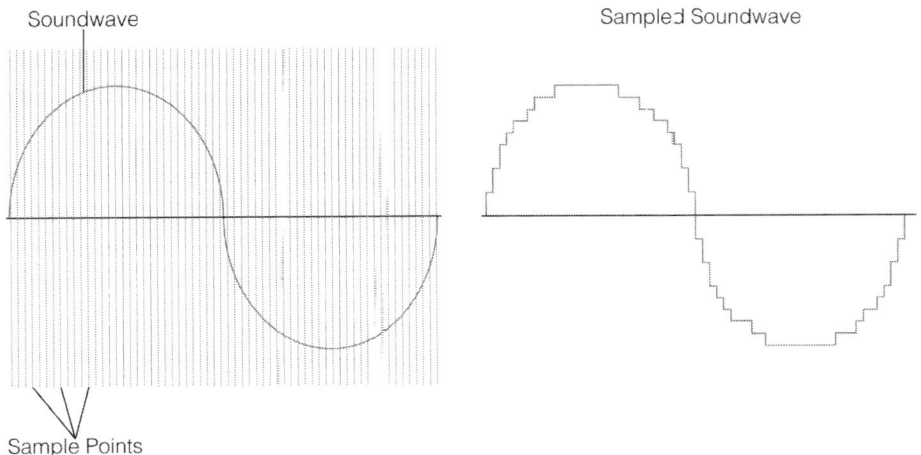

Figure 84: Digital Sampling of a Sound Wave

The highest possible recorded frequency on a digital recording is limited to one-half of the sample rate. A CD, therefore, will contain no frequencies above approximately 20 kHz. The Nyquist Theorem states that if a frequency of greater than half of the sample rate is introduced into a digital recording, inharmonic "ghost" frequencies will be created. For this reason, all analog to digital converters filter out all frequencies above their Nyquist cutoff point.

While the range of human hearing ends at approximately 20 kHz, the study of psychoacoustics suggests that we may be subconsciously affected by frequencies above our range of hearing. This suggests that the additional high frequencies captured by higher sample rates are not without merit.

While higher sample rates increase the quality of a digital signal and extend its frequency range, they also increase the size of audio files, in turn increasing the amount of digital storage needed. To save hard drive space, some people working in the home studio will limit the sample rate of their recordings to 44.1 kHz because they only plan to reproduce the recording on CD. Recording at higher sample rates does, however, leave the option open to reproduce the recording at a higher sample rate in the future.

See also *Nyquist Theorem, Appendix A: The Basics of Sound.*

Sampler

A sampler is an electronic musical instrument, available in both hardware and software forms, that can record or load short segments of audio to be played back on command. Users can record their own samples and play them back as is or transposed into a different key. Sample packs of prerecorded samples are also commercially available that can be loaded into a sampler. Samplers are particularly common in the production of hip-hop and electronica music.

SCMS

The Serial Copy Management System (SCMS) is a form of digital copy protection that was introduced in the early 1990s. It was created in response to the record industry's fear that the then-emerging DAT format and the S/PDIF digital protocol would lead to a significant rise in piracy because they would allow perfect copies of a digital recording to be made.

SCMS sets all digital recordings as one of three states of copy protection: copy allowed, copy prohibited, and single copy allowed. If a recording is set as copy allowed, the recording can be reproduced without restriction, if it is set to copy prohibited, digital copies cannot be made, and if it is set to single copy allowed, a copy can be made, but the resulting recording will be copy prohibited.

The SCMS (sometimes referred to as "Scums") was met with significant disapproval from the home recording community and many blame it for DAT's failure to succeed as a commercial format.

See also *DAT*, *S/PDIF*.

Scratch Track

Often engineers will start a session by recording scratch tracks. These are recordings of the performers that are not intended for the final recording, but instead serve as a guide for timing and feel when rerecording the instruments individually. Scratch tracks can be helpful because, when recording their parts in isolation, performers often lose track of where they are in the song or find the lack of other instruments disconcerting.

See also *Overdubbing*.

Send

See *Auxiliary Send*.

Sensitivity Rating

The sensitivity rating of a microphone indicates the amount of output that it will generate when it is fed a controlled standard level at its input. This rating is measured in volts and reflects how much gain is required from a preamplifier to bring it to line level.

See also *Gain*, *Microphones*, *Preamplifier*.

Sequencer

A sequencer is a piece of digital hardware or software that records and arranges MIDI notes. Many MIDI devices, such as workstation keyboards and drum machines, have internal sequencers. It is also common for digital recording software to have MIDI sequencing capabilities, allowing audio and MIDI to be used easily in the same song.

See also *MIDI*.

Serial Copy Management System

See *SCMS*.

Serial Effect

While a parallel effect processes a copy of the signal and blends it with the original, a serial effect is placed directly in a signal chain and routes the entire signal through its processor. Compressors and equalizers are examples of processors that must be run as serial effects to work properly. Serial effects are usually connected using the insert point on a mixing board or channel strip (see *Fig. 85*).

See also *Channel Strip, Insert, Parallel Effect*.

Servo-Driven Faders

See *Motorized Faders*.

Session

The term session is used to describe a period of work in a recording studio with a performer. Some recording workstations use the term session to refer to a single project file or song.

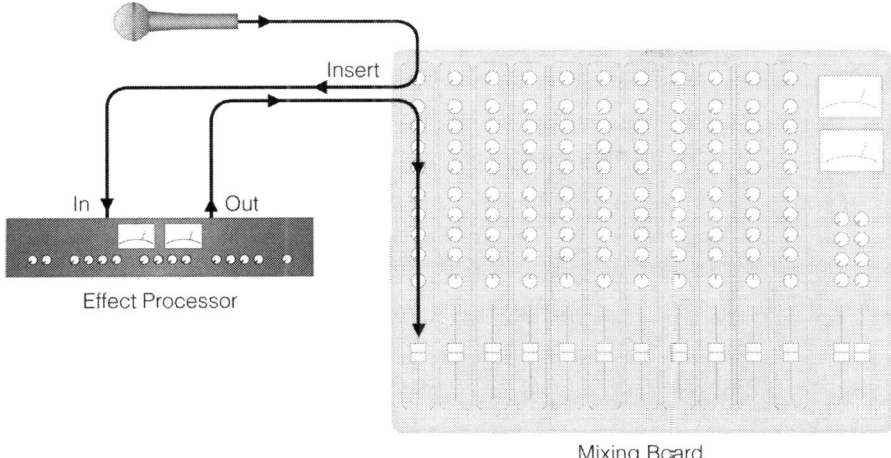

Figure 85: Signal Path of a Serial Effect Run on an Insert

Shelving Filter

On an equalizer, a shelving filter slopes to cut or boost the signal by the selected amount at the target frequency, then shelves off and boosts or cuts all frequencies to the end of the spectrum by the same amount (see *Fig. 85*). A shelving filter that affects all frequencies above the target frequency is called a high-shelf, and one that affects all frequencies below is called a low-shelf.

See also *Equalizer*.

Shock Mount

A shock mount, sometimes referred to as a mic cradle, holds a microphone in an elastic suspension to reduce vibrations in the stand from being transferred into the microphone. These are mainly used for condenser microphones, which are quite sensitive and prone to picking up extraneous noise. Some high-end condenser mics are internally shock-mounted, reducing the need for an external shock mount, though this is not very common.

See also *Microphones*.

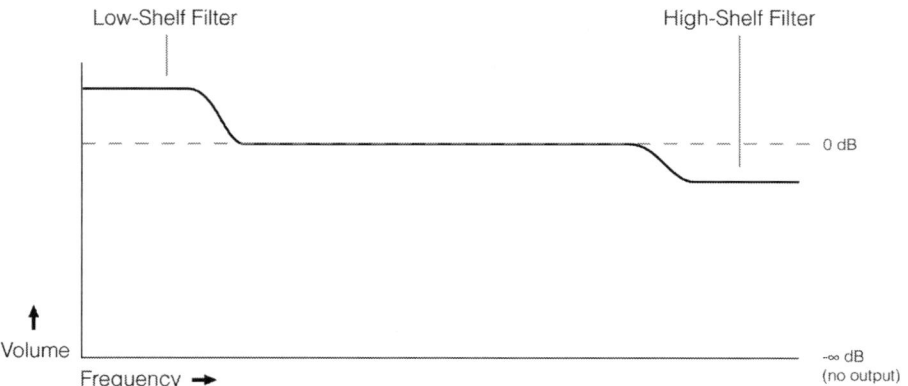

Figure 86: High- and Low-Shelf Filters

Sibilance

Sibilance is a loud gust of air created in the formation of certain consonant sounds such as *s*, *ch*, and *z*. Some vocalists have particularly strong sibilant sounds which can resonate unpleasantly in a recording, particularly in the range of 5–10 kHz. Ideally, this should be controlled through vocal technique, though its effects can be minimized by careful equalization or the use of a de-esser (a frequency specific compressor).

See also *De-esser*, *Plosive*.

Signal

A signal is an electrical impulse created by a microphone or device. Frequently we use the term hot to refer to a strong signal level.

Signal Flow

Signal flow is the path taken by an audio signal. Like water, audio signal flows in one direction. An example of a common signal flow would be from the output of a microphone, through the mic cable, to an input on a mixer's channel strip, then from the output of the mixer to the input of an amplifier, and from the output of an amplifier to a speaker (see *Fig. 87*).

Troubleshooting becomes much easier with a solid grasp on how the signal is getting from its origin to its destination. In the example above, if no sound was coming out of the speaker, finding the problem would be a matter of following the signal path back to find where the signal stops. So, if the amplifier was not receiving any signal, but the mixer is definitely sending signal out, the problem is probably the cable that connects them. If the input of the mixer is receiving signal and there is no signal coming out of the mixer, the problem must be somewhere in the mixer (perhaps the channel is muted, or the volume turned down).

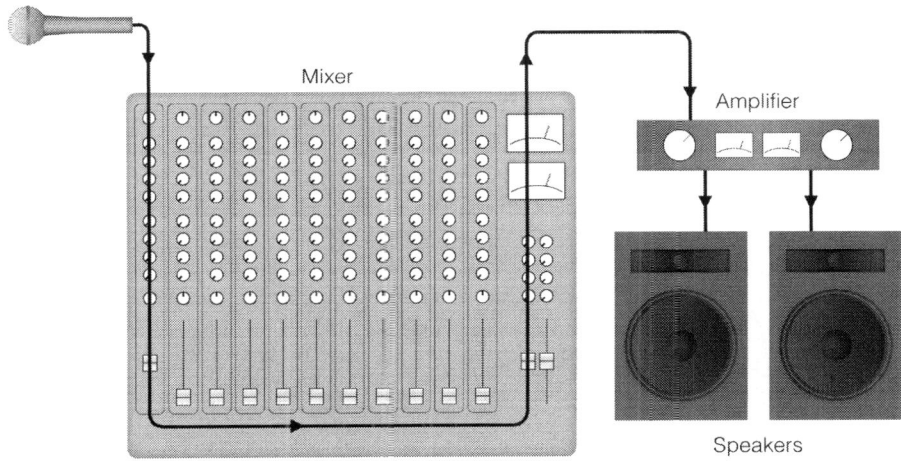

Figure 87: A Common Signal Flow

With a firm grasp of signal flow also comes the ability to use more complex routing. A more complex example of signal flow would be using one mixer to record and play back four tracks on a four-track recorder (see *Fig. 88*). In this situation the signal would start with four microphones, through the mic cables to four channels on the mixing board, those four channels are then routed to four separate outputs, which are connected to the four inputs of the recorder. To listen back, the four outputs from the recorder are run into four more channels on the mixer, which are assigned to a separate stereo buss. This buss combines the four channels into a stereo pair and sends them to the main outputs of the mixer, which are connected to an amplifier, which in turn is plugged into a pair of speakers.

In the above example, the manner in which the four input channels are run directly to the recording unit will vary depending on the mixing board. Some mixers have direct outputs on each channel for this specific purpose. When direct outputs are not available, unbalanced audio can be output through the insert or, as shown in *Fig. 88*, the channels can be run in pairs (panned hard left and right) to stereo busses. Either way, it is important to ensure that these channels are not assigned to the master buss.

See also *Buss, Channel Strip, Mixing Board, Appendix B: Studio Setup Guide*.

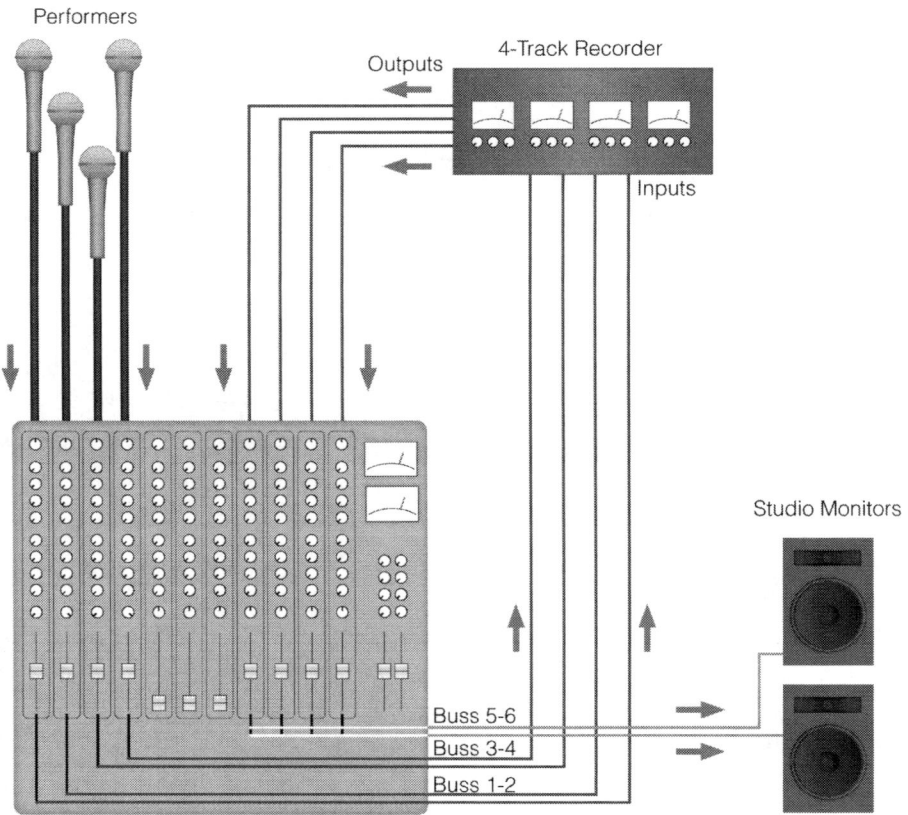

Figure 88: An Input Mix and an Output Mix for a 4-Track Recorder

Signal-To-Noise Ratio

A signal-to-noise ratio is the comparison of the level of desired sound in a recording or signal to the level of background noise. A higher ratio means less noise, and a lower ratio indicates more noise. Ideally, we want to use equipment that provides the highest signal-to-noise ratio possible.

Slope

On a pass filter, the slope refers to the rate at which the filter's cut increases. Because no filter can perfectly cut exactly a desired frequency, a pass filter slopes down until the target frequency is cut by 3 dB, then continues to cut on the same slope to the end of the frequency spectrum (see *Fig. 89*). This slope will usually be expressed in decibels per octave.

See also *Equalizer, Pass Filter*.

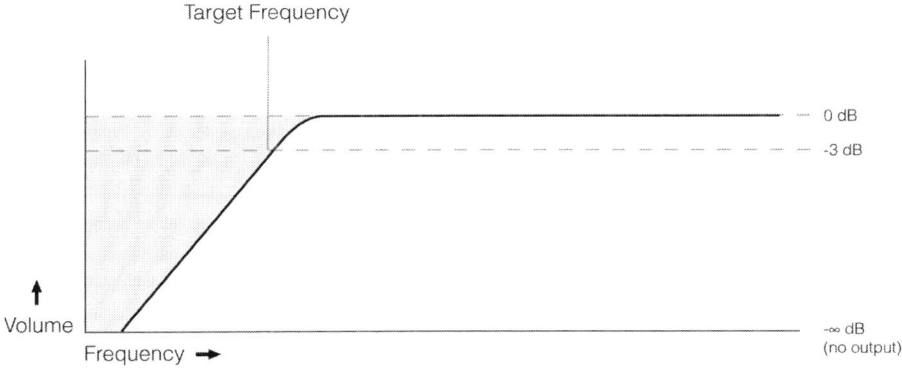

Figure 89: A High-Pass Filter

SMPTE Timecode

SMPTE timecode is a standard defined by the Society of Motion Picture and Television Engineers used to synchronize audio to film or video. The time code is recorded onto an available track on the audio device, allowing the engineer to reference the location on a recording to the frame rate of the video or film.

See also *Synchronization*.

Soft Clipping

Soft clipping is a form of distortion that occurs in analog magnetic tape and vacuum tubes. With transistor-based electronics and digital recording, when a signal becomes too strong for the circuit, the top and bottom of the sound wave are cut off with a sharp edge, resulting in unpleasant distortion. When the same process happens in a tube or on tape, the clipped edge is somewhat rounded off, and as a result the sound is less abrasive. Soft clipping is often used intentionally to add "sizzle" or "grittiness" to instruments such as drums, bass, or guitar. This is especially common in rock music.

See also *Clipping*.

Solo

Solo is a function on many mixers and audio workstations that allows a channel or track to be monitored individually, muting all other channels or tracks. Many workstations allow the solo function to work in groups, soloing grouped tracks together.

Sound Engineer

See *Audio Engineer*.

Sound Module

See *MIDI Module*.

Sound Pressure Level

Sound pressure level (SPL) is a measurement of the increased air pressure being caused by sound, which results in physical force against the eardrum (or the diaphragm of a microphone). This relates directly to volume, and is measured in decibels (dB SPL).

Silence (at least as far as the human ear is concerned) is expressed as 0 dB SPL. The range of human hearing is approximately 130 dB, which means that volumes greater than 130 dB SPL start to become painful to the listener.

Microphones are rated according to how much sound pressure level they can withstand without distorting. Mics with a high SPL rating are the best choice for high volume situations such as close miking drums or loud amplifiers.

See also *Decibel*, *Microphones*

Soundproofing

Soundproofing is the process of reducing or eliminating the transference of sound from one environment to another. This creates a state of acoustic isolation, where sound from inside does not escape, and sound from outside does not get in. Soundproofing is often confused with acoustic treatment, which affects how sound moves within a room. For information on acoustic treatment, see *Acoustics*.

Ideally, in a recording studio the live room (where the musicians perform) is completely isolated from the outside world to help prevent unwanted sounds from getting into the recording. It is equally important that the live room be isolated from the control room so that the engineer can clearly hear exactly what is coming from the speakers without being influenced by acoustic leakage.

Because proper soundproofing can be very expensive, it is a luxury rarely seen in the home studio. However, for those handy at home improvement, there are a number of things that can be done at a more modest expense to help reduce sound transfer. Care should be taken to adhere to home safety standards for your area when undertaking this type of project.

The Basic Concepts of Soundproofing

Because sound energy loses power with distance, space is a big factor in soundproofing. One of the most effective ways to soundproof a room is to build a room within a room. This means building a set of secondary walls spaced away from the existing walls, a "floating" floor, and a "floating" ceiling (all of which are covered below). This has the effect of decoupling the surfaces (meaning they no longer touch, so vibration is less easily transferred) as well as providing dead space to absorb the sound.

Mass is also very important in soundproofing because thick, dense materials are not easily moved by sound pressure. The thickest, heaviest materials available are often the best choices. Using more than one layer, with materials differing in density and thicknesses, can also increase transmission loss. These layers are best separated with a bit of dead space created by rubber blocks, silicone caulking, or similar material.

Soundproofing Walls

As mentioned above, the most effective soundproofing is the room-within-a-room scenario. The walls in this situation can be built with standard 2×4 studs, just as a normal wall is created. Spacing the studs wider apart than the standard 16", and staggering them so they do not line up with the studs of the existing wall, will help reduce sound transfer. The bottom plate, where the studs attach at the floor, should be raised off the floor with rubber blocks or caulk (see *Fig. 90*).

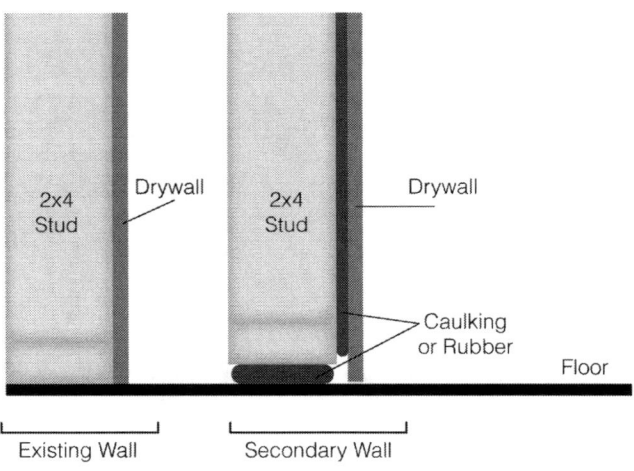

Figure 90: Cross-Section of a Secondary Wall for Soundproofing

When applying drywall, placing silicone caulking or rubber blocks between the drywall sheet and the studs will increase soundproofing. A second layer of drywall can be applied on top of the first layer, again separated by caulking or rubber.

If building a secondary wall is not possible, applying a second sheet of drywall to the existing wall can improve sound dampening (see *Fig. 91*). Just as with a new wall, caulking or rubber should be used to separate it from the existing drywall.

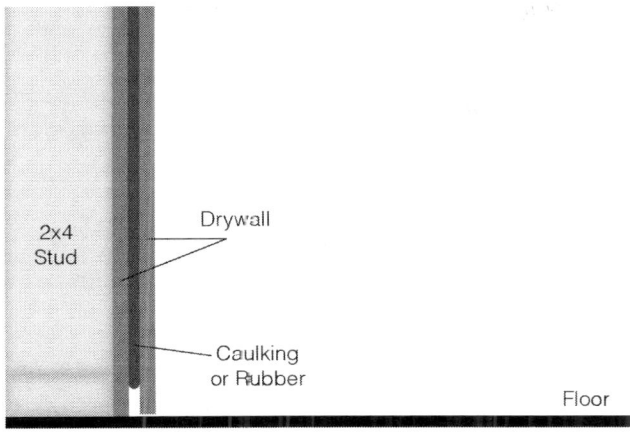

Figure 91: Cross-Section of an Existing Wall With Second Layer of Drywall

Soundproofing Ceilings

The simplest way to increase soundproofing on a ceiling is by attaching drywall spaced with caulking, just as on walls. Floating the floor of the room above will also help (see below).

As with walls, however, the most effective soundproofing is a "floating" ceiling. The term floating means it does not make direct contact with the existing ceiling or ceiling beams. A floating ceiling can be attached to secondary walls (as described above), or suspended from the existing ceiling using chains or other suspension brackets.

Soundproofing Floors

Soundproofing floors can be tough. In cases where budget is less of a concern and heavy construction is an option, a concrete floor can be poured on top of an existing floor, spaced with rubber and plywood. In the home studio, of course, this is usually a little drastic.

A basic floating floor can add acoustic isolation to a room. This is done by covering the floor with rubber underlay or spaced rubber risers. A plywood secondary floor can be laid overtop, followed by another layer of underlay, and finally carpet. The two layers of underlay help decouple the floor, reducing sound transference.

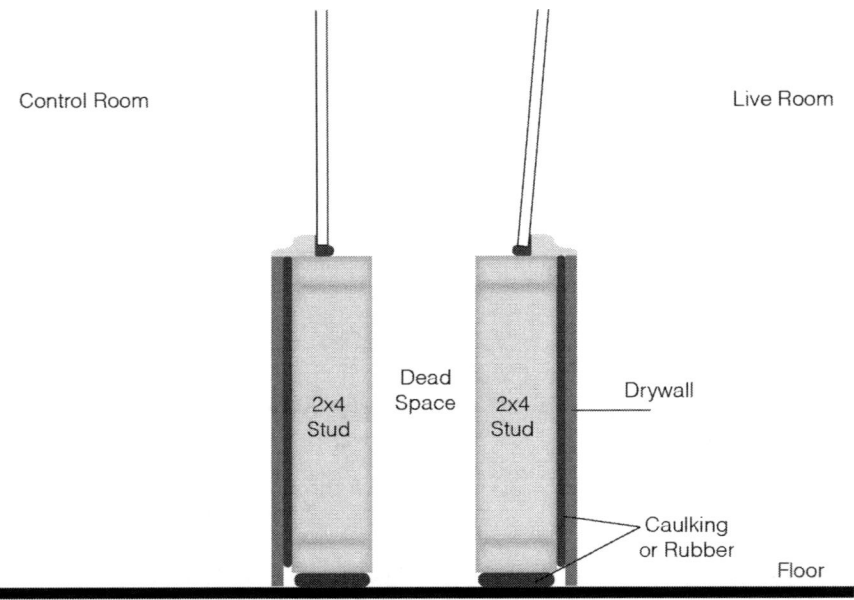

Figure 92: Mounting Windows Between Control Room and Live Room

Windows and Doors

Windows and doors can be sources of significant acoustic leakage and unfortunately can also be the hardest to control.

Windows to the outside world can be covered over, reducing transmission through them. Ideally, a secondary wall would also be in front of them. If covering these windows is undesirable, the windows can be treated as below.

Windows between the control room and live room can consist of two panes of thick glass. They should be mounted on rubber, to decouple them from the wall they are mounted in, and the edges sealed with silicone or acoustic sealant. Placing the pane on the live room side at an angle also reduces sound transfer (see *Fig. 92*).

Doors should be as thick and heavy as possible, with weather stripping on all edges. Creating a "sound lock", where two doors have a small room between them, can significantly increase acoustic isolation (see *Fig. 93*).

See also *Acoustics*.

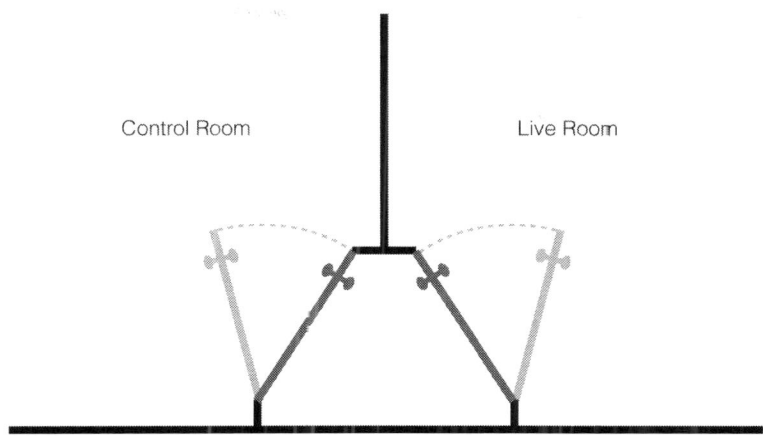

Figure 93: Creating a Sound-Lock with Two Doors

S/PDIF

The Sony/Phillips Digital Interface (S/PDIF) is a protocol for digital communication between devices that was designed as a consumer-level alternative to the AES/EBU protocol. S/PDIF can transmit a stereo digital audio signal along with track markers and copy protection information over a single 75Ω coaxial RCA cable or TOSLINK optical cable. A more recent application of S/PDIF is to digitally transmit compressed five-point surround sound for home theatre applications.

S/PDIF was first introduced with CD and DAT (digital audio tape) decks in mind. Some parties in the record industry feared that the introduction of a format capable of making perfect, loss-free copies, complete with all original track markers, would cause a huge increase in piracy, severely harming the industry. As a result, the Serial Copy Management System (SCMS) was created, allowing the creator to set a digital recording as copy protected, copy allowed, or single copy allowed. Some blame SCMS for the ultimate failure of the DAT as a commercial format.

See also AES/EBU, SCMS, TOSLINK.

Speaker Emulator

A speaker emulator is used in direct recording to mimic the tonal characteristics of an amplifier's speaker. When overdriven, an electric guitar generates some harsh harmonics, and guitar amps use deliberately unresponsive speakers to smooth out these tones. Without a speaker emulator, direct recording an electric guitar can often sound shrill.

Speaker emulators are sometimes found in DI boxes and guitar amplifiers' direct outputs, but the most common place they are found is in amp emulators. Amp emulators are direct recording devices that simulate the tone of classic amplifiers and speaker cabinets. The are very popular in the home studio because they provide versatile guitar tone without the expense of many amplifiers.

See also *Amp Emulator, Direct Injection/Direct Input (DI), Direct Recording.*

Speaker Phase

Speakers are said to be in-phase with each other when the drivers are moving in the same direction at the same time, and out-of-phase when they are opposite. Out-of-phase speakers can cancel each other out, causing major tonal problems. Keeping speakers in-phase is simply a matter of ensuring that the positive leads from the amplifier are connected to the positive leads on all speakers, and the negative to the negative.

See also *Phase.*

SPL

See *Sound Pressure Level.*

Spaced-Pair Miking

Spaced-pair is a stereo miking technique that uses two cardioid microphones placed apart. This could be two mics in the back of the room or close to the instrument, such as on the bridge and nut of a guitar (see *Fig. 94*). When miking with a spaced pair, it is recommended to follow the 3:1 rule to avoid phase issues.

The 3:1 rule says that spaced mics should be three times as far from each other as they are from the sound source. For example, if the mics are one foot from the instrument, they should be at least three feet apart.

See also *Microphones, Stereo Miking*.

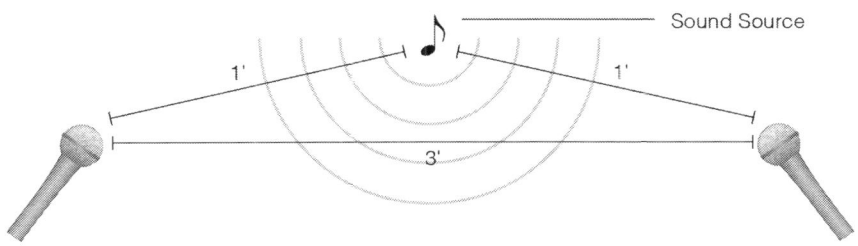

Figure 94: Spaced-Pair Microphone Placement

Spectrum Analyzer

A spectrum analyzer, also called a real-time spectrum analyzer or spectral analyzer, is used to measure the frequency content of a signal. The content is shown as a continually changing graph representing the volume of the signal at each frequency at any given time (see *Fig. 95*).

Spectrum analyzers are mainly used to measure the frequency response of a piece of equipment. To do this, pink noise (noise which is equal volume at all frequencies) is fed into the equipment, and its output is fed into a spectrum analyzer. The spectrum analyzer will show any difference in frequency content between the pink noise and device's output.

Acoustic spaces, such as the live room of a studio or a mixing environment, can be analyzed in the same way. To do this, the pink noise is played through speakers, and a flat-response microphone is used to pick up the sound in the room. Professional studios will often do this to make sure their recordings are not being affected too heavily by the frequency response of the room.

Some engineers will run a spectrum analyzer on the main mix during mixdown to provide a visual reference of the frequency content of the mix.

See also *Acoustics*.

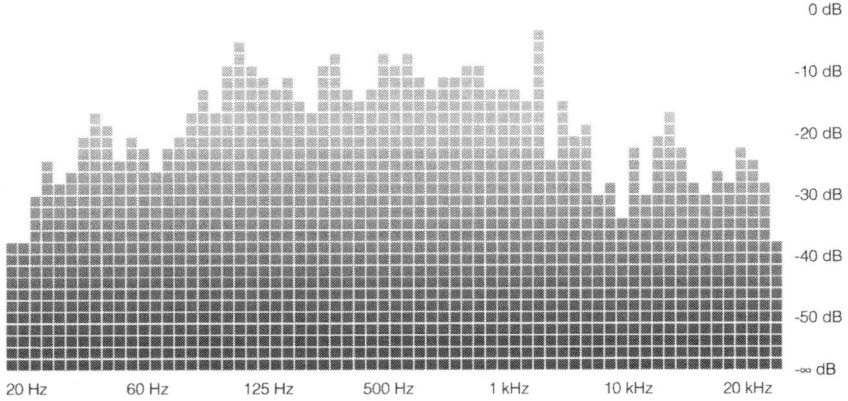

Figure 95: A Spectrum Analysis Graph

Spring Reverb

Spring reverb is a type of artificial reverb that, while no longer common in studio use, is still found in many guitar amplifiers because of its compact design and low cost. A spring reverberator uses a transducer to send audio signal through a set of suspended springs. At the other end of the springs, another transducer picks up the vibrations and converts this to an electrical signal. This signal is then combined with the original to give the illusion of reverberation.

See also *Reverberation*.

Standing Wave

Standing waves occur when a sound wave hits parallel walls and reflects back towards the center of the room. When the sound waves meet in the middle, they will begin to alternately cancel and reinforce each other, creating dips and boosts in volume (see *Fig. 96*). This phenomenon is also referred to as room modes.

As a result of standing waves, different frequencies will be louder and quieter in different areas of the room. The location of these boosts and drops of volume vary with frequency and the distance between the walls.

Standing waves can be reduced by avoiding parallel walls, parallel floor and ceiling, and other parallel surfaces. Unfortunately, in the home studio environment this is rarely possible. Diffusers, bass traps, and acoustic foam can be used to help break up reflections, minimizing issues with standing waves. One very inexpensive way to break up reflections is to use egg cartons, whose shape is perfect for increasing the complexity of sound reflections.

Even in a well diffused room, the volume of frequencies can vary from one spot to the next. Careful listening while moving around the room will help identify "sweet spots" for microphone placement.

See also *Acoustics, Bass Trap, Diffuser*.

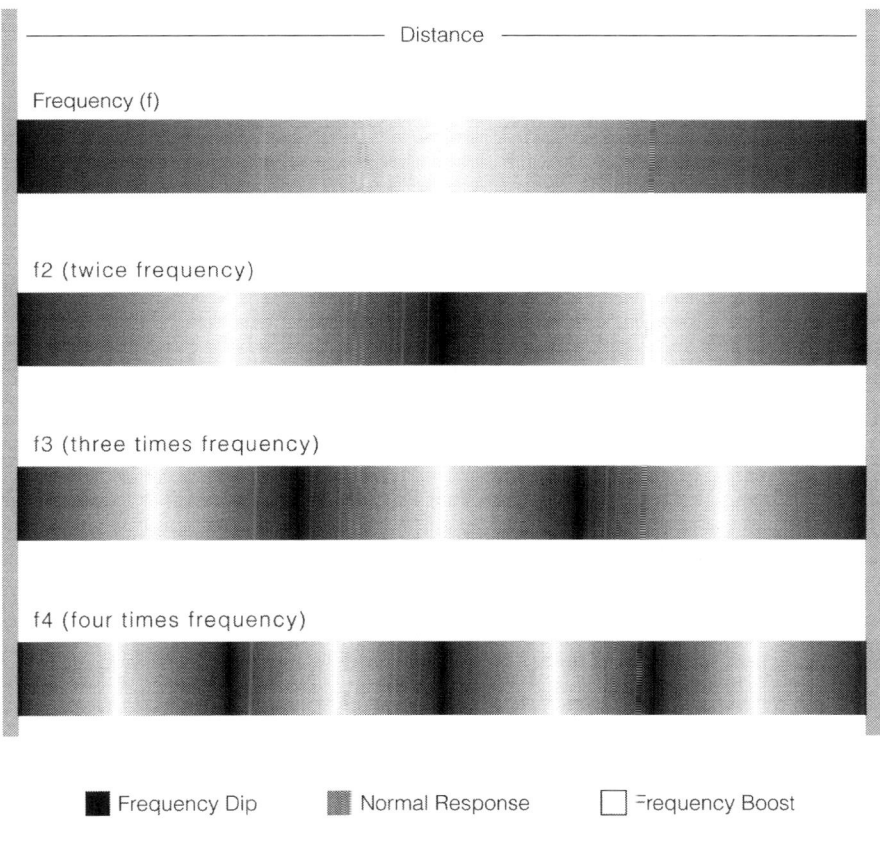

Figure 96: Frequency Response Patterns Caused by Standing Waves

Stereo Miking

Stereo miking is a technique that uses two or more microphones on the same instrument, or group of instruments, to create a stereo recording. There are a variety of stereo recording techniques in common use, and some manufacturers make stereo microphones – microphones with two capsules mounted in a specific configuration. When two mics are set up to mimic the placement of our ears, it is called binaural miking.

When using more than one mic on the same instrument, phase issues can be avoided by either using a coincident pair (meaning the mics are placed together), or by following the 3:1 rule. The 3:1 rule says that mics should be a least three times as far from each other as they are from the sound source. This means that if the mics are one foot from the instrument, they should be at least three feet apart.

A complete guide to stereo mic placement techniques, including diagrams, can be found in *Appendix C: Microphone Placement Guide*.

See also *Microphones, Pickup Pattern, Appendix C: Microphone Placement Guide*.

Stereo Mixing

Stereo mixing means mixing for two speakers. When mixing for stereo, all the same considerations apply as when mixing for mono (see *Mixing*), with the added dimension of the stereo field. Instruments can be placed at various points between the left and right speakers to create a more interesting mix.

Mixing in stereo is actually easier that mixing in mono because instruments that sit in similar tonal ranges can be separated by panning them to opposite sides of the stereo field. This is an easy way to deal with conflicting instruments in a mix, but it can be a bit of a false solution because it only works as long as the mix is played back in stereo. If the mix is played in mono, the problem will return.

Another potential pitfall with stereo mixing is the possibility of issues with phase cancellation going unnoticed. Phase cancellation occurs when two versions of the same signal (for example, two mics on the same instrument or a copy of a signal with an effect added) are played through the same speaker and the phase of the signals is out of line with each other. The result is that the signal is partially or completely cancelled out (see *Phase*). If the two signals are panned left and right, the cancellation may not occur, or it may be subtle enough to go unnoticed.

The rule of thumb to avoid both of the above problems is to always check mixes in mono. Some engineers choose to start a mix in mono and then add panning as the very last step. One of the benefits of this approach is that they can be assured a mix that will sound good in both mono and stereo.

See also *Mixing, Phase, Stereo Miking*.

Studio Design

Home studios can come in all shapes and sizes, from the corner of a bedroom to an entire basement or garage renovated for the specific purpose. While home studios usually have limitations on budget, space, and freedom to renovate, measures can still be taken to improve the quality of a studio space within these restrictions.

The three main considerations for improving the quality of a studio space are acoustic isolation, acoustics/reverberation, and comfort. Comfort may seem like a somewhat superficial factor, but recording often involves spending long periods of time in the studio with other people; increasing the comfort level for both the engineer and the performers will create a more enjoyable experience and encourage better performances from the musicians.

Acoustic Isolation

In an ideal studio environment, there are a minimum of two acoustic environments: a control room and a live room. The live room, where the artists perform for the recording, is completely soundproof to prevent outside noise from entering the recording. The control room, where the engineer operates the recording equipment, is separated from the live room by glass to allow for visual communication between the engineer and the performers but is acoustically isolated from the live room so that the engineer can hear exactly what is being picked up by the microphones. Ideally, the control room is also fairly soundproof to prevent outside noise from interfering with his or her decisions. Larger studios often have more than one live room as well as smaller isolation booths for recording amplifiers and vocals.

Because of the limitations mentioned above, home studios rarely have the luxury of multiple live rooms, and often the performance and recording must be done in the same room. In cases like these, movable dividers can be used to provide small amounts of isolation between performers and the engineer.

Proper soundproofing is costly and generally involves construction of secondary walls, ceiling, and floor that are "floated" with dead space in between them and the existing room. These surfaces are called floating because they do not directly touch the existing structure, which significantly reduces the amount of sound transferred though them.

For details on increasing acoustic isolation, please see the *Soundproofing* entry.

Acoustics and Reverberation

We use the term acoustics to refer to to how sound moves within a space. The amount of sound reflected and the frequency content of the reflections will affect how things sound in that space. The main factors that affect the acoustics of a space include its shape and size, the angles of the walls/ceiling and the material they are made of, as well as any objects that are placed within the space.

While some of these factors can only be changed through construction, carefully placing acoustically absorbent and reflective materials within the space can significantly affect the overall sound of a space. This is explored in greater detail under *Acoustics*.

It is important to consider acoustics and reverberation in both the live room and the control room environments. The tone of the instruments being picked up in the live room is heavily impacted by the acoustics of the space. Acoustics in the control room are also very important because they influence how we perceive the recordings being played back and therefore inform most of the decisions we make during the recording and mixing processes.

When a room is being acoustically treated in a professional studio, the frequency response of the room is usually measured using a real-time spectrum analyzer. To do this, pink noise (noise that is equal volume at all frequencies) is played into the room and then picked up with a flat-response microphone (a microphone that picks up equally at all frequencies). The spectrum analyzer then measures the differences between the pink noise and the sound picked up by the microphone to give the frequency response of the room. This is done in multiple locations within the space because the frequency response will be different at different points in the room (see *Standing Wave*).

Comfort in the Studio

As mentioned above, comfort can greatly impact the quality of the performance that is recorded. This is true of both physical and psychological comfort. For this reason, most large studios take great care to provide a comfortable environment for their clientele. This often includes comfortable seating in the control room and a green room with some entertainment options for members of the band when they are not actively tracking.

In the home studio, when recording for yourself or friends, it is still highly beneficial to take comfort into consideration to help encourage great performances.

See also *Acoustics, Control Room, Live Room, Soundproofing, Spectrum Analyzer, Standing Wave*.

Studio Monitors

See *Monitors*.

Submix

A submix is a set of tracks that have been routed to the same buss then to an individual channel, or stereo pair of channels, on the mixing board (see *Fig. 97*). In effect, this is like running multiple signals into one mixing board then running the mixed output into a separate mixing board.

One reason for using a submix is to run multiple tracks through a single effect or processor. This is generally only used for serial effects, such as a compressor or equalizer, which require the entire signal to be run through it. Parallel effects, which mix the wet signal (with effect) with the original dry signal (no effect) are best applied through an auxiliary send.

Other reasons for submixing include making mix groups (e.g., running all drums to a submix so that the volume of all drum tracks can turned up and down with a single control) or to run multiple signals into a single input on a recording device. The latter is a handy workaround when the recording device has limited inputs but has the drawback that once it is recorded, the signals within the submix can only be manipulated as a group. All effects, equalization, and volume changes will apply to the entire submix.

See also *Buss, Mixing, Mixing Board, Parallel Effect, Serial Effect.*

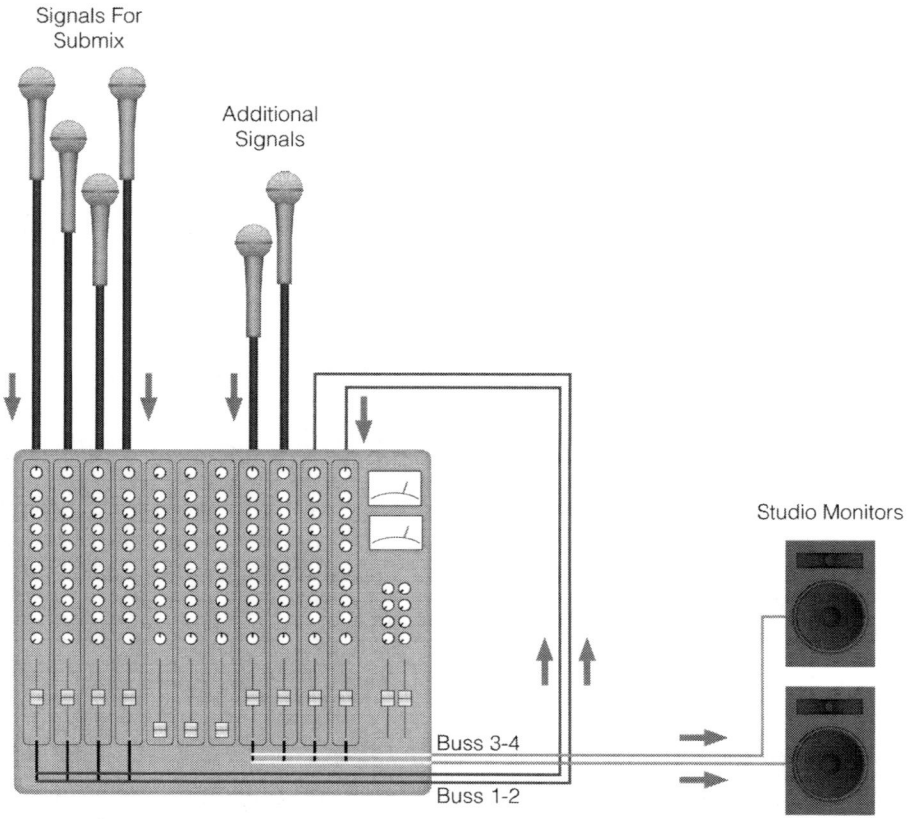

Figure 97: Routing of a Submix

Subwoofer

Subwoofers are speakers dedicated to reproducing very low bass frequencies. The exact frequency range reproduced varies from one subwoofer to the next, but the frequency response is commonly in the range of 20–100 Hz.

A studio subwoofer can be added to a pair of studio monitors to increase the bass response of a monitoring system. While it can be a good idea to check mixes using a subwoofer, many engineers choose to leave them off during the most of the mixing process because they can give a false sense of bass response.

See also *Monitors*.

Super-Cardioid Pickup Pattern

The super-cardioid pickup pattern is a directional microphone pattern similar to hyper-cardioid. Like the hyper-cardioid pattern, super-cardioid picks up in a slightly heart-shaped pattern at the front of the microphone with a small lobe of sensitivity from the rear. The difference between these two patterns is that the super-cardioid pattern has a greater degree of rejection from the rear and is slightly more sensitive from the sides than the hyper-cardioid (see *Fig. 98*).

See also *Cardioid Pickup Pattern*, *Hyper-Cardioid Pickup Pattern*, *Microphones*, *Pickup Pattern*.

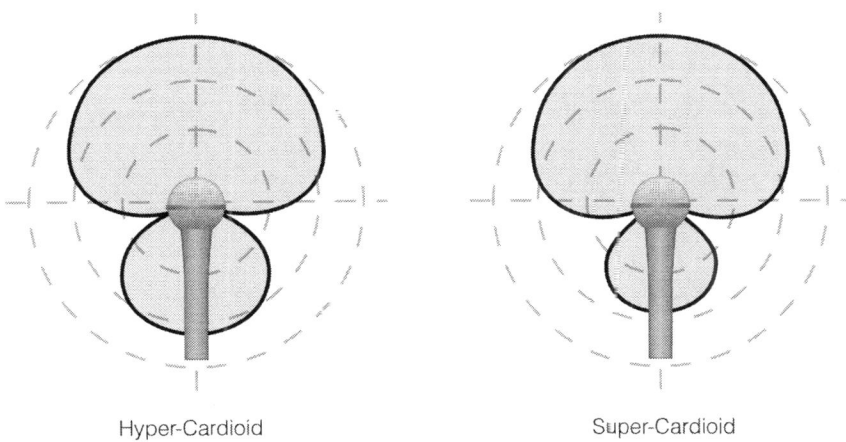

Figure 98: Hyper-Cardioid and Super-Cardioid Pickup Patterns

Synchronization

In order for multiple digital devices to be controlled in unison, they must be synchronized. This is done by means of a master-slave relationship where one device (the master) sends instructions to one or more recipient devices (slaves).

There are various means of synchronization, each used for different purposes. For synchronizing audio to video, SMPTE (Society of Motion Picture and Television Engineers) timecode is generally used. The time code is recorded onto an available track on the recording workstation (called "striping" the track) allowing other devices such as video transports to be synchronized to it.

MIDI devices can be synchronized using MIDI Time Code (MTC). While MTC is not as accurate other synchronization methods, it is commonly used to link MIDI devices.

Digital word clock synchronization locks slaved devices to the sample rate of the master. This information can be transmitted along with digital audio using digital formats such as S/PDIF, AES/EBU, and ADAT Lightpipe, or it can be communicated directly via a 75Ω coaxial cable (usually using a BNC connector).

Talkback

A talkback mic, or talkback system, is an intercom system used to allow the engineer, or others in the control room, to communicate with performers in the live room or isolation booth. A talkback system usually has an inexpensive microphone, sometimes on a gooseneck, that is muted except when the "talkback" button is pressed. The talkback signal may be compressed to help make speech from all parts of the control room more audible.

Tape

While digital recording has become the standard because of its many advantages for editing and processing, many studios still record some, or all, tracks to tape. The performance is recorded on a reel-to-reel deck, then re-recorded from the tape into a digital workstation for editing, processing, and mixing.

This is done because tape has a couple of distinct advantages over digital recording. Many people prefer the warm tone that comes from recording to tape due to its inefficiencies in recording high frequencies. The other advantage is the "soft clipping" that comes when a signal is a little too strong for the tape to properly record. The result is added "grit" or "sizzle" in the recording rather than the unpleasant distortion that comes from digital clipping. This effect is very desirable for some styles of recording.

There are many disadvantages to tape as a recording medium as well, including cost, difficulty to back up, and degradation over time. These drawbacks make recording to tape uncommon in the modern home studio.

See also *Soft Clipping*.

Tape Delay

A tape delay is a device that creates a delay effect using magnetic tape. A continuous loop of audio tape is fed through a transport, first past a record head and then multiple play heads. The signal is recorded onto the tape by the record head then played back as it passes the play heads (see *Fig. 99*), creating the delay. The speed of the tape and which play heads are active affects the length and number of delays.

Tape delays are coveted for their warm, "vintage" tone, but they can be hard to come by and pricey to maintain. Many digital delays and software delays have a tape delay simulation modes which achieve similar results at lower cost.

See also *Delay, Tape*.

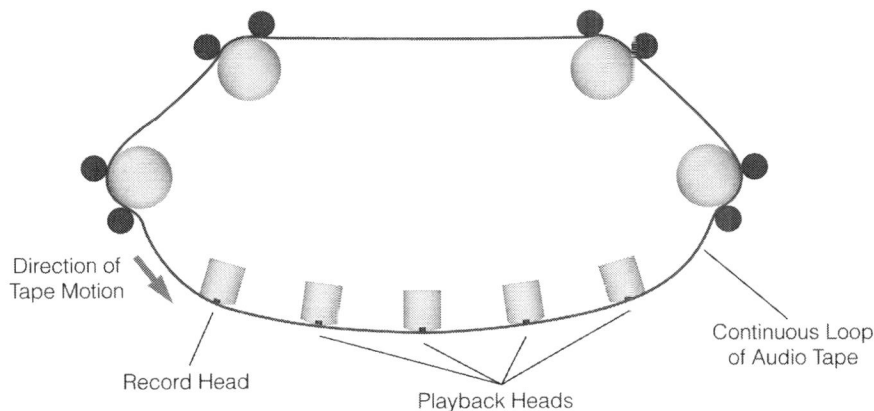

Figure 99: Transport of a Tape Delay

Three-to-One (3:1) Rule

The 3:1 rule is a guideline for stereo microphone placement that helps reduce or prevent issues with phase cancellation. The rule states that if two or more microphones are used on the same instrument, they should either be a coincident pair, meaning the mics are placed together (e.g., X-Y technique), or they should be a minimum of three times as far from each other as they are from the instrument itself. This means, for example, that if the microphones are 1' from the instrument, they should be at least 3' apart; if they are 2' from the instrument, they should be 6' or more apart. When this rule is followed, phase issues rarely occur.

See also *Phase, Stereo Miking, Appendix A: The Basics of Sound, Appendix C: Microphone Placement Guide*.

Threshold

Some effects and processors use a threshold to determine the point at which the effect starts to work. The most common of these include compressors, gates, and pitch correctors.

Threshold (compressor)

On a compressor, the threshold is the signal level at which the compressor begins to compress. When the input signal level is lower than the threshold, the compressor is inactive. Once the signal level exceeds the threshold, the compressor engages and continues to compress until the signal level falls below the threshold again.

How soon the compressor begins to work once the threshold is surpassed, and how quickly it stops after the signal drops below the threshold, is determined by the attack and release settings of the compressor. Some compressors have a fixed threshold, in which case the amount of compression is controlled by the input volume level.

See also *Compression*.

Threshold (gate)

Gates use a threshold to determine when the gate opens and closes. When the input signal is below the threshold, the gate is closed (no signal passes through).

When the signal level is above the threshold, the gate is open (signal passes through unaffected).

See also *Gate*.

Threshold (pitch correction)

Pitch correction processors usually have an assignable threshold, or margin of error. This determines how far off-key the signal needs to be in order for the pitch corrector to work. This is an important setting because if the margin of error is set too low, it will remove any vibrato and intentional changes in pitch from the performance; if it is set too high, it will have little or no effect, and off-key notes will not be corrected.

See also *Pitch Correction*.

Thru

Many MIDI devices and interfaces have a Thru port in addition to the standard In and Out ports. The Thru port outputs an exact copy of the signal as it is received by the unit's In port. This is mainly used when controlling multiple devices from the same controller in a daisy-chain manner. This would be done

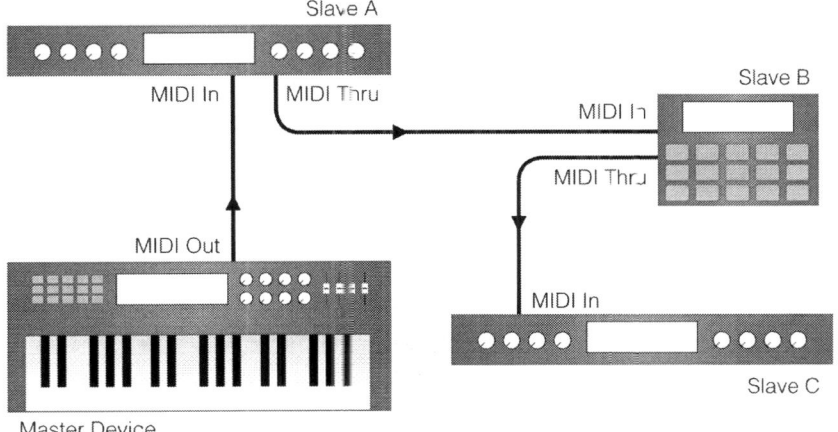

Figure 100: A Controller with Three Slave Devices

by connecting the Out from master device (controller) to the In of slave A, then connecting the Thru of slave A to the In of slave B, etc. (see *Fig. 100*).

See also *MIDI*.

Timbre

Timbre (pronounced "tam-ber") refers to the tonal characteristics of an instrument or voice. The difference in timbre between different instruments is the result of the presence and relative volume of harmonics above the fundamental frequency. These harmonics are one of the reasons why the same note sounds different played on different instruments.

See also *Fundamental Tone, Appendix A: The Basics of Sound*.

Time Code

See *SMPTE Timecode*.

Time Stretching and Compression

Time stretching and compression is a digital process that changes the duration of a segment of audio without affecting the pitch of the recorded sound. The process is related to pitch correction and pitch shifting, where the duration of the segment stays the same, but the pitch is altered.

Uses for time stretching and compression include matching the tempo of a sampled audio loop to an existing project or lengthening/shortening the sustain of an instrument.

The effectiveness of time stretching and compression depends on the quality of the software performing the process. The process is most effective when used to make small changes in duration and when used on sounds where exact pitch is not crucial (such as many percussion instruments).

See also *Pitch Shifting, Pitch Correction*.

TOSLINK

TOSLINK is a connection system used to connect digital audio devices by use of fiber optic cabling. Originally designed by Toshiba to connect their CD player and other devices, the format was later adopted by other companies. The primary use of TOSLINK cables is to optically transmit digital audio using the S/PDIF format. The same cabling can be used to transmit 8 channels of audio using the ADAT Optical format.

See also *ADAT Optical Interface, S/PDIF*.

Transducer

A transducer is a device that converts one type of energy into another. A microphone is a transducer because it changes sound pressure into electrical signal. Other examples of transducers include speakers, tape heads, and our ears.

Transient

Momentary boosts in sound pressure or signal levels are called transients. They are often caused by a sudden change in performance, such as an overly exuberant drum hit or a vocal plosive.

Because transients are fleeting and somewhat unpredictable, they are common causes of clipping and distortion. Often engineers will use a bit of compression while tracking to help reduce the chances of clipping caused by transients. This minimizes the risk of an otherwise good take being ruined by clipping.

Transient Response

How quickly a microphone or speaker is able to respond to a sound or signal is called its transient response. The prime factor that affects the transient response is the mass of the diaphragm; lighter diaphragms react more quickly, reproducing the initial attack of the signal more accurately than heavier diaphragms. For this reason, moving-coil dynamic mics tend to have a lower transient response than ribbon mics, and condenser mics generally have a better transient response than either.

Transient response is an important factor in the tone of the recorded signal and can inform decisions when choosing a microphone for a specific application. Better transient response is not always the best choice for an instrument, however, as lower response can often smooth out harsher tones or provide a bolder, more robust sound.

See also *Microphones, Appendix C: Microphone Placement Guide*.

Triggering

Triggering is the act of using a MIDI sensor to trigger an audio sample. This is most often used for drums, where a MIDI trigger can be attached to the drum itself, triggering a sample each time it is hit. This technique is mainly used to provide a tone that is not available acoustically or as a special effect.

Using a trigger for the kick drum is especially common in very fast styles of metal where the kick drum is being played so fast that the beater strikes from a very short distance, limiting its volume and tone.

See also *MIDI*.

TRS

TRS (short for tip, ring, and sleeve) is a type of ¼" audio connecting jack. While a standard ¼" patch cable has two leads (tip and sleeve), a TRS jack has three (see *Fig. 101*). TRS cabling can be used for balanced signals (the third lead runs the ground though a separate wire), or it can be used for unbalanced stereo signals.

See also *Balanced Cabling*.

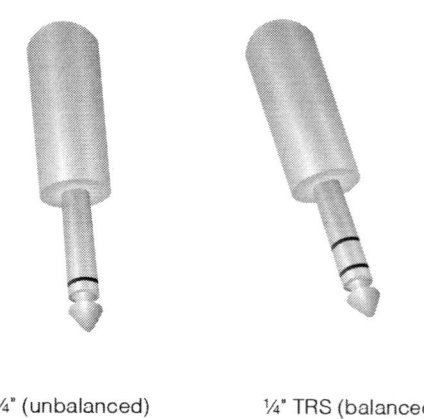

¼" (unbalanced)   ¼" TRS (balanced)

Figure 101: Standard ¼" Jack and TRS Jack

Tubes

See *Vacuum Tube*.

Tube Microphone

At one point in time, all condenser microphones had tube-driven preamps in them to boost the signal to an acceptable level. In the '60s and '70s, manufacturers began to use FETs (field effect transistors) instead of tubes on most designs because of their greater reliability and longer lifespan.

In recent years, tube microphones have risen in popularity because of the warm tone they produce, and many manufacturers are making tube mics again. Using tube mics and/or preamps in digital recording helps to "warm up" the tone of the recording. This is particularly attractive to those who find the perfect reproduction of digital recording sterile or harsh sounding.

The functionality of a tube microphone is the same as for FET condenser mics with the exception that tube mics usually have their own power supply that goes between the mic and the preamp and connects to the microphone with a 5-pin cable. In some models of tube mics, the polar pattern of the microphone can be switched from this power supply.

See also *Microphones*, *Vacuum Tube*.

Tube Preamplifier

A tube preamplifier uses vacuum tubes to boost the level of an audio signal. While tube preamplifiers were once the only option, most modern preamps are built with transistors instead. There are, however, still many options for tube preamps available from a variety of manufacturers.

While transistors are less finicky (and more reliable) than tubes, tube preamps can be a good choice in digital recording because they tend to produce a warmer tone than transistors. Another benefit of tube preamps is that, when the tube is being driven hard, they add a bit of "grit" to the tone of the signal. This is particularly beneficial for styles of music such as rock or blues, where "dirty" tone is desirable.

See also *Preamplifier*, *Vacuum Tube*.

Unbalanced Cabling

See *Balanced Cabling*.

Vacuum Tube

A vacuum tube, also called a valve (particularly in the UK), is a device with a sealed, low-pressure space that regulates the movement of electrons in order to modify an electrical signal. Before the invention of the transistor, vacuum tubes were used in radios, televisions, and even early computers. With a few notable exceptions, particularly in the realm of audio, almost all modern electronics now use transistors rather than tubes.

In recording, however, tubes still see regular use in devices such as amplifiers, preamplifiers, and microphones because of the warm tone and pleasant distortion that they provide. Many engineers and home recordists use tube devices to help offset the almost sterile tone that can come from digital recording.

While tubes have their tonal benefits, they also have shortcomings. The lifespan of a vacuum tube is much shorter that that of a transistor, meaning that tube devices have the ongoing maintenance cost of replacing tubes. Tubes are also less reliable and can be damaged by jostling and changes in temperature or humidity. For this reason it is often advisable to have replacement tubes on hand, particularly for devices that are critical to a session.

See also *Tube Microphone*, *Tube Preamplifier*.

Valve

See *Vacuum Tube*.

Virtual Studio Technology

Virtual Studio Technology (VST) is a software plug-in format developed by Steinberg. It is used to add effects and virtual synthesizers to audio editing software that supports the VST format.

See also *Plug-In*.

Vocal Booth

See *Isolation Room*.

VST

See *Virtual Studio Technology*.

VU Meter

VU, or Volume Units, are a measurement used to indicate perceived loudness. In contrast to a peak meter, which indicates the highest signal peaks reached, a VU meter ignores transient peaks because they do not contribute to our perception of loudness. This is an important distinction as a VU meter is not an effective way to monitor for potential signal overload and clipping.

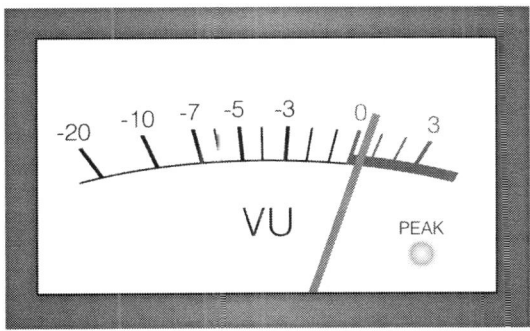

Figure 102: A VU Meter

VU meters generally show a scale that runs from -20 VU to +3 VU, with standard operating level being 0 VU (see *Fig. 102*). This means that levels should be set so that the meter rarely passes the 0 VU mark and does so only for brief instances.

See also *Peak Meter*.

WAV File

WAV, pronounced "wave", is an audio file format developed by Microsoft and IBM. Windows-based systems use WAV as their default format for uncompressed audio, though the file type is compatible with Macintosh and Linux operating systems as well.

See also *File Compression*.

Waveform

A waveform is a visual representation of the amplitude or volume of a signal over time (see *Fig. 103*). Waveforms show a number of characteristics of a sound, including its amplitude, frequency, and acoustic envelope.

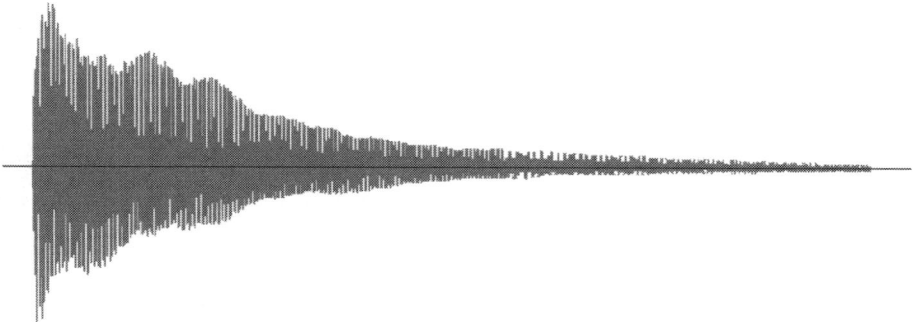

Figure 103: A Waveform

On the vertical axis, waveforms display the amplitude of the signal. This is the amount of voltage in an electrical signal or the amount of compression (increased sound pressure) and rarefaction (reduced sound pressure) in a physical environment. How far the waveform extends above or below the signal shows how intense the signal is, or the volume of the sound. The period where the sound wave moves from the baseline into positive amplitude (above the baseline), then into negative amplitude (below the baseline), and back to the baseline again is called a cycle.

The horizontal axis of a waveform graph represents time. This shows us how the signal changes over time. The number of cycles that occur per second is the frequency of the signal, and the change of intensity over time is called its acoustic envelope. How the acoustic envelope looks varies greatly with different sounds and (along with timbre) is one of the factors that gives different instruments their own individual character.

See also *Acoustic Envelope, Amplitude, Appendix A: The Basics Of Sound*.

Wavelength

Wavelength is the distance a sound wave travels in a single cycle. Lower frequency sounds have longer wavelengths, and higher frequency sounds have shorter wavelengths. When a frequency is doubled, creating an octave, the wavelength is cut in half. Because of variations in wavelength, our perception of a signal can change depending on the distance it is heard from.

See also *Acoustics, Cycle, Appendix A: The Basics of Sound*.

Wet Signal

The term wet is used to describe a signal with an effect applied to it, while a signal with no effect is called a dry signal. When running an effect through an auxiliary send, the wet signal is blended with the original dry signal. The level of the auxiliary send will control the relative volumes of the wet and dry signals, allowing for control over how wet the final signal is.

See also *Auxiliary Send, Dry Signal*.

Word Clock

A word clock is a signal used to synchronize digital devices. This is done by locking the sample rate of slaved devices to that of the master device. The signal can be sent on its own between devices with word clock connectors, or it can be transmitted along with digital audio on some formats, including S/PDIF, AES/EBU, and ADAT Lightpipe.

See also *Synchronization*.

XLR

XLR, sometimes referred to as a canon jack, is a connector for cabling that uses a cylinder-shaped plug (see *Fig. 104*). XLR jacks can have different numbers of pins for different applications, but by far the most common style is the 3-pin XLR used for balanced audio signals.

Most microphones and microphone cables use XLR jacks, and many other audio devices use them as well. It is important to note that XLR is merely a type of connector, and the signal that is sent or received may be microphone level, line level, or even a digital signal in the AES/EBU format.

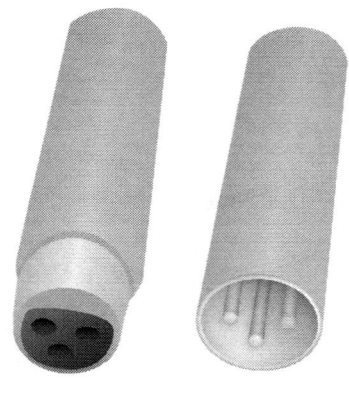

Figure 104: Male and Female XLR Jacks

See also *AES/EBU, Balanced Cabling, Line Level, Microphones*.

X-Y Mic Technique

X-Y is perhaps the simplest stereo miking technique. Two cardioid microphones are placed at a 90° angle with their capsules together and almost touching (see *Fig. 105*). The mic on the left picks up the right half of the sound source and the mic on the right picks up the left half. The two signals are sent to two channels on a mixing board that are then panned hard left and right.

See also *Pickup Pattern, Stereo Miking, Appendix C: Microphone Placement Guide*.

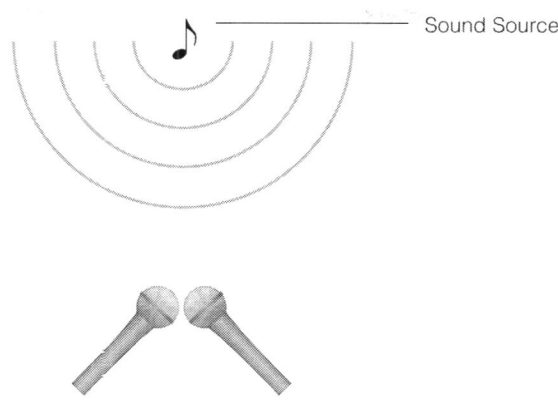

Figure 105: X-Y Microphone Technique

Z

The letter Z is often used as an abbreviation for the word impedance. For example, a microphone may be labelled as "Lo-Z" to indicate it has a low impedance output, and a high impedance input may be labelled "Hi-Z".

See also *Impedance*.

Appendix A: The Basics Of Sound

To gain a thorough understanding of recording, we must start with a fundamental understanding of how sound and hearing work. In this section we'll look at the basics of how sound propagates, its fundamental characteristics, and how we perceive it.

How Sound Works

Sound is created by vibration and is propagated by the movement of air. Let's use the example of a vibrating string (such as a guitar string) to illustrate this concept. When the string is plucked and begins to vibrate, it moves the air surrounding it, causing a space of increased pressure where the air molecules are compressed together. This increased pressure moves outward from the string and is directly followed by an area of decreased pressure. In this area of decreased pressure there are fewer air molecules than the normal air pressure of the space. This is called rarefaction.

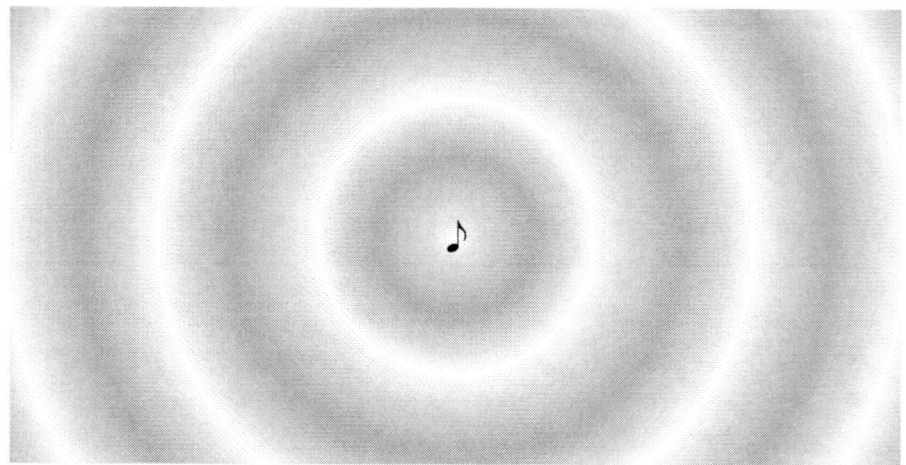

Figure 106: Patterns of Compression and Rarefaction Caused by Sound

The pattern of compression and rarefaction repeats over and over, sometimes hundreds or thousands of times per second, until the string stops vibrating (see *Fig. 106*). This is how sound is created.

This pattern is more easily visualized by thinking of ripples created when a stone is dropped into water. The stone displaces water, causing ripples to move outward. These ripples work in the same way that sound does (see *Fig. 107*).

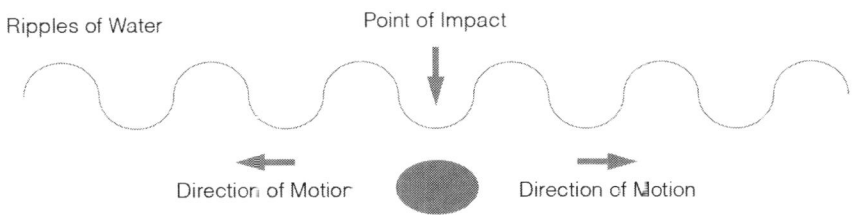

Figure 107: Propagation of Ripples in Water

Characteristics Of A Sound Wave

Amplitude

When we look at a waveform graph, such as the sine wave in *Fig. 108*, the line through the middle, called the zero line or centerline, represents silence. In the acoustic world this means normal atmospheric air pressure, and in the realm of electrical signal, it means an absence of signal.

How far above or below the centerline the waveform is at any given time is called its amplitude and tells us how strong the signal is or how loud the sound is. When it is in positive amplitude (above the centerline) it represents compression or higher air pressure, and when it is in negative amplitude (below the centerline) it represents rarefaction or lower air pressure. The farther above and below the centerline the waveform is, the greater the variation in air pressure.

Frequency and Wavelength

When the waveform moves from the centerline into positive amplitude, past the centerline to negative amplitude, and back to the centerline, this is referred to as one cycle (see *Fig. 109*). The number of cycles a soundwave goes through

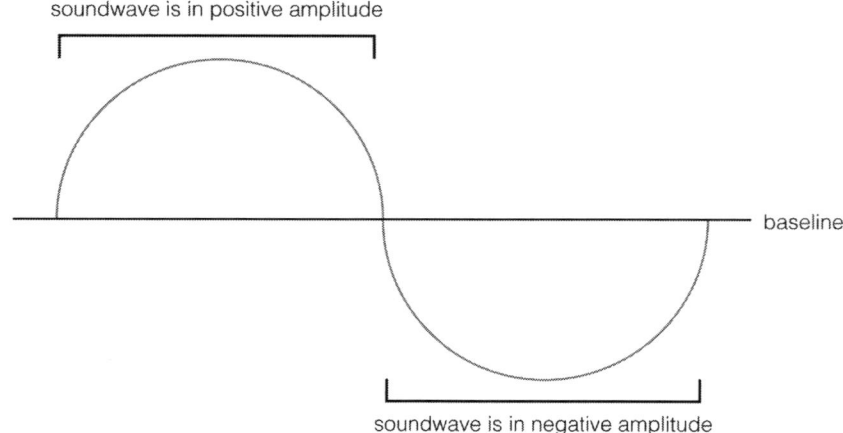

Figure 108: A Basic Sine Wave

in a second is called its frequency, and is measured in Hertz (abbreviated as Hz). When the frequency of the signal gets into the thousands of cycles per second, it is common to use kilohertz instead (kHz) which means "thousands of cycles per second". So, 1000 Hz is equal to 1 kHz and 2500 Hz is 2.5 kHz. The frequency of a signal determines its pitch. The higher the frequency, the higher the pitch of the sound.

When the frequency of a signal is doubled, the pitch raises one octave (see *Fig. 110*). For example, the A string of a guitar, or A above middle C on a

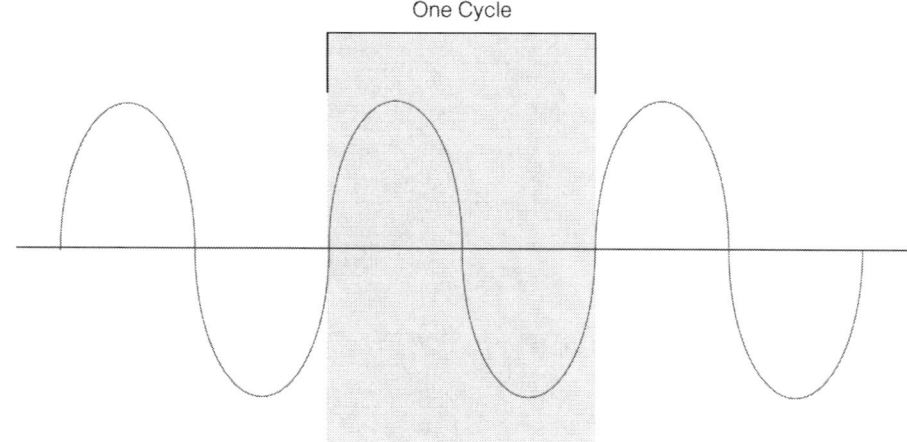

Figure 109: The Cycle of a Soundwave

piano, has a fundamental frequency of 440 Hz. One octave above that is 880 Hz, and two octaves above is 1760 Hz (or 1.76 kHz).

The distance that a sound wave travels in one cycle is called its wavelength. Lower frequency sounds have longer wavelengths, and higher frequencies have shorter wavelengths. In fact, when a frequency is doubled (one octave above), the wavelength is half as long.

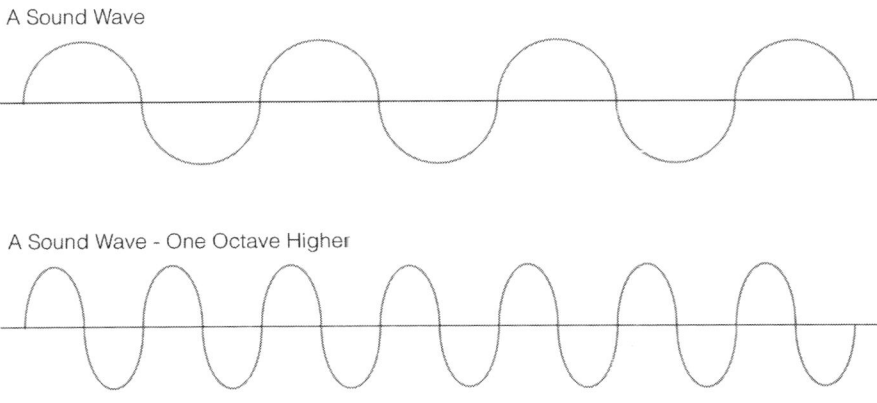

Figure 110: Doubling the Frequency of a Sound Wave

Phase

We use phase to describe the progress of a sound wave in its cycle. Locations along the cycle are referred to in degrees, with a full cycle being 360° (see *Fig. 111*). It may help to think of these points as the would relate to a circle; a 90° arc is one quarter of a circle, just as 90° is one quarter of the cycle of a sound wave. In fact, a sine wave (such as show in *Fig. 111*), can easily be visualized as a circle that has been cut in half with the bottom half reversed, making the circle analogy a little more clear.

If we take two copies of the same signal and combine them with the phase lined up in perfect synchronization, then the two signals will amplify each other. If, however, there is a slight time delay on one of the signals, the phase will not be lined up and they are said to be "out-of-phase". In this case, the two signals will amplify each other when they are both in positive amplitude or both in negative amplitude, but they will cancel each other out when one is in each (see *Fig. 112*). How far out of phase two signals are is also measured in degrees. As *Fig. 112* shows, when the signals are partially out-of-phase, the resulting sound will be

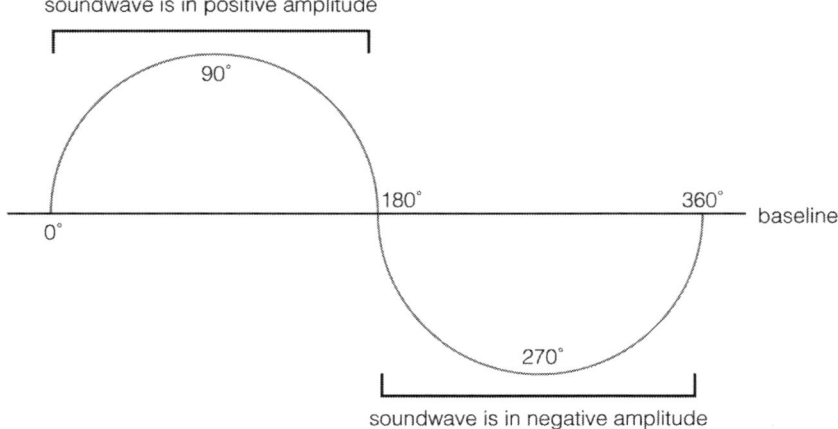

Figure 111: Phase

washy or hollow-sounding, and when two identical signals are 180° out-of-phase, the result is silence.

Most problems with out-of-phase signals come from delay effects or from poor stereo mic placement. When phase problems result from delay effects, the solution is usually as simple as adjusting the delay time until the phasing stops. Phase issues from mic placement are usually eliminated by using coincident pairs (mics placed with the capsules together), or by following the 3:1 rule (mics should be three times as far from each other as they are from the instrument). These techniques are covered in greater depth in *Appendix C: Microphone Placement Guide*. Because phase problems only show up when the two signals are being played through the same speaker, it is very important to always check mixes in mono.

When two mics are used on the same instrument from different sides, for example miking the top and bottom of a snare drum, the resulting signals will usually be 180° out-of-phase from each other. This can be remedied by reversing the phase on one of the signals. Many devices have phase reversal circuits, and they are usually labelled with the "Ø" symbol. If a phase reversal circuit is not available, a mic cable can be made to reverse the phase by swapping its hot and cold leads at one end. This is usually a last resort because it makes the cable unusable for any other application.

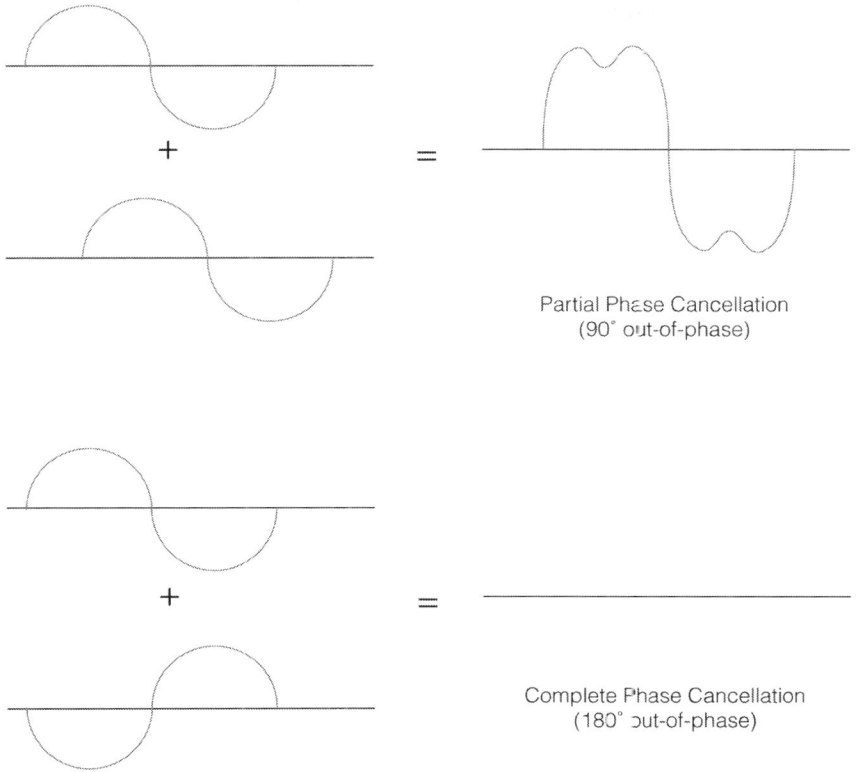

Figure 112: Phase Cancellation

Timbre

As mentioned above, we say that A above middle C vibrates at 440 Hz, but when this note is played, there are actually many frequencies occurring at once. This is true of all naturally occurring sounds. The only time a single frequency is created in isolation is by an artificial waveform generator.

We name a note, such as A 440, for its fundamental tone, which is the lowest and most prominent frequency in the sound. While the string (or reed, etc.) is vibrating, it also creates other, higher pitches at mathematical intervals. These are called harmonics or overtones, and they occur at multiples of the fundamental frequency. For example, harmonics of A 440 will include 880 Hz (2x the fundamental), 1320 Hz (3x the fundamental), 1760 Hz (4x), 2.2 Khz (5x), etc.

The relative volume of these tones creates the tonal character of a specific instrument, called its timbre (pronounced "tam-ber"), which is why two different instruments playing the same note will sound different.

Acoustic Envelope

The acoustic envelope refers to how the volume of a sound changes over time. All sounds follow the same pattern of attack, decay, sustain, and release (see *Fig. 113*). Differences in the volume, length, and intensity of these four sections of the acoustic envelope are part of what gives different instruments their own unique characteristics.

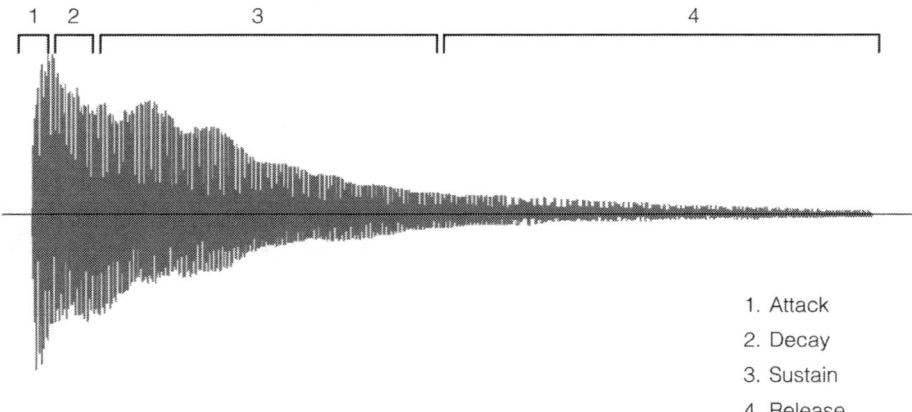

Figure 113: The Acoustic Envelope

The initial rise in volume of a sound is called its attack. The attack lasts from the moment the sound begins to the point where it reaches its greatest volume. While the attack generally only lasts a matter of milliseconds, its duration can vary quite a bit from one sound to another.

Once the sound has reached its initial peak of intensity, the volume drops off. This is called the decay, and it can be subtle or dramatic depending on the sound.

The decay then levels into the sustain of the sound, where the volume decreases gradually as the sound rings out. As the volume of the sound wanes, it eventually decreases to silence. This final drop in volume is called the release.

The acoustic envelope can be manipulated using a compressor (see *Fig. 114*). By carefully setting the attack and release settings on the compressor, the engineer can select which part of the acoustic envelope to compress and which to leave uncompressed (see *Compression*).

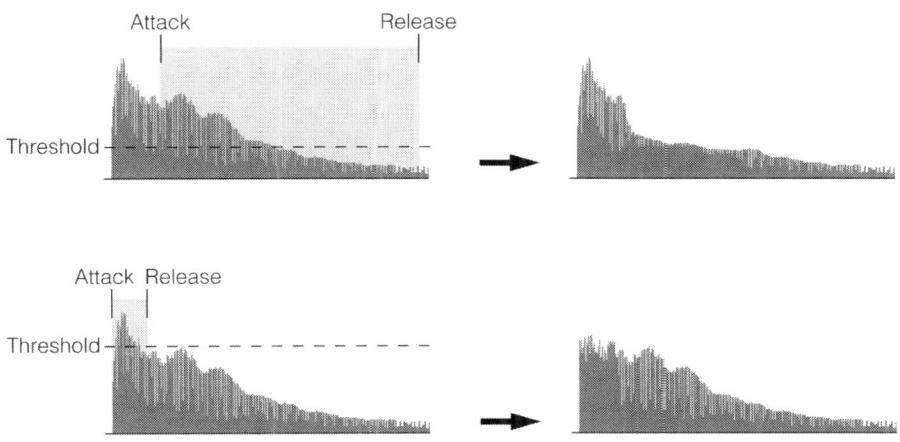

Figure 114: Controlling the Acoustic Envelope with Compression

Hearing

The typical range of human hearing is approximately 20 Hz–20 kHz. This varies a bit between individuals, and most people slowly lose hearing at the high end with age.

Perception Of Loudness

Our ears do not react equally to all frequencies at all volumes. In fact, as sound pressure increases, we become more sensitive to very high and very low frequencies. This was discovered by scientists Harvey Fletcher and W. A. Munson, who charted this phenomenon with a series of graphs that are referred to as Fletcher-Munson Curves. More recent studies have refined these curves, resulting in what are referred to as Equal Loudness Contours.

Because of this non-linear response in our ears, engineers are careful to check their recordings at a variety of volumes. Optimal average mixing volume is considered to be 80 dB SPL, as this yields a mix that will vary the least at common listening volumes.

This phenomenon is used by some home stereo manufacturers who offer a "loudness" feature which uses the equal loudness contours to make music seem louder than it actually is.

Hearing Loss and Hearing Fatigue

Hearing loss is a danger for anyone who frequently spends time in loud environments. Musicians, particularly those that play louder styles of music, are at increased risk of damaging their hearing if precautions are not taken. Hearing loss can be a career-breaker for musicians and especially recording engineers because their perception of the tonal qualities of sound are compromised.

There are two simple ways to prevent hearing loss. The first is to limit exposure to loud environments. At the volume of an average rock concert, permanent damage can occur in less than half an hour. Working musicians and live sound engineers, of course, need to expose themselves to that volume in order to perform, so they must rely on the second method of prevention combined with limiting exposure to loud volume outside of performances.

The second way to prevent hearing damage is to use proper hearing protection. Foam earplugs are very inexpensive and can reduce volume by up to 25 dB. These should be used whenever attending loud concerts or using loud machinery. Those wishing to avoid the "muffling" effect of foam earplugs can purchase flat-response "musician's" earplugs. These have much less effect on the tone of the sound than foam plugs, though they are significantly more expensive. They must be custom moulded to your ear and can be bought through most companies that provide hearing tests and hearing aids.

Long-term exposure to sound, even moderate volumes, can result in a phenomenon called hearing fatigue, where the ear begins to tune-out repeated sounds and frequencies. While the effect is temporary, hearing fatigue can drastically reduce an engineer's ability to make objective decisions about tone. Regular breaks from recording and low monitor volume are the best ways to avoid this problem. Headphones tend to increase problems of fatigue, so they are best used sparingly when spending long hours in the studio.

Transducers and Signal Flow

Turning acoustic sound into a form we can record, reproduce, or manipulate is the job of a transducer. Simply put, a transducer is something that converts one form of energy into another. A good example of this is a speaker, which turns electrical signal into acoustic sound. The type of transducers we're most interested in here, however, are those that turn acoustic sound into an electrical signal, such as microphones and instrument pickups.

Once an acoustic sound has been turned into an electrical signal (for details on how this is done see *Microphones*), we need to concern ourselves with where it's going and how it gets there. This is called signal flow.

Signal flow, like the flow of water, only travels in one direction. *Fig. 115* shows the signal flow of a basic stereo recording setup. The signal originates at the microphone and travels down the microphone cable into the mixing board. In the mixing board, the signal travels down the channel strip, through the master buss, and to the main outputs (for greater details see *Mixing Board*). From the outputs of the mixer, the signal travels though audio cables to the recording device.

Because the signal only travels one direction, the type of recording device being used will not affect what happens at the mixing board, and the settings on the mixer will not affect what happens at the microphone, just as your home's hot water tank will not be affected by what you put in your kitchen sink.

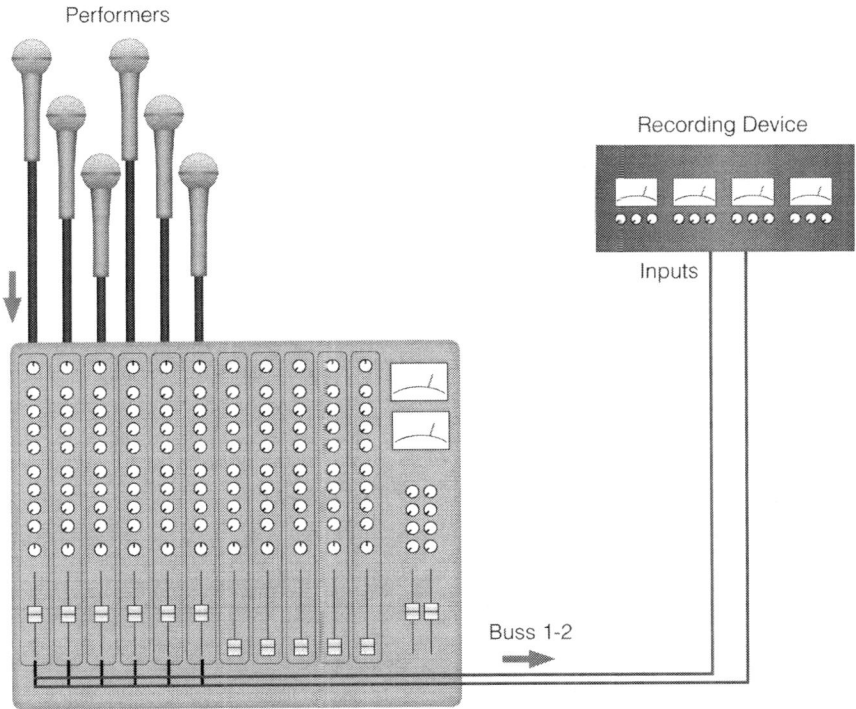

Figure 115: Signal Flow of a Basic Recording Setup

The Encyclopedia of Home Recording

Understanding this concept makes trouble-shooting much easier. For example, in the scenario above, if we were not getting signal to the recording device, we'd need to figure out where our signal flow was breaking down. We can determine this by backtracking from the recorder until we find the last place we successfully had signal. First we would check if there was signal getting to the outputs of the mixer. If the answer is yes, we know we have faulty cables, or they are not hooked up correctly. If there is no signal getting to the outputs, we can check the input of the mixer and make sure we're getting signal there. If there is signal at the input, we know that the problem is happening somewhere in the mixing board, and so on, until we find the source of the problem. This process works on systems of all sizes and levels of complexity.

Digital Audio

When we work in the digital realm, the electrical signal provided by the microphone or pickup must be turned into digital information. This is done by an analog to digital converter, also called an A/D converter. A/D converters and their opposites, D/A converters (for playback), are generally built into dedicated digital recording devices, while in computer-based recording setups, the A/D and D/A converters are part of the soundcard or audio interface.

The A/D converter takes the electrical signal and converts it into a stream of binary code, which is made up of a series of 1s and 0s or ons and offs. This is done by taking a series of evenly-spaced samples of the analog waveform. Much like how film uses static images in quick succession to fool our eyes into perceiving movement, digital audio uses a series of static samples to recreate an analog waveform (see *Fig. 116*).

Sample Rate

The sample rate of a digital signal describes how many digital samples are used for every second of audio. CDs, for example, have a sample rate of 44.1 kHz, which means that for every second of audio there are 44,100 digital samples. Sample rates of some devices can even be as high 192 kHz (192,000 samples per second) or higher, though sample rates that high are less common. Higher sample rates result in a more accurate reproduction of the original signal.

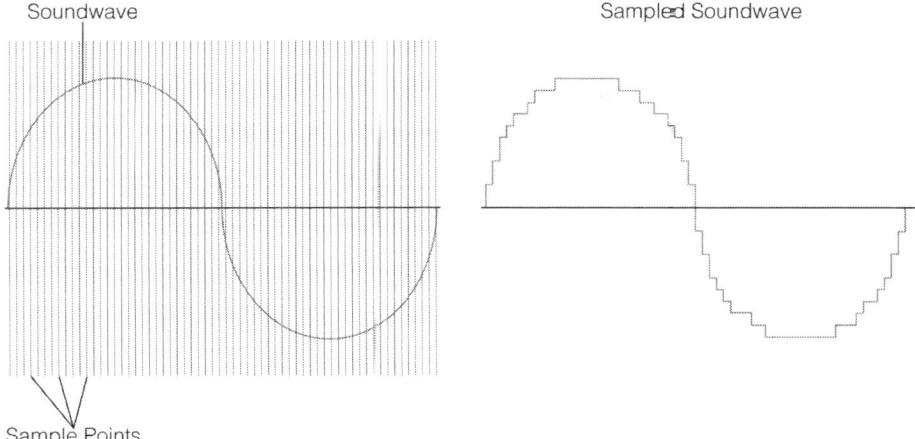

Figure 116: Digital Sampling of a Sound Wave

The highest possible recorded frequency on a digital recording is limited to one-half of the sample rate. A CD, therefore, will contain no frequencies above approximately 22 kHz. The Nyquist Theorem states that if a frequency of greater that half of the sample rate is introduced into a digital recording, inharmonic "ghost" frequencies will be created. For this reason, all analog to digital converters filter out frequencies above their Nyquist cutoff point. While the range of human hearing ends at approximately 20 kHz, the study of psychoacoustics suggests that we may be subconsciously affected by frequencies above our range of hearing.

While higher sample rates increase the quality of a digital signal and extend its frequency range, they also increase the size of audio files, therefore increasing the amount of digital storage needed. To save hard drive space, many people working in the home studio will limit the sample rate of their recordings to 44.1 kHz because they plan to reproduce the recording on CD. Recording at higher sample rates does, however, leave the option open to reproduce the recording at a higher sample rate in the future.

Bit Depth

As mentioned above, digital audio signal is made up of a series of 1s and 0s. Each of these digits is called a bit. A set of bits that make up a discrete piece of information, for example a single sample, is called a digital word. The number of 1s and 0s used to make up each digital word is called the signal's bit depth (see *Fig. 117*).

A 16-Bit Digital Word: 1001100001001101

A 24-Bit Digital Word: 011001001101001001000100

Figure 117: Digital Words

The bit-depth of CD audio is 16-bits. This means that each sample contains sixteen 1s and 0s. At a sample rate of 44.1 kHz, that means that there are 705,600 bits (1s and 0s) for every second of CD-quality audio. Some recording devices can use higher bit-depths, though currently most do not exceed 24-bit recording.

There are two practical benefits to using higher bit depths for recording. First, the longer digital word allows for a more precise measurement of the amplitude of the signal at the time of the sample. This results in a more accurate recording.

The second reason is that any errors in the recording or playback will be less significant. If there is an error resulting in 2 of the bits in a 16-bit recording being completely lost then 1/8 of the sample is missing. In a 24 bit recording, losing 2 bits would only be 1/12 of the sample. A lower ratio of signal-to-error effectively means less noise in a recording.

Like higher sample rates, the tradeoff of a higher bit depth is increased file size. As mentioned above, one second of 16-bit, 44.1 kHz audio contains 706,600 bits. One second of 24-bit, 96 kHz digital audio has 2,304,000 bits, meaning it requires triple the storage space. As hard drives and other digital storage mediums get cheaper, however, this becomes less and less of an issue.

Appendix B: Studio Setup Guide

Home recording studios can come in many forms. They can be a pocket-sized recorder, a standalone workstation, a mixing board and a recording deck, a computer-based workstation, or a variation on any of the above.

While every style of workstation is set up a little differently, and different manufacturers often have their own terminology for different components, all modern workstations are based on the same traditional multitrack studio setup.

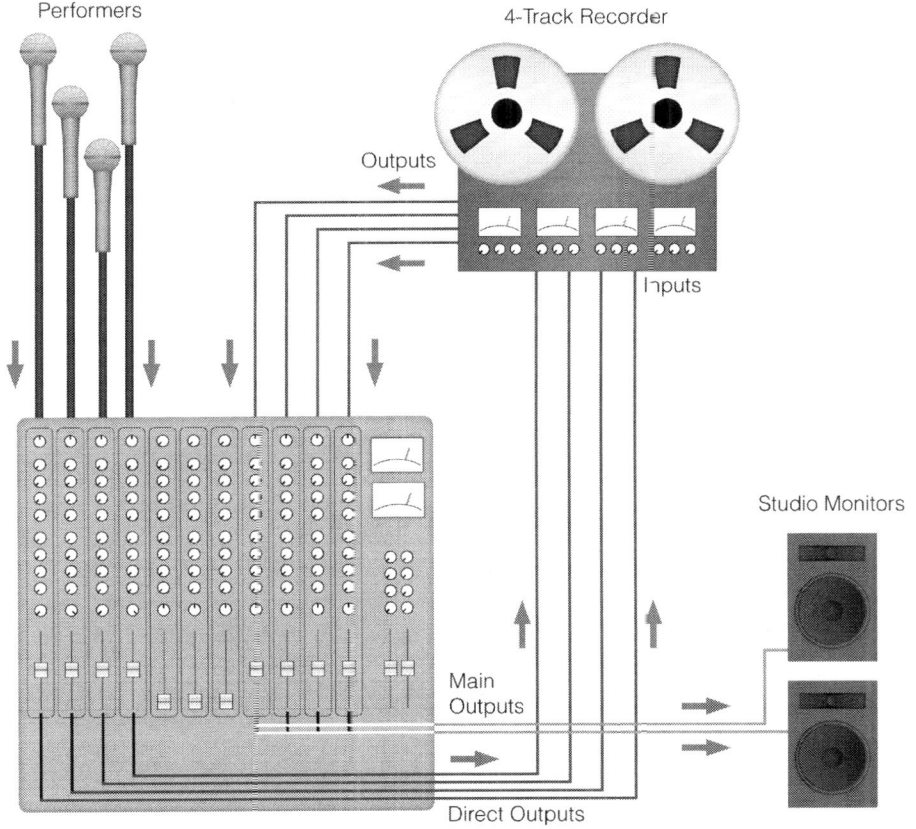

Figure 118: A Traditional Studio Setup

We'll start off by looking at this traditional setup then look at the most common variations that we see in modern workstations.

This section will be most useful to those with a working knowledge of how a mixing board works. It is recommended that you read the *Mixing Board* entry in the alphabetical portion of this book before continuing with this section.

The Traditional Setup

In the early days of multitrack recording, a studio setup consisted of a mixing board, outboard effects, a reel-to-reel tape deck, and a set of studio monitors (see *Fig. 118*). The mixing board is separated into two sections: an input section (for

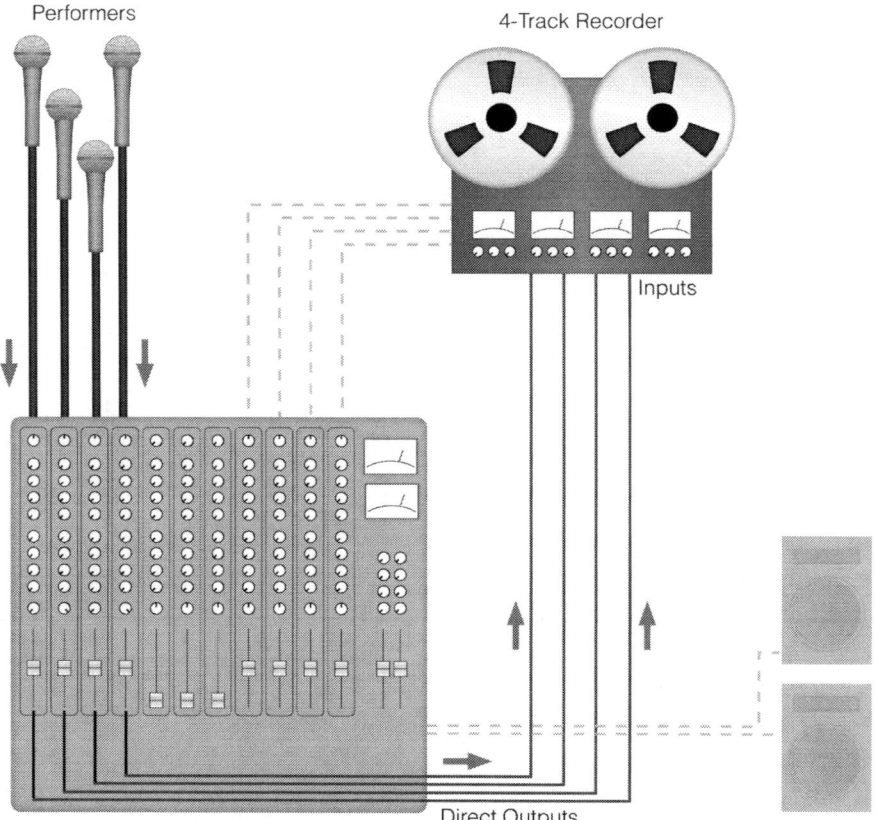

Figure 119: The Input Section of a Traditional Studio Setup

controlling the signal that will be recorded) and an output section (for monitoring and mixing). Using two separate mixing boards is also an option.

The Input Section

Microphones and other signal sources are run into the input channels of the mixing board, giving access to mic preamps, equalizer, and volume control (see *Fig. 119*). Adjustments made in this section of the mixer will be recorded to tape and therefore are permanent. If desired, effects can be added to a signal using the auxiliary sends or inserts on these channels. These, too, will be permanent and so should be applied carefully.

Direct outputs from each of these channels are then connected to the inputs of the reel-to-reel deck where the signal is recorded.

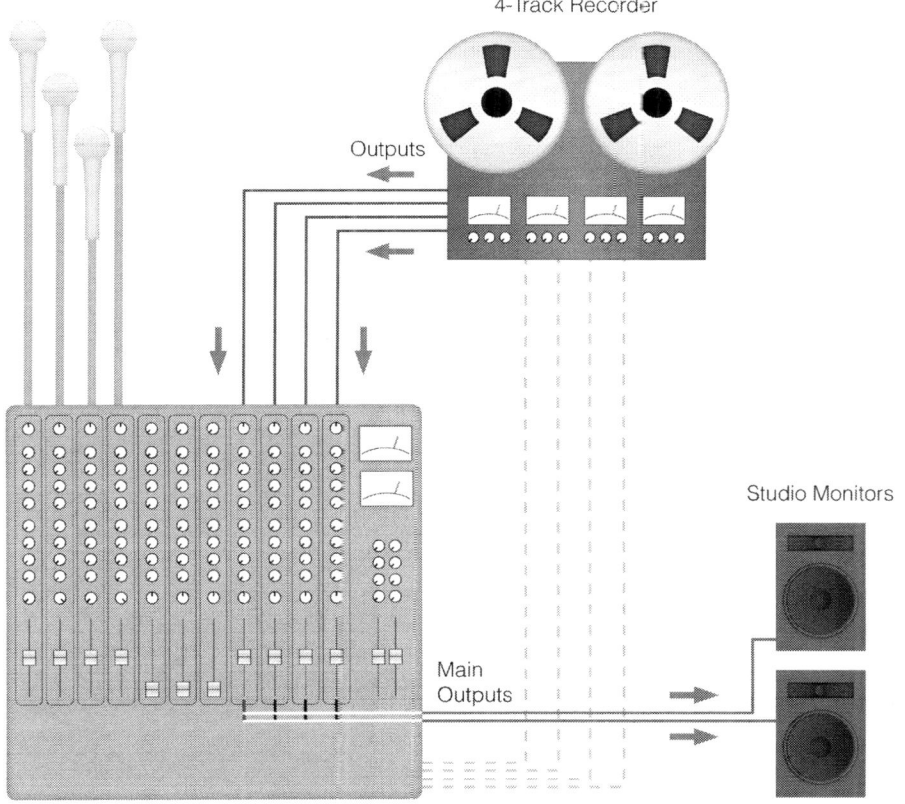

Figure 120: The Output Section of a Traditional Studio Setup

The Encyclopedia of Home Recording

The Output Section

So that the recording can be monitored and mixed, the outputs from each track of the tape deck are routed to individual tracks on the mixing board (see *Fig. 120*). These channels are used for mixing. Adjustments and effects applied here can be changed as often as necessary until final mixdown.

The main outputs of the mixer are fed into an amplifier that powers a pair of studio monitors. Self-powered monitors (also called active monitors), which have the amplifier built into the speaker box, are now very common, eliminating the need for a separate amplifier.

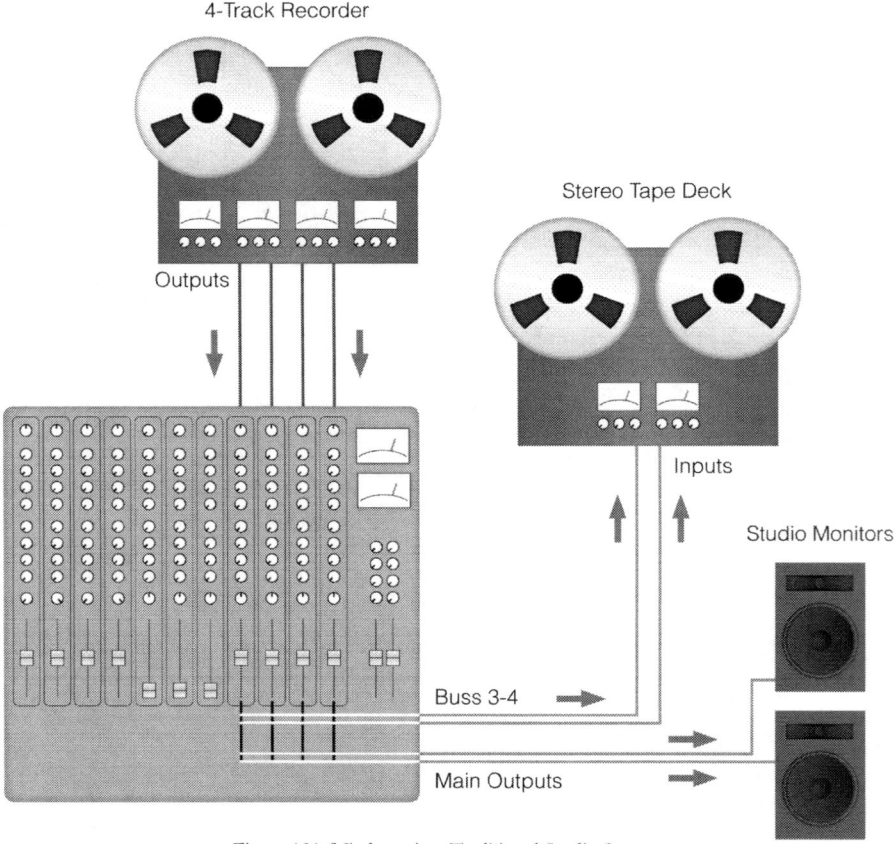

Figure 121: Mixdown in a Traditional Studio Setup

Mixdown

In this setup (see *Fig. 121*), the final mix is recorded onto a separate stereo device. The resulting tape is called a "mixed master" and can be sent to a mastering suite to be prepared for reproduction. This would have traditionally been a stereo reel-to-reel tape deck but is done digitally in modern studios.

Modern Workstation A: Mixing Board And Deck

The "mixing board and deck" setup works in the same manner as the traditional setup, with a few small variables (see *Fig. 122*). While the traditional

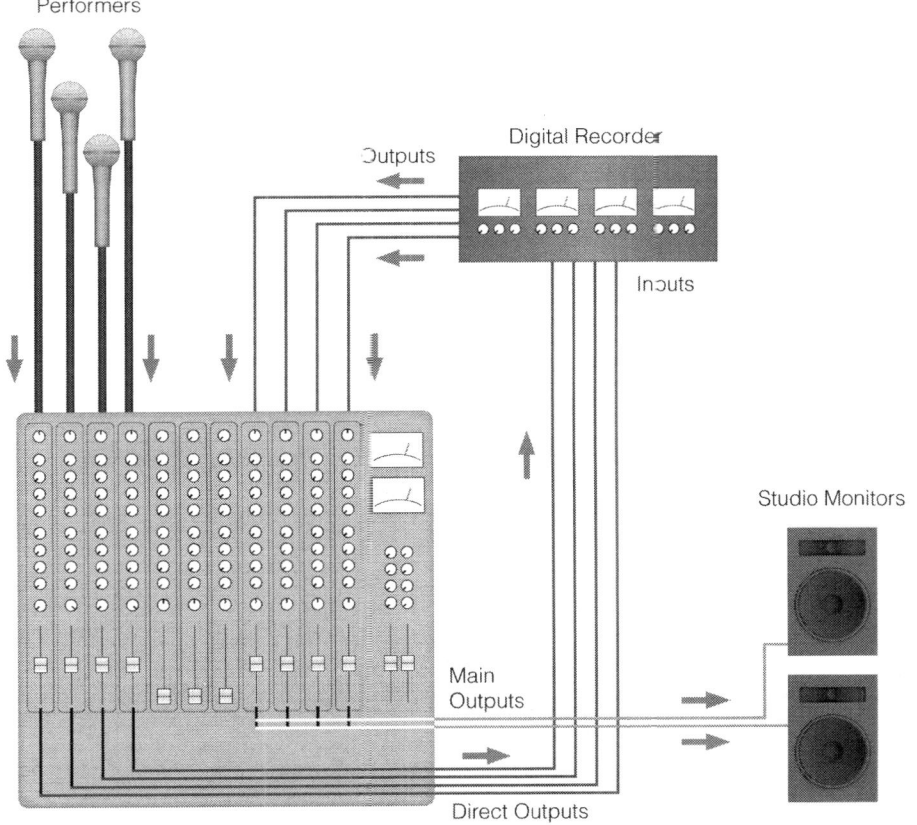

Figure 122: A "Mixing Board and Deck" Studio Setup

setup would record to a reel-to-reel tape deck, in a modern setup the recording device is generally a digital unit such as a multitrack hard disk recorder, which may even have a graphical software interface to allow for easy digital editing. Tape-based digital multitracks, such as ADAT recorders, also work in this setup, though these units are less common than they once were.

A digital mixer can be used in this setup to reduce signal loss from analog cabling and connections. These connect to the recording device digitally and in some cases may have effects built in to allow for a more compact setup.

Mixdown in this setup still requires a separate device, such as a CD recorder or DAT deck, to create a stereo mixed master.

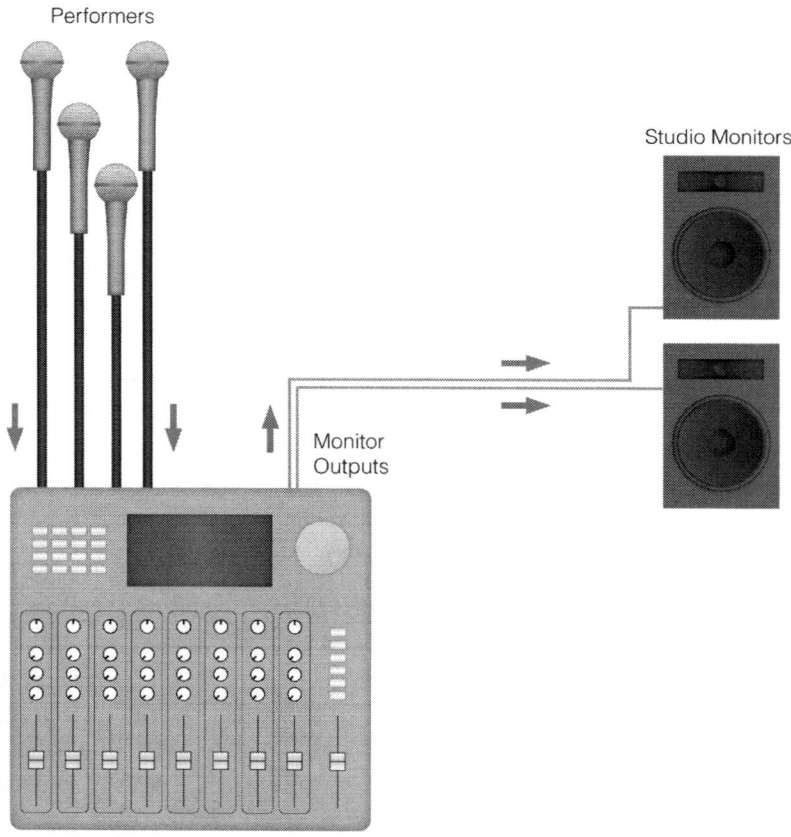

Figure 123: A Standalone Workstation

Modern Workstation B: Standalone Workstation

Standalone DAWs (digital audio workstations) have become extremely popular for home recording. These devices have all the necessary components contained in a single unit, making them completely portable. The only additional equipment needed are microphones, monitors, and headphones (see *Fig. 123*). Functionally, these units are very similar to computer-based workstations, though they tend to be more stable because their processors are dedicated to the single function of recording.

The basic routing for these units is the same as the traditional setup, though because all components are contained in one unit, it is usually less obvious. Any routing and adjustment that would be done on the mixing board in the traditional setup are done on a software "virtual mixer" in a standalone workstation. These virtual mixers usually still have both an input and an output section, though they may share a set of controls that can be toggled between input and output.

Mixdown in standalone workstations usually comes as a "bounce down" or "bounce to disk" function. This function exports a stereo audio file such as a WAV or AIFF file that can then be exported or burned to a CD or DVD.

Modern Workstation C: Computer-Based Workstation

The computer-based workstation is the most common home studio setup. This is likely because they are one of the most accessible. Most people already have a personal computer, introductory software is often very inexpensive, and peripheral items can be added as needed, so getting started often does not require a huge investment.

Computer-based systems offer more flexibility than standalone workstations because individual components can be added or upgraded independent of each other to add functionality or to increase the number of inputs and outputs. In contrast, for most standalone workstations, the only way to upgrade is to replace the entire device.

The number of options available for computer-based workstations does, however, increase the potential for conflict. Compatibility between recording software, operating systems, recording hardware, and computer hardware should be checked before making any purchases.

Any computer-based recording system must consist of a minimum of two basic pieces: recording software, and hardware to get sound in and out of the computer. The hardware can be as simple as the computer's stock soundcard, though better quality and more inputs/outputs can be achieved by using an audio interface designed for recording.

Audio interfaces come in a variety of sizes, from one input and one output to 24 channels of ins and outs. Some interfaces have mic preamps built into them and some do not. When using an interface without preamps, a preamp or mixing board should be placed before the interface if microphones are to be used.

Because computer-based systems are so flexible, the configuration can vary

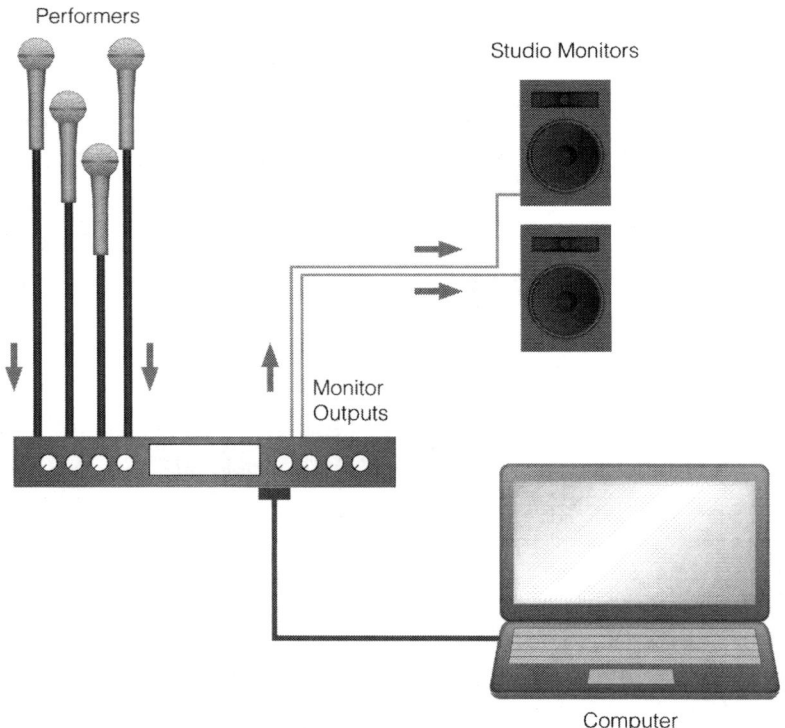

Figure 124: A Computer-Based Workstation

quite a bit, but the setup shown here (*Fig. 124*) is pretty standard. The setup shown consists of an audio interface, a computer with recording software, a pair of headphones, and a set of powered studio monitors. The signal flow of the input section of this setup goes from the microphones, into the inputs of the audio interface, then to the recording software. In the output section, the signal comes from the recording software, through the outputs of the interface, to the monitors and headphones.

Effects can be applied to the recorded tracks using software plug-ins or by using external effect units. Plug-ins are far more convenient but can be limited by the speed of the computer's processor. Most recording software will come with some basic effects, and additional plug-ins can be purchased to add effects and functionality.

All mixing and routing is done using a software mixer controlled with the mouse. Control surfaces can be added to a workstation to control the software mixer with actual physical knobs and faders. This form of tactile control often feels more natural, though all functionality can also be controlled using a mouse.

Like standalone workstations, mixdown in most software is done by exporting a stereo audio file. This command will usually be called "bounce down" or "bounce to disk".

Installing Software and Hardware Drivers

The number of possible variations between recording software, hardware, operating system, and versions of all of the above means that installing software and hardware drivers can be a minefield of potential hiccups when setting up your studio. These variations also make it hard to provide detailed instructions here, but below are a few tips that may help the process along.

Installing Software

The process of software installation will vary depending on the software and the operating system its being installed on. For most software, installation should be as simple as putting the disc into the computer, finding and running the installer program on that disc, then following any instructions that come up as a result.

Programs with more complicated installation processes should always include installation instructions.

If you have installed the program and cannot get it to run, then it is time for troubleshooting. This can be a frustrating process, especially when you are excited to get recording, but keep calm and remind yourself that you only have to do this once.

The first thing to check is the software's compatibility with your operating system. Ideally you want to do this before purchasing the software, as most stores will not accept returns on software products. If the software is compatible with your operating system, then check the website for the product. Often, small updates to your operating system and/or to the software you've purchased can occur between the time the product was packaged and the time you bought it. In these cases, updates will usually be available as a free download.

If, once you have established that you have the latest version of the software, it still will not run, try checking the company's website for an online "answer base" or tech support forum. These are places where users post questions or problems they are having, and the company's tech support will post the answer publicly. Often, other people have had the same problem that you are, and the solution will be posted here.

If you have tried the above solutions and still cannot get the software to run, then it is time to contact the software company's tech support. Options for tech support may include email, an online form, a toll-free phone call, or in some cases even online instant messaging. The process for initiating tech support service will be listed on the software's website and often in the manuals and documentation that accompanied the software.

Setting Up New Hardware

When adding new hardware to your computer-based setup, the computer will usually require drivers to be installed. Drivers are small pieces of software that allow the computer and the new hardware to communicate with each other. These will be included on a disc in the hardware's packaging. It is often advisable to go to the manufacturer's website to download the drivers instead of using the supplied disc, as this will ensure that the drivers you install are the latest version.

If you have the latest version of the driver and the hardware does not seem to work, check the preferences for your recording software as well as the preferences for your operating system to see if there is a place to select the hardware for use. For example, if the hardware is an audio interface, check that your operating system and software have selected it as its source for audio input and output.

If the hardware still does not work, check the manufacturer's website. As with software, most manufacturers will provide an answer base or tech support forum where they will post solutions to known problems and conflicts. If the solution cannot be found on their website, then it is time to contact their tech support.

Appendix C: Microphone Placement Guide

It is fair to say that recording starts at the microphone; everything before it is performance. The quality of the sound you get out of the microphone affects every other step in the recording process. While it is easy to fall into the mindset that any tonal issues can be "fixed in the mix", in actuality, trying to clean up a poorly captured sound can be very time consuming and often provides less than satisfactory results. Taking the time in the tracking process to pick the right microphone and the right mic placement usually takes less time in the long run, and the result is far better. In this section we'll look at how to choose a microphone and placement for your recording.

This section presumes a working knowledge of how microphones work. It is recommend that you read the *Microphones* entry in the alphabetical portion of this book before continuing with this section.

Before We Mic Anything

Before we look at microphones and where to place them, there are some factors we need to think about. These are the context the instrument will be placed in, the instrument itself, and the room being recorded in. These factors will inform our decisions and the tone we get from our recordings.

Context

Most people's instinct when recording an instrument is to make it sound great. This is a perfectly reasonable attitude, but many people concentrate on how that instrument sounds on its own without thinking about how it will fit into the overall mix. This brings us to an important axiom of recording: how an instrument sounds on its own only matters if it is heard on its own. If the instrument never plays on its own, all that matters is how it sounds in the mix.

Approaching a recording this way can drastically change how we approach miking an instrument. For example, if we are recording an acoustic guitar for a song that is just guitar and vocals, it needs it to be full and rich to fill the mix. If the acoustic guitar is part of a ten-piece band that includes electric guitar, keyboard, and a horn section, then any body and fullness in the acoustic guitar will be masked by other instruments and will just make the mix muddy. In the ten-piece band, the acoustic guitar is likely there to provide bright, sparkly rhythm, so that is the only important part of the instrument's tone, and choice of microphone and placement should enhance these characteristics.

Taking the time to consider how the instrument fits in to the arrangement and the mix will inform our decisions when choosing a microphone and placement, and it will reduce the amount of effort needed to make the recorded track sit nicely in the mix.

The Instrument

Obviously we want to use the best-sounding instrument available to us at any given time, but we also need to take time to ensure that the instrument we use is sounding its best. Small bits of preparation such as replacing guitar strings, tuning drums, and getting rid of any mechanical buzzes or rattles from instruments will save time, energy, and frustration, and will improve the overall quality of your recording.

We also want to make sure we're choosing the right instrument for this particular recording. A Les Paul guitar sounds different from a Stratocaster, and a 16" kick drum sounds different from a 24" kick drum. Choosing the right instrument for the situation will make getting it to sit nicely in the mix much easier.

The Room

The context of the instrument in the mix will also help inform which acoustic qualities we need from the room we record in. Every room will have its own tonal characteristics and reverberation, and different spots in the same room can even give drastically different tone. It is well worth taking the time to experiment with available recording environments before setting up microphones. If possible, try putting the performer in different rooms and different spots in each room. Listen to them play in these different rooms and positions to find the best available spot to record.

For greater detail on the acoustic qualities of a room, see the *Acoustics* entry in the main section of this book.

Choosing A Microphone

The tone and quality of a recording can be greatly affected by the microphone used. Factors to consider when choosing a microphone for a recording include the type of transducer (e.g., condenser or dynamic microphone), its pickup pattern, its frequency response, and its maximum SPL rating. Even when the specifications of two microphones are similar, they may produce quite different tones when miking the same instrument in the same position, so taking the time to try different microphones can help you get the best tone possible in your recordings. All the factors below are explained in the *Microphones* entry in the main section of this book.

Transducer Type

There are three main types of microphones that are used in the studio: condenser, moving-coil dynamic, and ribbon. Each has their own set of characteristics that will affect how they are best used. Like all areas of recording, there are no rules, only guidelines. The best results, and certainly the most unique, often come from deliberately working contrary to these guidelines.

Condenser mics are very popular in the studio because they provide a clear, natural sound. They are generally more sensitive than dynamic microphones and pick up more of the sound of the room. This can actually be problematic when miking a quiet instrument in an environment with extraneous background noise (such as computer fans, air conditioning, and fluorescent lighting). Common uses for condenser microphones include miking vocals, acoustic instruments, drum overheads, and ambient room miking.

Moving-coil dynamic mics are more rugged than condenser mics, which is why they are more for common in live sound situations. Their rugged nature also makes them a good choice for close miking drums because there is always a small a possibility of them taking an errant hit from a drum stick. Dynamic mics are less sensitive to room sound, so they generally need to be placed close to the sound source to provide decent tone and signal level. They also generally have higher maximum SPL ratings than condenser mics, making them a good choice for high-volume instruments. Common uses for moving-coil dynamic mics include close miking drums, amplifiers, and brass instruments.

Ribbon mics are often prized for their warm, vintage-sounding tone. Traditionally, ribbon mics have been more fragile because high sound pressure or sudden gusts of air can tear the thin metal ribbon of the diaphragm; however, modern designs are usually more rugged, making them more versatile than their predecessors. Common uses for ribbon mics include miking vocals and acoustic instruments.

Pickup Pattern

The pickup pattern of a microphone will affect how much of the acoustics of the room are picked up and can be used to specifically reject unwanted sounds. Narrower pickup patterns such as hyper-cardioid and super-cardioid will pick up less room sound than wider patterns such as cardioid, figure-8, and omnidirectional.

The angle of most rejection for each pattern should be noted, and unwanted sounds placed at that angle. This angle is 180° off-axis (directly behind) for a cardioid mic, 90° off-axis for a figure-8 microphone, and approximately 135° off-axis (45° from the rear of the microphone) for the hyper-cardioid pattern. This technique can be very helpful for isolating individual pieces of a drum kit. For example, a mic on the snare drum can be placed so that the hi-hat is in its angle of most rejection in order to minimize the amount of hi-hat in the snare mic.

When choosing a pickup pattern it is also important to remember that all unidirectional microphones are subject to proximity effect, meaning they will produce more bass response the closer they are to the sound source.

Frequency Response

When choosing a microphone, we want it to be sensitive in the instrument's important frequency ranges. For example, when choosing a mic for a bass or kick drum, it is important to look at its low frequency response because the frequency response on many microphones declines steeply in low frequencies. At the same time, care should also be taken not to select a microphone that accentuates unwanted frequencies for the instrument. Again, context is important as it will tell us which frequencies to accentuate and which to downplay.

Maximum SPL Rating

On louder instruments such as drums and amplifiers, it is a good idea to check the maximum SPL rating of microphones before placement. This is especially true when close miking these instruments. Sound pressure reduces with distance, so SPL rating becomes less of an issue as the mic is placed farther away.

Microphone Placement Techniques For Any Instrument

Before we look at mic placement for specific instruments, we'll take a look at some methods for finding mic placements for any instrument and some tried-and-true techniques that yield decent results for most instruments. The best results come from taking time to experiment with different mics and placements, but these techniques offer a good place to start.

Finding the Instrument's Tone

Many people's first instinct is to mic the loudest part of an instrument. This will provide a healthy signal level, but this is not necessarily the place with the best tone. For example, a mic placed at the embouchure (mouthpiece) of a flute will have plenty of volume, and may sound quite nice, but it will not pick up any of the tone created at the instrument's keys. One way to find new and creative mic placements for an instrument is to first take the time to understand how the instrument's tone is created.

To illustrate this, let's look at an acoustic guitar. Sound is created when the guitar's strings are plucked or strummed and begin to vibrate. The vibration of the stings is transmitted into the body of the guitar at the two points of contact: the bridge and the nut. Vibrations transmitted through the nut vibrate the entire top of the guitar, which vibrates the bracing on its underside, and is then amplified by the body of the instrument.

Looking at the above information, a few ideas present themselves. The bridge and nut, as contact points for the string, are both interesting spots to try miking. The top of the guitar, as the main resonating part of the body, is also a spot to consider. A less obvious, though quite effective, placement is the 12th fret because it is the half-way point in the length of the string.

This method of analysis can be used on any instrument to identify mic placement options. Because every individual instrument, microphone, and room are different, the results from any of these positions can vary greatly. Taking time to try different combinations of these variables will lead to more effective results.

The 1:1 Technique

Perhaps the simplest mic placement, the 1:1 (one-to-one) technique uses one microphone placed at a distance equal to the width or height (whichever is greater) of the instrument. An instrument that is 4' wide, for example, would be miked from 4' away (see *Fig. 125*). The 1:1 technique will usually yield a balanced overall tone in most situations, but because of the microphone's distance it can be heavily affected by the acoustics of the room.

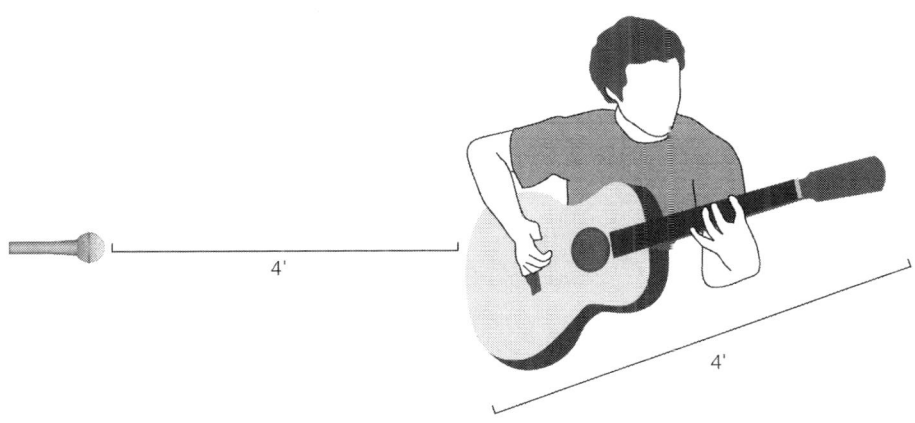

Figure 125: The 1:1 Technique

Miking At the Performer's Ear

Placing a microphone next to the performer's ear can have some pleasant results (*Fig. 126*). The theory behind this technique is that performers work towards making their instrument sound good to their own ear, and if the instrument sounds good to the performer, it should sound good to the microphone. This technique can also pick up much of the tone of the room, so it is most effective in a room with pleasant acoustics.

Figure 126: Miking At the Performer's Ear

Miking The Points of Contact

For most instruments, sound is created at the point where the player connects with the instrument (see *Fig. 127*). Take the keys and reed of a saxophone, the skin of a drum, or strings of a double bass for example. Miking the instrument at these points of contact is another placement that can be effective. It should be noted that in some cases the point of contact is extended by a mechanism of some

Figure 127: The Points of Contact

sort, such as a drumstick, the lever of a piano key, or the bow of a violin. In these cases, the mic should be placed where the extension meets the instrument (the drumhead, for example).

Microphone Placement Techniques for Specific Instruments

Below we'll look at some common mic techniques for a variety of instruments. When reading the placement tips below, it's important to remember that there are no true rules when it comes to recording. There are a few guidelines to help avoid problems, such as "cut narrow, boost wide" (see *Equalizer*) and the 3:1 Rule (see *Three-To-One Rule*), but most advice for recording – especially when it comes to microphone choice and placement – are more like suggestions, and are subject to individual taste and the context of the recording. The suggestions below are common placements and offer a great place to start, but great recordings come from taking the time to experiment with many placement options.

Vocals

Common practice for miking a single vocalist is to use a wide-diaphragm condenser mic with a cardioid pickup pattern. The mic is placed approximately 6" from the singer and slightly above the vocalist's mouth (see *Fig. 128*). The distance can be adjusted to alter the tone, moving the mic farther away to reduce bass response and closer to add bass.

Some engineers will use a dynamic microphone for certain vocalists or musical styles to get a more direct, punchy sound. Usually a closer mic distance is appropriate in these situations.

Figure 128: Common Placement for a Single Vocalist

Vocal Ensembles

When recording multiple vocalists at once, the choice of mic placement will depend on the size of the group, the style of music, and how the track will be used.

For small groups of 2–4 vocalists, often a single large-diaphragm condenser mic placed 3–4' from the vocalists can be enough to mic the group (see *Fig. 129*). The group should stand in a semi-circle around the microphone. If the group is experienced, they should have no problem self-mixing to make sure no individual is overpowering the group. Experimenting with mic distance will allow control of the amount of presence in the track.

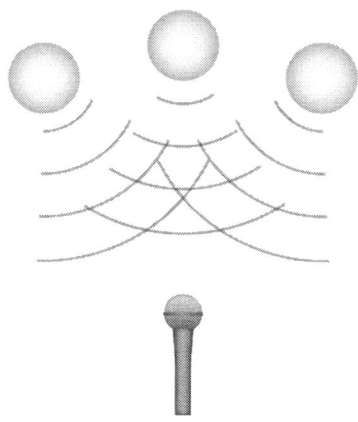

Figure 129: Miking a Group of Vocalists

For larger groups and choral ensembles, stereo miking is often a good option. Techniques such as X-Y, ORTF, and the Decca Tree can be used. These techniques are all explained below under *Stereo Miking Techniques*.

In some cases, miking each vocalist or each vocal section, if it is a larger group, separately can provide more versatility during mixdown.

Acoustic/Classical Guitar

Many novice recordists fall into the pitfall of recording an acoustic guitar by placing the mic directly in front of the soundhole. While this placement provides plenty of volume, it rarely offers great tone. Below are a few popular placements (see *Fig. 130*). Most engineers will choose a bright-sounding condenser mic for these applications.

- Pointed at the top of the body, just below the bridge an a distance of 5–6".
- Pointed at the 12th fret with distance of 3–5".
- Miking the nut at a distance of roughly 1" offers a very bright sound. On its own this placement rarely has much body but can be blended with another mic placement to add sparkle. This can be done with a clip-on style condenser mic designed for drums or horns – but be sure to cut low frequencies, as the vibrations through the clip can cause some deep rumble.

- Some recording engineers will record a feed directly off an acoustic pickup and blend it in with the miked sound. This can add brightness and help the acoustic cut through a mix. Recording the pickup, however, rarely sounds natural on its own.
- Stereo techniques such as X-Y and ORTF can be very effective as well. These techniques are explained in the Stereo Miking Techniques section below.

The most common mic to use on acoustic instruments is a condenser mic. The choice of pickup pattern will depend on the acoustics of the room and if there are any other instruments or sounds in the room that you are trying to avoid. Cardioid or hyper-cardioid patters are safest, though in a nice-sounding room it can be beneficial to experiment with bi-directional or omnidirectional microphones

Figure 130: Miking an Acoustic Guitar

Electric Guitar

When miking a guitar amplifier, the most common mic choices are a moving-coil dynamic or a wide-diaphragm condenser in a cardioid or hyper-cardioid pickup pattern. The Shure SM-57 has long been a standby as a workhorse dynamic mic and is a popular choice for close miking guitar amps. When using a condenser mic in a close placement, it's advisable to check the SPL (sound pressure level) rating of the mic to make sure that it can handle the volume that is coming out of the amp.

Close miking an amplifier can be done on- or off-center to the speaker (see *Fig. 131*), meaning that it can be directed either at the center or the cone of the speaker. Miking the center will give a brighter tone, with the tone becoming more mellow as the mic is moved towards the edge of the speaker.

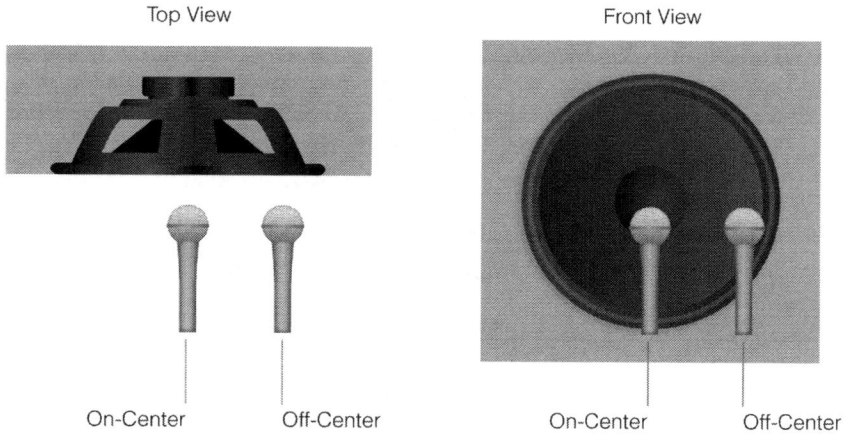

Figure 131: On- and Off-Center Placement for a Guitar Amp

Placing a mic inside the back of the speaker cabinet provides thick, full tone from some amplifiers. Note that this placement will be 180° out-of-phase with mics placed on the front of the amp, so if they are being blended together, the phase will need to be reversed on this signal (see *Phase*).

Placing mics at a distance of a few feet from the amp can also create a big sound, although the tone will be heavily affected by the room this is done in.

Recording the output of the guitar directly is also an option but has its own set of considerations. For clean, jazzy styles of music, the direct signal can be recorded by running the output of the guitar into a DI box. An overdriven electric guitar, however, creates some harsh sounding harmonics, which are smoothed out by the amplifier's deliberately unresponsive speakers. For this reason, it is usually best to use an amp or speaker emulator when direct recording for rock, blues, and other gritty styles of music. Amp and speaker emulators can be found as standalone units or in software.

There are two main benefits of recording electric guitar in this manner. First, setup is more convenient and problems of signal bleed are reduced or eliminated when recording multiple instruments in the same room. The second benefit is that amp emulators offer the tone of a wide range of amplifiers, adding tonal versatility at a relatively low cost.

Upright Bass

The desired tone for an upright bass will depend on the style of music being played. Common microphone choices are a large-diaphragm condenser mic or a large-diaphragm dynamic mic, usually in a cardioid pickup pattern. It is important that the mic chosen have a good low-frequency response.

Getting the right tone from an upright bass can be tricky, so it is important to take time to try different mic positions. Here are some places to start:
- 6–12" from the F-hole on the treble side of the instrument.
- Pointed directly at the bridge from a distance of 6–12".
- The point where the neck meets the body.
- Pointed at the fingerboard from about 1' away. This position will not have a lot of body, so it is best used in conjunction with another placement.

Electric Bass

It is very common to record electric bass directly by running it into a DI box (see *Fig. 132*). The main advantages of this are ease of setup and prevention of sound bleed from other instruments recorded at the same time. Additionally, the

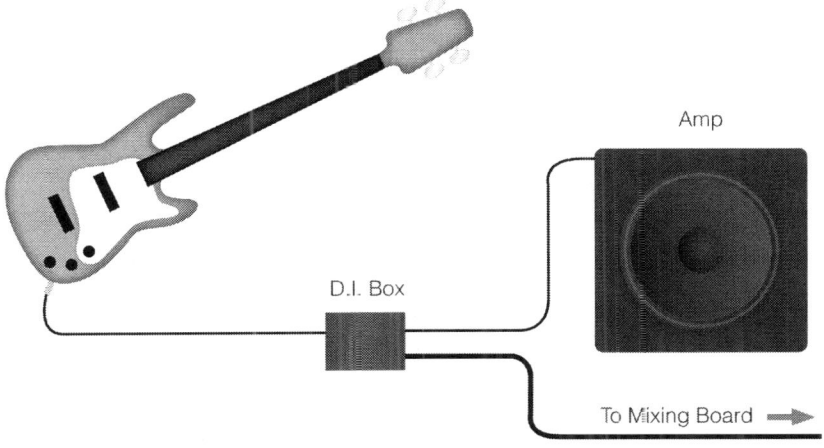

Figure 132: Direct Recording a Bass Guitar

tone from direct recording an electric bass is usually quite good, so many choose to stick with this method.

When direct recording, the performer can have their signal run through headphones, though some bass players prefer to have their amp running because they are used to feeling its rumble as they play.

If a bass amp with desirable tone is available, miking the amp is also a great option and in many cases can result in a better tone and solid low-frequency response. As with miking a guitar amp, the mic can be placed very close (1–2") to the amp, and placing the mic at the center of the speaker will result in brighter tone, while placing it towards the edge provides mellower tone.

Figure 133: A Minimal Drum Mic Setup

Drum Kit

The drum kit is arguably the hardest instrument to mic because it is really several instruments together. Drums are also a very important instrument to record well for many types of music because they provide the drive that moves the song forward. It is a good idea to allow plenty of time in a session for experimenting with mic placement on the drum kit.

The importance of properly tuning the drums before recording is often underestimated, but the effect can be significant. The tuning of the drum will affect its pitch, sustain, and tone. Additionally, poorly tuned drums often have a high-pitched ringing sound that follows the note, which is difficult to get rid of in a recording.

Figure 134: A More Elaborate Drum Mic Setup

The best approach for miking drums will depend greatly on the style of music and the tone you are looking to achieve. In softer styles, such as jazz, a somewhat minimal setup is generally used that involves a mic, or pair of mics, placed above the kit (referred to as "overheads") that are responsible for picking up most of the kit. This is usually reinforced by a mic on the kick drum and possibly the snare (see *Fig. 133*).

For heavier styles, like rock, it is more common to mic each piece of the kit individually with "close mics". In this setup, the overheads are used to pick up the cymbals, to add some "air" to the tone of the kit, and to fill out its tone (see *Fig. 134*). Below we'll look at some common placements for the individual pieces of the drum kit.

Kick Drum

Because of the huge amount of sound pressure being created by the kick drum, it is important to use a mic with a high SPL rating. By far, the most common mic to use is a wide-diaphragm dynamic mic, though some condenser mics are rugged enough to handle a kick drum. The mic also needs to have a good low-frequency response, particularly when recording heavier styles of music.

Placement options for a kick drum mic include:
- 1–2" outside the hole in the resonant head, or from the head itself if there is no hole.

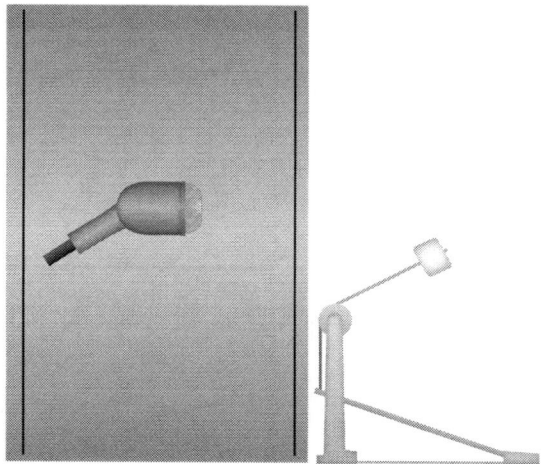

Figure 135: Mic Inside Kick Drum

- Inside the drum at a distance of 2–3", pointed at the spot where the beater makes contact with the batter head (see *Fig. 135*).
- Below the drum throne, pointed at the spot where the beater makes contact with the batter head.

Another interesting technique that is quite popular is making a drum mic from an old speaker. This is traditionally done with the woofer from a Yamaha NS-10 monitor, though any woofer will work. Results will vary from one speaker to the next. The speaker is removed from its cabinet, wired to a mic cable, and mounted to a stand placed 1–2" from the resonant head of the kick drum. This generally results in a signal with plenty of low end thump. There are many ways to build such a mic, and there are plans readily available on the internet.

Low-end thump can be added to an existing recording by playing the kick drum track through a subwoofer, then miking the subwoofer and recording it onto a separate track. The recorded subwoofer track then has a low-pass filter placed on it and is blended with the original kick drum track.

Snare Drum

Snare drums are commonly miked with a cardioid or hyper-cardioid dynamic microphone. Common placement is to place the mic slightly above (approximately 1") and inside the rim of the drum pointing towards the drum head at an angle of approximately 30–60° (see *Fig. 136*). Care needs to be taken to place the mic where

Figure 136: Common Placement for Miking a Snare Drum

The Encyclopedia of Home Recording

it won't receive any blows from errant drumsticks, and it is usually a good idea to place it so the hi-hat is in the pickup pattern's angle of most rejection.

It is also common to use the same placement on the bottom skin of the snare drum to pick up more of the sizzle of the snares. Miking both the top and bottom skins will allow flexibility when mixing. It's important to note that the signal from the bottom head will usually be 180° out-of-phase with the mic on top and the overheads, in which case it is necessary to reverse the phase of the bottom mic signal (see *phase*).

Toms

Toms are usually miked with a cardioid or hyper-cardioid dynamic mic. On larger toms, a mic should be used that is fairly sensitive in lower frequencies. When miking toms individually, the mic is usually placed 1–2" from the skin, just inside the rim. As with all drums, care should be taken to avoid the possibility of the mic being struck by the drumsticks.

More than one tom can be picked up with the same mic by placing a cardioid or bi-directional microphone above and between them (see *Fig. 137*).

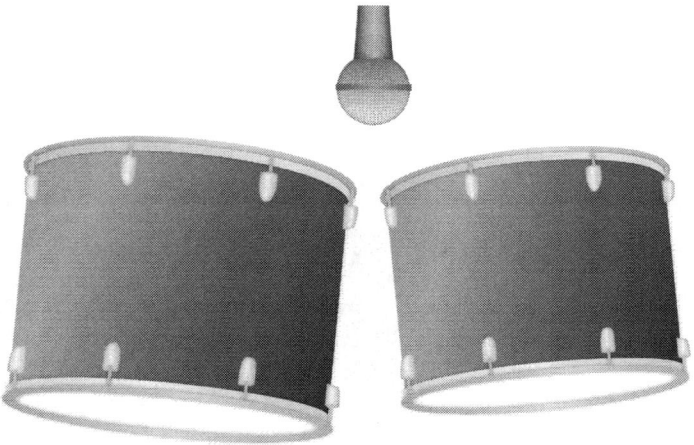

Figure 137: Miking Two Toms with One Mic

Hi-Hat

In many cases it is unnecessary to mic the hi-hat as it is often very present in the overheads. When a mic is needed on the hi-hat, a small diaphragm, or "pencil", condenser can be placed above it at a distance of 3–4" (see *Fig. 138*).

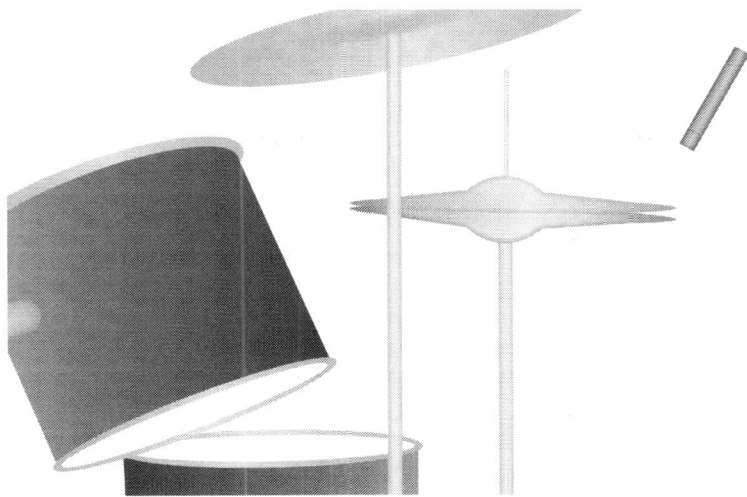

Figure 138: Miking Hi-Hats

Cymbals

As with the hi-hat, cymbals are usually present enough in the overheads that miking them individually is not necessary. If individual mics are needed or desired, small-diaphragm condenser mics are usually a good choice. They can be placed at a distance of 3–4", but clearance should be checked so they are not hit by a swinging cymbal.

Drum Overheads

In a simple setup, a single overhead mic can be placed above the drummer's head. A more interesting drum sound comes from a pair of overheads panned hard left and right to create a stereo drum sound. The two overhead mics should be the same make and model and have a cardioid pickup pattern. Small-diaphragm condensers are most common, though wide-diaphragm condensers are also a good choice.

Overheads can be set up as a spaced pair, with one mic over each half of the drum kit, or a coincident pair can be used in an X-Y pattern by placing the two mics together at a 90° angle to one another. The mic on the left will pick up the right side of the kit, and the mic on the right will pick up the left (see *Fig. 139*).

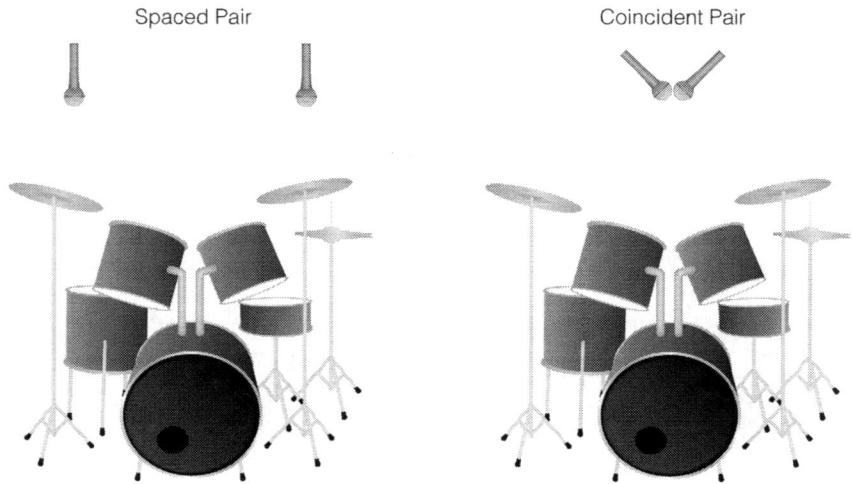

Figure 139: Spaced Pair and Coincident Drum Overheads

Distant Miking Drums

Experimenting with distant mics on a drum kit can yield big, fat drum sound. This can take some trial and error and is heavily affected by the acoustics of the room, but the results are often worth it. A few possibilities include:

- Mics placed at the other end of a large loading bay (or other large open space).
- Placing a mic down the hall from the kit.
- A mic placed at the the top of a tall stairwell when the drum kit is at the bottom.
- Mic placed on the other side of a closed door.

Violin or Viola

A wide-diaphragm condenser mic is a typical choice for miking violins or violas, though a ribbon mic can be also be a very good choice for certain styles of music. The cardioid pickup pattern is usually best for this application, but a bi-directional or omni pattern can be very effective when recording in a flattering room.

For classical music, a distance of 3–8' above and away from the performer is generally used for a nice, smooth tone. For fiddle music, the same technique can also be used, or the mic can be placed closer (6–8") for a more raw, folky tone. In both cases, the mic should be facing the top of the instrument (see *Fig. 140*).

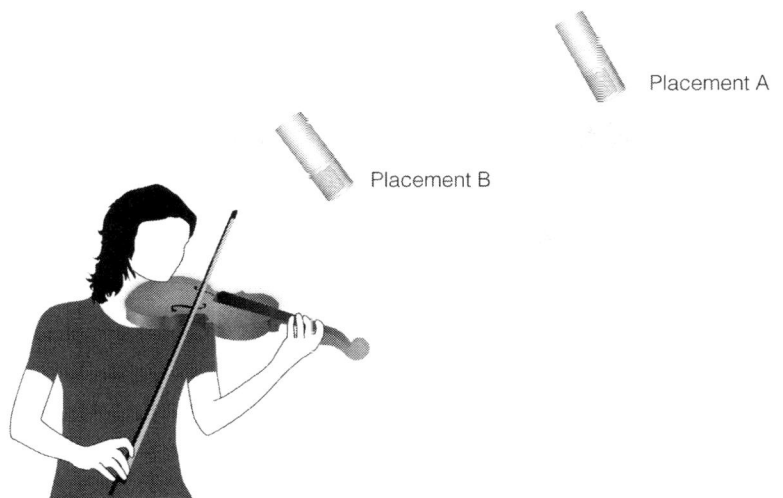

Figure 140: Mic Placements for a Violin or Viola

Cello

The most common placement for miking a cello is to place a wide-diaphragm condenser mic directed at the F-holes of the instrument. A distance of anywhere from 6" to 3' is appropriate, depending on the desired amount of room sound and bass response. As with the violin, a cardioid pickup pattern is usually a good choice, or omni and bi-directional patterns can be used when recording in an acoustically pleasing room.

Trumpet or Trombone

When miking a trumpet or trombone, a standard mic choice for the studio is a wide-diaphragm condenser mic. Ribbon mics are another popular choice, though care should be taken because the thin diaphragm of many ribbon mics can be damaged by quick blasts of air.

Modern musical styles tend to favor a distance of 2–12", whereas 3–4' is more common for classical music. To avoid distortion from gusts of air, the mic should be placed off-center from the bell and can be turned slightly off-axis (see *Fig. 141*). A pop filter can also be placed between the horn and the microphone to further protect from plosive blasts of air.

When miking a horn section or ensemble, the performers can be placed in a semi-circle and miked with a single mic or with a stereo pair of mics in an X-Y or Blumlein pattern (see *Stereo Miking Techniques* below).

Figure 141: Mic Placement for a Trumpet or Trombone

French Horn

The french horn is generally played with the horn facing backwards so the sound reaches the listeners by reflecting off of the rear wall. This presents a couple of good options for mic placement. One is to seat the performer 6–10' from the wall and place an omni or bi-directional microphone halfway in between, catching the direct as well as the reflected sound. The other option is to place a cardioid, omni, or bi-directional mic in front of the performer to pick up only reflected sound (*Fig. 142*). In either position, wide-diaphragm condensers or ribbon mics are good choices.

Figure 142: Mic Placement Options for French Horn

Saxophone or Clarinet

The tone of a saxophone or clarinet is created along its entire length, from the mouthpiece, bell, and keys of the instrument. A good starting placement is a wide-diaphragm condenser or ribbon mic directed at the midpoint between the bell and the keys (see *Fig. 143*). For modern musical styles, 1–2' is an appropriate distance, while classical music usually calls for a greater distance of 4–8'. Close placement can result in picking up the clicking of keys during the performance. This can be remedied by moving the mic farther from the instrument.

For clarinet and soprano sax, where the bell of the instrument points away from the keys, using two mics, one over the keys and one at the bell, is also an option.

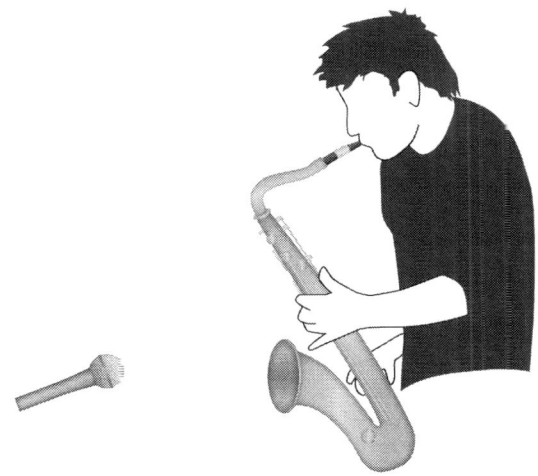

Figure 143: Mic Placement for a Saxophone

Flute

Like other woodwinds, the tone of a flute comes from both the keys and the embouchure (mouth piece). When using a single microphone on the instrument, a wide-diaphragm condenser can be placed directed at the midpoint between the keys and the embouchure. A cardioid or bi-directional pattern can be used depending on how much room sound you would like in the recording.

For classical music, it is common to place the mic at a distance of 3–6', whereas modern styles tend to benefit from a closer placement of 6"–2'. If the clicking of the keys is too prominent in the recording, try moving the mic farther back.

For a stereo recording, a pair of mics can be placed in an X-Y pattern in the same placement as above (see *X-Y Technique* below).

Upright Piano

The piano has the greatest range of any instrument, so it's best to use a microphone that has a wide frequency response. Condenser mics are usually the best choice for a clean, natural sound. The choice between wide-diaphragm or pencil condensers is a matter of taste, but pencil condensers are a little more common.

Here are some placement options for an upright piano:
- Over the open lid of the piano, place either a single mic, a spaced pair, or a coincident pair.
- With the piano pulled away from the wall so the soundboard is facing the room, a pair of mics can be placed at a distance of 6–8" (see *Fig. 144*). These can be either spaced with one at each end of the soundboard or together in an X-Y pattern (see *X-Y Technique* below).
- A stereo pair in an X-Y or ORTF pattern can be placed above the pianist's head (see *Stereo Miking Techniques* below).
- With the kickboard removed (there is usually a metal latch holding it in place), one mic is placed at each end. This position can, however, be problematic on an instrument with squeaky pedals.

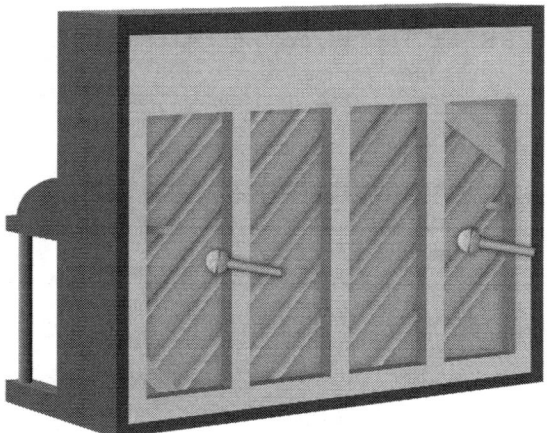

Figure 144: Miking the Soundboard of an Upright Piano

Grand Piano

For the grand piano, like the upright, condenser mics with a wide frequency response are a good choice, but the different shape and layout of the instrument requires that it be miked differently. Having the lid is open, closed, or taken completely off will affect the tone of the instrument. It is worth experimenting with the lid in different positions, but as with any instrument, if the performer has a preference, it can be worth catering to them to encourage the best performance possible.

Figure 145: Miking Outside the Lid on a Grand Piano

Below are a few options for miking a grand piano:
- X-Y or ORTF pair at distance of 4–6' (see *Stereo Miking Techniques* below).
- One mic over treble strings and one over bass strings at a distance of 1–2'.
- With the lid up, a mic or pair of mics can be placed just outside the lid facing either the strings (for brighter sound) or lid (for mellower, reflected sound) (see *Fig. 145*).
- An X-Y or ORTF pair placed above the pianist's head.
- An X-Y pair placed 2–3" over the point where the high and low strings cross. This delivers a punchier sound, so it is often favored for rock and similar styles of music (see *Fig. 146*).

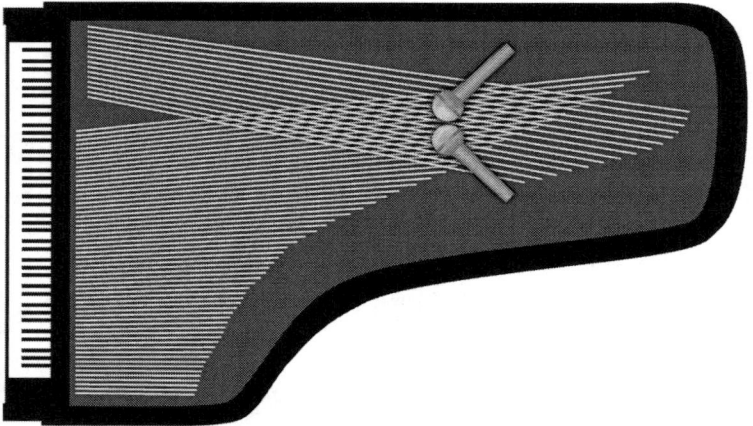

Figure 146: Miking a Grand Piano Over Crossed Strings

Stereo Miking Techniques

Stereo miking is the use of more than one microphone on the same instrument or group of instruments. The resulting signals are panned left and right to create a stereo image. Some stereo microphones and stereo miking techniques are designed to approximate as closely as possible the placement of human ears. These are called binaural microphones or binaural mic techniques.

When placing more than one mic on the same instrument, there is always potential for problems with phase cancelation (see *Phase Cancelation* or *Appendix A: The Basics of Sound*). Phase problems can be minimized or eliminated by following the three-to-one (3:1) rule.

The 3:1 rule states that if two or more microphones are used on the same instrument, they should either be a coincident pair or they should be a minimum of three times as far from each other as they are from the instrument itself. This means, for example, that if the microphones are 1' from the instrument, they should be at least 3' apart; if they are 2' from the instrument, they should be 6' or more apart. When this rule is followed, phase issues rarely occur.

Spaced and Coincident Pairs

As the name implies, spaced-pair miking involves two microphones placed apart from each other. Examples of spaced-pair miking are two mics placed in opposite corners at the back of a hall, mics placed over the bass and treble strings of a piano, or miking a guitar at the bridge and the nut.

A coincident pair is just the opposite of a spaced pair. In a coincident pair, the microphones are placed together. Coincident pair techniques include X-Y Technique, ORTF, Blumlein Pair, and Mid-Side techniques (all of which are explained below).

X-Y Technique

The X-Y technique uses two cardioid microphones placed at a 90° angle to each other, with their capsules pointing inward (see *Fig. 147*). The pair is oriented so that each is at a 45° angle to the instrument or instruments. The result is that the microphone on the left picks up sound from the right and the microphone on the right picks up sound from the left. The resulting signals are then panned hard left and right.

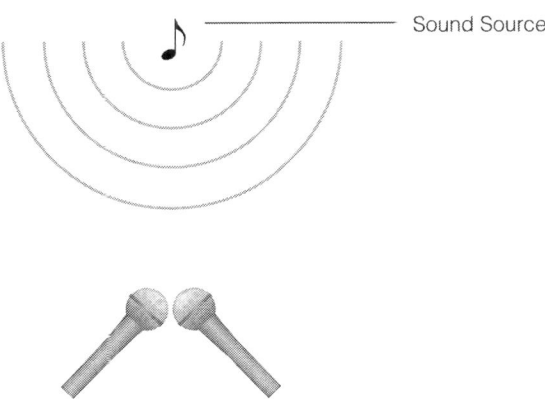

Figure 147: X-Y Microphone Technique

Blumlein Pair

A variation on the X-Y technique is the Blumlein pair. This technique uses two bi-directional microphones placed together and rotated 90° in relation to each other (see *Fig. 148*). One microphone picks up the front left and rear right of the

The Encyclopedia of Home Recording

room, while the other picks up the front right and rear left of the room. This technique works best when recording in a room with flattering acoustics.

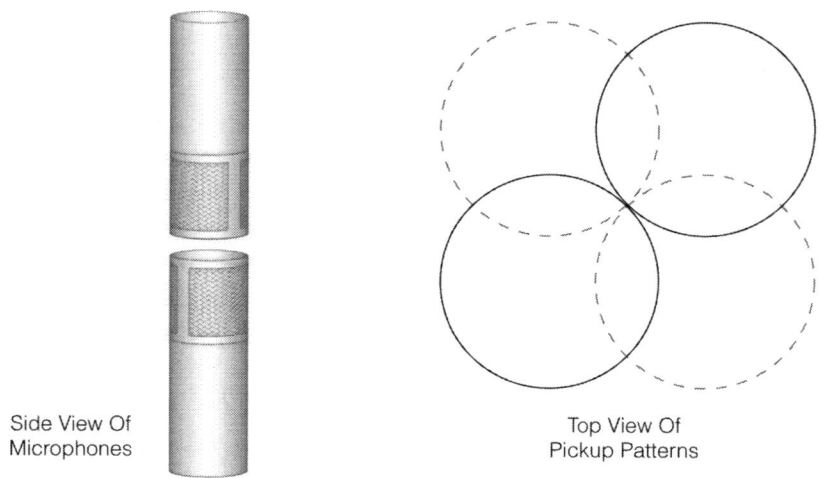

Figure 148: Blumlein Microphone Placement

ORTF

The ORTF technique is named after the French television and radio commission that invented it (Office de Radiodiffusion-Télévision Française). This is a binaural mic technique, which means it is meant to approximate the response of a pair of human ears. In the ORTF technique, two cardioid mics are placed at an angle of 110° with the heads 17 cm (7") apart (see *Fig. 149*). The beauty of this

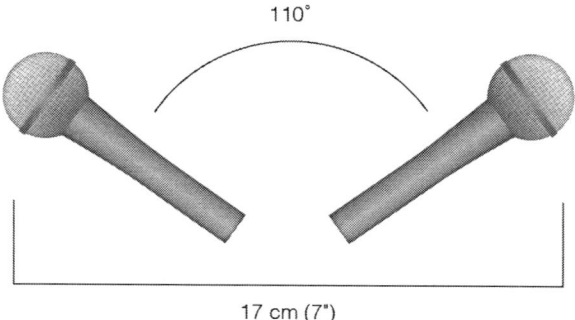

Figure 149: ORTF Stereo Miking Technique

technique is that choosing a mic placement can be as simple as moving around the room until it sounds good and then placing the ORTF pair where your head was.

Mid-Side

Mid-side (or M-S) is a stereo miking technique that uses one cardioid microphone and one bi-directional microphone. The cardioid mic is placed facing the sound source and a bi-directional mic is placed perpendicular to the cardioid mic so it is picking up the sides of the room (see *Fig. 150*). They are each recorded onto a separate track.

The track with the bidirectional microphone is then copied to a third track and the phase is inverted on the copy. The two bi-directional tracks are then panned hard left and right while the cardioid mic is panned to the center. By adjusting the relative volume of the cardioid mic to the sides, we can control how close or far away the recorded instrument sounds.

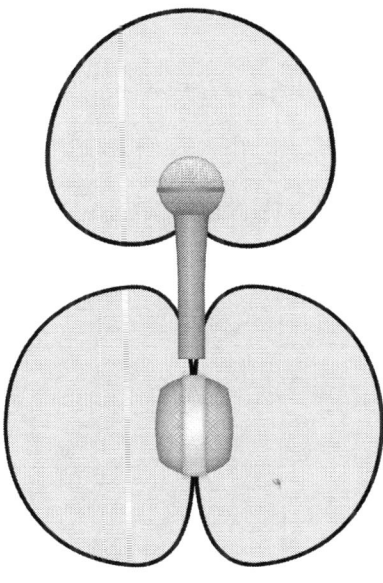

Figure 150: Mid-Side Microphone Technique

It is important to note that this technique only works in stereo. If this is played back in mono, the two tracks from the bi-directional mic will cancel each other out completely.

Decca Tree

The Decca Tree is a stereo recording technique used mainly for recording orchestras, which was developed in the 1950s by engineers at Decca Records. The Decca Tree traditionally uses a special T-shaped mic stand suspended above the conductor's head, though the same effect can be achieved using three mic stands with booms.

On the T-shaped stand are three cardioid microphones: one facing left, one right, and one center. The tracks recorded from these mics are then panned to match their configuration, providing a stereo image from the conductor's point of view (see *Fig. 151*).

There are no fixed measurements for the distance between the microphones, but the standard seems to be around 5–7". The mics are usually placed closer together for smaller orchestras and farther apart for larger ones.

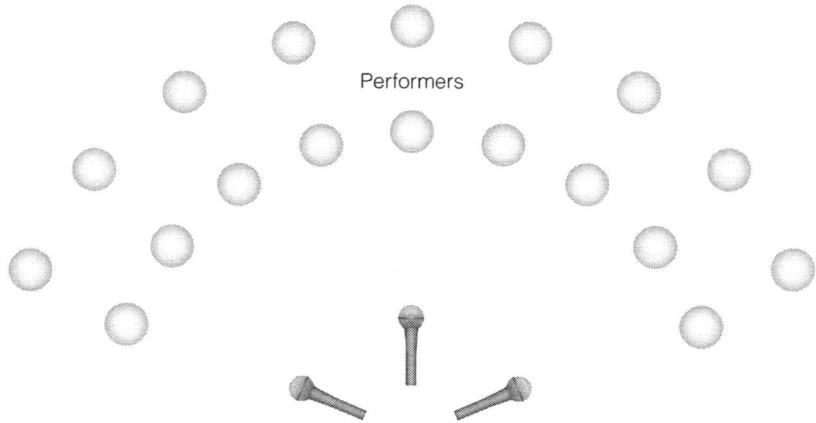

Figure 151: Decca Tree Mic Placement (Overhead View)

Index

A/D Converter **15**, 62, 64, 210
Absorption **5**, 6–7
Acoustic Envelope **9**, 16, 42-43, 53-54, 154, 196-197, 206
Acoustic Foam 5-6, **9**, 24, 49, 179
Acoustic Guitar 65, 76, 225, 228, **232–233**
Acoustic Isolation **10**, 86, 153, 171-174, 181
Acoustics **5–8**, 18, 48, 119, 125, 181–182, 227, 229, 233, 242, 250
Active DI 11, **64**, 132, 146
Active Monitors **11**, 216
ADAT **11–12**, 60, 84, 113, 218
ADAT Optical Interface **12**, 18, 191
ADSR **12**
AIFF **13**, 94, 219
Ambient Microphone Placement **13**, 100
Amp Emulator **13**, 65, 176, 235
Amplitude **14**, 29, 38, 133, 135, 150–151, 160, 161, 196–197, 201, 203, 212
Analog to Digital Converter **15**, 62, 64, 69, 123, 150, 162, 210–211
Angle of Most Rejection **15**, 26, 88, 102, 137–138, 227, 240
Attack (Acoustic Envelope) 9, **16**, 43, 54, 191, 206
Attack (Compressor Control) **15–16**, 42–44, 58, 83, 154, 188, 206

Attenuate **16**, 56, 73
AU **19**, 63, 142
Audible Range **17**, 56, 87, 123, 162, 171, 207, 211
Audio Engineering **17–18**
Audio Interface **18**, 52–53, 64, 65, 93, 210, 220–221, 223
Audio Units **19**, 63, 142
Aural Exciter **19**
Auto-Tune **141**
Automation **19–20**, 115
Auxiliary Return **20**, 21–22, 37, 111, 128
Auxiliary Send **20–22**, 36, 67, 71, 91, 110, 128, 144, 145–146, 183, 197, 215
Balanced Cabling **23**, 89, 132, 192, 198
Band-Pass Filter **24**, 73, 130
Bass Guitar 38, 64, 66, 77, 107, 118, 141, 170, 227, **235–236**
Bass Trap 6, 10, **24–25**, 179
Bed Track **25**, 40, 126–127
Bi-Amplification **26**
Bi-Directional 15, **26**, 29, 101, 103–104, 137–139, 224–252
Binaural Miking **26–27**, 126, 180, 248, 250
Bit Depth **28–29**, 67, 150, 211–212
Blumlein Technique **29**, 39, 243, 249
Bouncing **30–31**
Boundary Mic **31**

Buss **32–33**, 34, 36–37, 97, 110–112, 119, 167–168, 183, 209

Buss Assign **34**, 36–37, 110–111

Cardioid Microphone 15, 27, **34**, 53, 88, 101–102, 103–104, 126, 137–139, 148, 176, 195, 224–252

Cello **243**

Chamber Reverb **35**, 156–157

Channel 20–22, 32–33, 34, **36–37**, 50, 58, 63, 64, 91–92, 97, 104, 110–112, 115, 128, 132, 144, 145, 146, 168, 166–168, 170, 183

Channel Strip 20–21, **36–37**, 91–92, 110–111, 128, 146, 164, 166, 209

Choral 232

Choir 107

Chorus **37–38**

Clarinet **245**

Classical Guitar **232**

Click Track 33, **38**, 40

Clipping 36, **38–39**, 45, 46, 66, 96, 111, 127, 170, 186, 191, 195

Coincident Pair 29, **39**, 134, 180, 188, 204, 241, 246, 248, 249

Companson **39**, 77

Composite Track **40**

Compression 9, 15–16, 21, 36, 39, **40–46**, 50, 57–58, 69–70, 77, 82, 92, 96, 97, 106, 116–117, 146, 154, 164, 166, 183, 188, 191, 206

Compression Ratio 42, 43-46, **46**, 96,

Condenser Microphone **47–48**, 56, 71–72, 97–102, 132, 146, 165, 192, 193, 224–252

Control Room 10, **48**, 92, 96, 153, 171–174, 181–183, 186

Control Surface 20, **49**, 115, 221

Convolution Reverb **49**, 157

Crossfade **49–50**, 77

Crossover 26, **50**

Crosstalk **50**

Cue Mix **51**

Cycle **51**, 80, 87, 92–92, 133, 197, 201–203

Cymbals 238, **241**

D/A Converter 15, 62, **64**, 210

DAT **52**, 60, 84, 151, 162–163, 175, 218

dBm **53**

dBu **53**

dBv **53**

dBV **53**

De-esser **57–58**, 166

Decay (Acoustic Envelope) 9, 16, **53–54**, 206

Decay (Reverb) **54**, 157, 158,

Decca Tree **54–55**, 232, 251

Decibel 53, **55–57**, 102, 170–171

Delay 21, 54, **58–60**, 62, 67, 71, 139, 158, 187

Destructive Editing **60**, 120

Destructive Recording **60**, 94, 120–121, 149

DI 11, **64–65**, 89, 132, 176, 234, 235–236

Diffuser 7–8, 48, **61**, 179

Digital Audio Tape **52**, 60, 84, 151, 162–163, 175, 218

Digital Audio Workstation 15, **52**, 64, 219
Digital Delay **62**, 187
Digital Mixing Board 20, **62**, 218
Digital Signal Processing **62**
Digital to Analog Converter 15, 62, **64**, 124, 210
Direct Injection/Direct Insertion 11, **64–65**, 89, 132, 176, 234, 235–236
Direct Recording 13, **65**, 176, 233, 234, 235–236
Directional Response 101, 137
Distortion 38, 41, 46, 56, , 57, **65–66**, 85, 86, 142, 143, 170, 186, 191, 194, 243
Distribution Amplifier **66**, 86
Dither **67**
Doubling 59, **67**
Drums 39, 48, 66, 68, 98, 160, 170, 171, 192, 204, 225, **237**
Dry Signal 21, 36, **67**, 111, 218, 144, 197
DSP **62**
Dynamic Microphone 48, 56, **68**, 97–102, 116, 160, 192, 224–252
Dynamic Range 45, 46, **69–70**, 77, 122
Dynamics 39, 40–46, 70, 107
Dynamics Processor **70**
Early Reflections 6, **70–71**, 145, 155, 157
Echo 35, 58, 62, **71**
Effect Loop **71**
Effect Send **71**
Electret-Condenser Microphone **71–72**

Electric Guitar 13, 23, 38, 48, 64–65, 176, **233**
Engineer **17-18**, 148
Envelope **9**, 16, 42–43, 54, 154, 196–197, 206
Equalizer 36–37, 45, 58, **72–77**, 82, 83, 110–111, 117, 129–130, 149
Expansion 39–40, **77**
Fade 49–50, **77**
Fader 20, 22, 37, 49, 50, 57, **78**, 111, 115, 144, 145
Far-Field Monitors **78**, 114, 119
Feedback Loop **78**
Figure-8 Microphone **26**, 101, 137, 138, 227
File Compression **79**, 94, 116
Flanging **79**, 136
Fletcher-Munson Curve 56, **79–80**, 207
Flute 228, **245–246**
Foley **80**
French Horn **244**
Frequency 51, 72–77, **80**, 81, 82, 87, 92–93, 127, 149, 201–205
Frequency Response **81**, 85–86, 102, 108, 113, 136, 177–178, 226
Frequency Response Curve **81**
Front of House 32, **82**, 103
Fundamental Tone **82**, 127, 190, 203, 205
Gain 36, **82**, 110, 130, 146
Gate **82–83**, 188–189
General MIDI **83**
Grand Piano **247**
Graphic Equalizer 75, **83**, 130

The Encyclopedia of Home Recording

Guitar 13, 23, 38, 64–65, 76, 89, 122, 170, 176, **232–235**
Guitar Amplifier 13, 23, 48, 56, 65, 68, 98, 176, **233–235**
Hard-Disk Recorder 60, **83–84**, 113, 120, 151, 218,
Harmonic Distortion **85**
Harmonics 13, 19, 65, 82, 85, **127**, 176, 190, 205, 234
Headphone Amplifier **86**
Headphones 10, 38, 51, 66, **85–86**, 108, 115, 208, 219, 221, 236
Headroom 67, **86**, 131
Hearing 17, 27, 56, 87, 149, **207**
Hertz 51, 80, **87**, 92–93, 202
High-Pass Filter 24, 73, **87**, 95, 130, 146
Hyper-cardioid Microphone **88**, 101–102, 137–139, 148, 185, 224–252
I/O 18, 64, **91**
Impedance 11, 64–65, 86, **88–91**, 124, 199
Insert 20–21, 36, **91–92**, 111, 164, 168, 215
Isolation Room 10, **92**, 96, 153, 181, 186
Kick Drum 77, 96, 107, 116, 141, 192, **238–239**
Kilohertz 80, 87, **92–93**, 202
Latency 63, **93**, 142, 148
Lightpipe **12**, 186, 198
Limiting 42, 44–45, 69, 70, **96**
Line Level **96**, 136, 147, 163, 198
Live Room 10, 48, 92, **96**, 153, 171, 174, 177, 181–182, 186
Loop **93–94**

Loop Record **94**
Lossless 13, 79, **94**
Lossy 13, 79, **94**, 116
Loudness 56, 80, 149, 195, 205
Low-Pass Filter 24, 73, **95**, 130, 239
Masking 45, 69, **96–97**, 225
Master Buss **97**, 112, 168, 209
Mastering 45, 46, 52, 69, **97**, 106, 116, 217
Microphone Placement 124, 127, 188, **224–252**
Microphone Snake **103**
Microphones 26, 31, 34, 47, 68, 71, 88, **97–102**, 116, 125, 132, 160, 185, 193
Mid-Side Mic Technique 39, **103–104**, 249, 251
MIDI 18, 36, 83, **104–105**, 150, 164, 186, 189–190, 192
MIDI Interface **105**
MIDI Machine Control **105**
MIDI Module **105**
Mix Automation **19–20**, 115
Mix Position 48, 78, **109**, 140
Mixdown 19–20, 45, **106–110**, 177, 216–219, 221
Mixing 46, 56, 78, 80, 85, **106–110**, 114, 119, 180, 183, 207
Mixing Board 32, 34, 36–37, 62, 97, **110–113**, 115
Modular Digital Multitrack Recorder **113**
Monitor Mix 20–21, 37, **51**, 111
Monitors 11, 26, 78, 108, **113–115**, 119

Mono 67, 104, **115**, 117, 134, 180, 204, 251
Monophonic **115**, 143
Motorized Faders 20, 49, **115**
Moving-Coil Microphone 99, **116**, 160, 192, 226–227
MP3 13, 64, 79, 94, **116**
Multi-band Compression 45, 50, 97, **116–117**
Multitimbral **117**
Multitrack Recording **117–118**
Mute 22, 32, 37, 78, 82, 111, **119**
Near-Field Monitors 78, 108, 114, **119**
Noise Gate **82–83**, 188–189
Noise Reduction 39, **120**
Non-Destructive Editing 60, **120**
Non-linear Editing **151**
Normalizing **121–122**
Notch Filter **122**
Null Point **15**, 137–139
Nyquist Theorem **123–124**, 162, 211
Off-Axis 34, **124**, 13–139, 227, 243
Ohm 88, **124**
Omnidirectional 101, **125**, 137–139, 224–252
Orange Book **125**, 154
ORTF 27, 39, **126**, 232, 233, 246, 247, 249
Outboard Equipment 83, **126**, 214
Overdubbing 25, 118, **126–127**
Overhead Mics 100, **127**, 237–241
Overtones 82, 85, **127**, 205
Pad 16, 56, **127**, 146
Pan 34, 37, 106, 111, **128**

Parallel Effect 21, 37, 63, 111, **128**, 164, 183
Parametric Equalizer 58, 72–77, **129–130**
Pass Filter 24, 72–77, 87, 97, **130**, 146, 169, 239
Patch Bay **131**
Peak Meter **131**, 195
Pencil Condenser **132**, 240
PFL **145**
Phantom Power 11, 48, 64, 69, 72, 99, 100, **132–133**, 146, 160
Phase **133–135**, 136, 176, 180, 188, 203–204
Phase Cancellation 67, **135**, 180, 188, 248
Phase Reversal 134, **135–136**, 204
Phaser **136**
Phono Preamp **136**, 147
Phrase Looping 58, **136–137**
Piano 31, 246–**247**
Pickup Pattern 15, 26, 31, 34, 88, 101–102, 125, **137–139**, 185, 227
Ping-Pong Delay 58, **139**
Ping-Ponging 30, 118
Pink Noise **139–140**, 177, 182
Pitch 51, 80, 82, **140**, 141, 190, 202, 205
Pitch Control **140**
Pitch Correction 107, **141**, 189, 190
Pitch Shifting **141**, 190
Plate Reverb **141**, 156
Plosive **141–142**, 143, 191, 243
Plug-In 19, 53, 63, **142**, 144–145, 152, 195, 221
Polar Pattern 101, **137**

Polyphony **143**
Pop Filter 142, **142–144**, 243
Post-Fader Send 22, 37, 111, **144**
Potentiometer 78, **144**
Powered Plug-ins 63, **144**
Pre-Delay **145**, 157
Pre-Fade Listen **145**
Pre-Fader Send 22, 37, 111, **145–146**
Preamplifier 11, 15, 16, 18, 36, 48, 64, 66, 82, 89, 96, 110, 127, 132, 136, **146–147**, 193, 194
Pressure Zone Microphone **31**
Pro Tools **147–148**, 152
Producer 17, **148**
Project Studio **148**, 153
Proximity Effect 26, 102, 139, **148**, 227
Psychoacoustics 18, **149**, 162, 211
Punch-In **149**
Punch-out **149**
PZM **31**
Q 24, 58, 73–77, 122, 129–130, 149
Quantization **150–151**
Random Access Editing 84, **151**
Ratio (Compression) 40–46, **46**, 96
Real-Time AudioSuite 63, 142, **152**
Real-Time Effect 62, **152**,
Real-Time Spectrum Analyzer **177**, 182
Recording Engineer **17-18**, 148
Recording Studio 48, 96, 148, **153**, 171–174, 181–183
Red Book 125, **153–154**
Release (Acoustic Envelope) 9, **154**, 206

Release (Compressor Control) 42–43, 58, **154**
Return **20**, 20–22, 37, 71, 111, 128,
Reverb Time 157, **158**
Reverberation 6, 35, 49, 54, 61, 70–71, 141, 145, **154–157**, 158, 178, 182
Reverse Delay 58, **158**
Reverse Reverb **158–159**
Reverse Tracking **159–160**
Ribbon Microphone 68–69, 99–100, 132, **160**, 192, 224–252
RMS **160**
RTAS 63, 142, **152**
Sample **161**, 211–212
Sample Rate 12, 28, 52, 93, 123–124, **161–162**, 186, 198, 210
Sampler 117, **162**
Saxophone **245**
SCMS 52, **162–163**, 175
Scratch Track 127, **163**
Send **20–22**, 37, 67, 71, 91–92, 111, 128, 144, 145–146, 197, 215
Sensitivity Rating **163**
Sequencer 104–105, 150, **164**
Serial Copy Management System 52, **162–163**, 175
Serial Effect 21, **164**, 183
Session **164**
Shelving Filter 73, 129, **165**
Shock Mount **165**
Sibilance 57–58, **166**
Signal Flow **166–168**, 208–210
Signal-to-Noise Ratio 56, **169**
Slope 73, 87, 95, 130, **169**
SMPTE Time Code **169**, 186

Snare Drum 134, 204, 227, 238, **239–240**
Soft Clipping 39, 66, **170**, 186
Solo 145, **170**
Sound Engineer **17-18**, 148
Sound Module **105**
Sound Pressure Level 55–56, 68, 102, **170–171**, 228
Soundproofing 153, **171–174**, 181–182
Spaced Pair Miking
S/PDIF 12, 18, 162, **175**, 186, 191, 198
Speaker Emulator 65, **176**, 234
Speaker Phase **176**
Spectrum Analyzer **177**, 182
SPL 55–56, 68, 102, **170–171**, 228
Spring Reverb 156–157, **178**
Standing Wave 7–8, 61, 153, **178**
Stereo Miking 26–27, 29, 39, 103–104, 126, 127, 134, 176–177, **180**, 188, 198, **248–252**
Stereo Mixing **180–181**
Studio Design **181–183**
Studio Monitors 11, 26, 78, 108, **113–115**, 119
Submix 32, **183–184**
Subwoofer **184–185**, 239
Super-Cardiod Pickup Pattern **185**, 227
Synchronization 12, 113, 169, **185–186**, 198
Talkback 10, 33, **186**
Tape 39, 41, 50, 66, 120, 170, **186–187**, 214–217
Tape Delay 58, **187**

Three-to-One Rule 134, 177, 180, **188**, 204, 231, 248,
Thru **189–190**
Timbre 82, 127, **190**, 205
Time Code **169**, 186
Time Stretching and Compression 190
TOSLINK 12, 175, **191**
Transducer 14, 141, 156178, **191**, 208–209, 226
Transient 16, 42, 43, 86, **191**, 195
Transient Response 132, **191–192**
Triggering 104, **192**
Trombone 99, **243**
TRS 23, 92, **192**
Trumpet 99, **243**
Tube Microphone **193**
Tube Preamplifier 66, 146, **193–194**
Tubes 66, 146, 170, 193–194, **194**
Unbalanced Cabling 11, **23**, 64, 89, 92, 192
Upright Bass **235**
Upright Piano **246**
Vacuum Tube 66, 146, 170, 193–194, **194**
Viola **242**
Violin 44, 231, **242**
Virtual Studio Technology 63, 142, **195**
Vocal Booth 10, 92, 96, 181, 186
Vocal Ensemble **232–234**
Vocals 7, 8, 38, 48, 57–58, 141–142, 143–144, 166, **231–232**
VST 63, 142, 195
VU Meter 57, **195–196**

WAV File 13, 94, **196**, 219
Waveform 38, 49, 66, **196–197**, 201, 210
Wavelength **197**, 201, 203
Wet Signal 20–22, 37, 67, 91, 111, 128, 144, 183, **197**
Word Clock 18, 186, **198**
X-Y Mic Technique 13, 39, 188, **198**, 224–252
XLR 12, 23, 48, 89, 100, 103, **198**
Z (Impedance) 88, **199**

Made in the USA
Charleston, SC
25 June 2011